Breaking the Silence

Breaking the Silence

The Education of the Deaf in Ireland

1816 - 1996

Edward J. Crean

Irish Deaf Society Publications

Dublin

Irish Deaf Society
30 Blessington Street
Dublin 7

First published February 1997

Copyright © Edward J. Crean, 1997
All rights reserved

ISBN 0 9529206 0 3

Book design Terry Monaghan
Cover design Terry Monaghan
Printed and bound in Ireland
by Colour Books Ltd, Dublin
Index by Author

The Arts Council
An Chomhairle Ealaíon

Your children are not your children.

They are the sons and daughters of Life's longing for itself.

They come through you but not from you,

And though they are with you yet they belong not to you.

You may give them your love but not your thoughts,

For they have their own thoughts.

You may house their bodies but not their souls,

For their souls dwell in the house of tomorrow,

which you cannot visit, not even in your dreams.

You may strive to be like them,

but seek not to make them like you,

For life goes not backward nor tarries with yesterday.

You are the bows from which your children as living

arrows are sent forth.

Let your bending in the archer's hand be for gladness.

Khalil Gibran, *The Prophet* (1923)

Contents

Foreword	xi
Acknowledgements	xiii
Preface	xv

1 Early History of Education of the Deaf — 1
- The American experience — 2
- Early schooling in Spain — 3
- British efforts — 5
- Enlightenment influences — 7
- The French oral school: Pereire — 8
- The British oral schools: Braidwood — 10
- The first signing school: Epée — 10
- The German oral school: Heinicke — 12
- Epée's successors — 13
- Itard, professional analyser — 15
- Bébian — 18

2 The Battle of the Methods in the Nineteenth Century — 20
- Milan Congress on the Deaf, 1880 — 22
- The British Royal Commission, 1889 — 29

3 Early Irish Endeavours — 35
- Claremont School and provision for minority religions — 35
- O'Dowd's history of the Cabra schools — 37
- Cork School for the Deaf, 1822 — 38
- The Cabra schools, 1846 — 38
- One language for the girls and another for the boys — 41
- The religious orders and nineteenth-century Irish society — 41

4 Recent Developments in Ireland — 46
- The Cabra establishment — 46

	Fair weather for reform	47
	The Dominicans' fact-finding tour	48
	Oralism for the boys' school	50
	Audiological clinics	50
	Teacher training	51
	The visiting teacher service and mainstreaming	53
	Rationale for the changeover to oralism	53
	The Department of Education report, 1972	57
	Forum on the Education of Hearing-Impaired Children, 1991	62
	The NAD v. the IDS	64
	Attempt by the IDS to reform education, 1991–92	68
	The chaplaincy of the deaf	70
	Social services for the deaf	73
5	**The American Picture**	78
	The fact-finding tour of Thomas Gallaudet, 1816	79
	The first school: Hartford, Connecticut, 1818	81
	Edward Gallaudet	83
	Horace Mann, "Father of the Common Schools"	83
	Alexander Graham Bell: friend of the deaf?	86
	The return of the professionals	89
6	**Philosophical Approach to the Education of the Deaf**	94
	The quest for integration	96
	The oralist method	96
	Some observations on language	98
	Curriculum for the deaf	100
	Teachers' experience	102
	A process of decline	104
	Apathy among the deaf community	105
	Changes, good and bad	107
	Early intervention	112
	Mainstreaming and the visiting teacher service	112
	The multi-handicapped child	115
	The lip-reading myth	119
	The deaf community	120
7	**Epilogue: the Swan Report, 1994, and a Modest Proposal**	123

Appendixes

A	Speech Methodology at St Mary's School for the Deaf (address by Sister Nicholas Griffey to International Congress for the Oral Education of the Deaf, Northampton, Mass., 1967)	131
B	Deafness or Language Disorder: Differential Diagnosis (address by Sister Nicholas Griffey to International Congress for the Education of the Deaf, Stockholm, 1970)	137
C	Oralism versus Signing (address by Sister Nicholas Griffey to seminar organised by Royal National Institute for the Deaf, London, 1975)	141
D	From a Pure Manual Method via the Combined Method to the Oral-Auditory Technique: Educating Profoundly Deaf Children: Experience in Thirty Years' Teaching Deaf Children (address by Sister Nicholas Griffey to International Congress for the Education of the Deaf, Hamburg, 1980)	149
E	Fifty Years of Teaching Deaf Children: Thomas Watson Memorial Lecture by Sister Nicholas Griffey, Manchester University, 1988	158
F	Headstart in Deafness: Early Home Environment (address by Prof. Hilde S. Schlesinger to 44th Meeting of Convention of American Instructors of the Deaf, 1969)	166
G	Deaf Studies in the Year 2000: New Directions (address by M J. Bienvenu to National Conference on Deaf Studies, Chicago, 1993)	176
H	Stan Foran's recollections of his days in the Boys' School, Cabra	187
I	Reading Assessment of Deaf Children	188
J	Survey of past pupils by Irish Deaf Society, 1988	194
K	Questionnaire prepared by Irish Deaf Society for Forum on Education of the Deaf, 1991	198
L	Interchange of views between Pat Quinlin, Director of the National Association for the Deaf, and E.J. Crean	199
M	A letter from Grover Odenthal and some replies, November 1986	206
N	The Irish Sign Language Project, 1995	215
O	Dialogue of the deaf: what Gallaudet won't teach, by Lew Golan and Response from Gallaudet president, Dr. I. King Jordan	217
Glossary		223
Bibliography		227
Index		230

Foreword

The title itself is an excellent analogy describing the book's purpose. The book is a brave and much awaited venture recording the general perspective of the Deaf community on the Irish provision of education for the benifit of the Deaf community.

Many publications and journals had previously published perspectives on the area. However, it must be pointed put that the vast majority of these arise from the vested interests of those professionals or concerned individuals who seriously lack the advantage of empirical experience by Deaf people. The book, *Breaking the Silence,* attempts to redress or balance the debate by including the Deaf perspective which has been, and indeed still is, largely ignored.

The book is a serious attempt to record in writing, a view which is well known and long-standing through decades. The author, Edward J. Crean, is himself a parent of a Deaf son, whose links allowed the author gain access and obtain invaluable insights of the the Deaf perspective. The book contains the author's own opinions which he acquired through experience of past years.

The Irish Deaf Society proudly associates itself with this venture and its author, Edward J. Crean. The Irish Deaf Society hopes the book, *Breaking the Silence,* will be enjoyable reading and educational for the readers. It is hoped that the book will open and widen the domain of the debate on the education provision, and more importantly provide food for thought for those who are involved in the policy-making process.

We as publishers thank the author for the immense amount of energy and time he put into the book all at his own expanse, without any researchers or typists to assist him. He regularly submitted proofcopies to us for approval to ensure he was expressing what he felt was in the hearts and minds of the Deaf. We thank him in particular for giving us the benefit of the royalties of the publication.

The Irish Deaf Society wish to acknowledge the financial help received from the Brazil and Lynch families towards the publication costs of the book.

Kevin Stanley, Chairperson
John Bosco Conama, Hon. Secretary
Irish Deaf Society

Acknowledgements

I am grateful to those who helped me in their various ways: Seán English, Fr. Brendan Duddy S.J., Fergus Dunne, John Bosco Conama, Br. Hannon, David Breslin, Terry Brady, Pat McDonnell, and to my wife, Ethna, and family for their patience and for keeping me on track.

Seán aroused my interest in peace and conflict studies, which was the original reason for writing this book. Having recently retired from a lifelong career in engineering, I was introduced by Brendan to the works of Bernard Lonergan and other philosophers and thereby inspired with important new interests that I found particularly satisfying.

Fergus and John kept me abreast of current feelings in the deaf community. Br. Hannon gave me the bebefit of his knowledge learned from over thirty years as teacher and later as principal of St. Joseph's School for Deaf Boys in Cabra. Pat provided insights from his experience as a progressive teacher of the deaf. A special note of thanks to Dr. I. King Jordan, President of Gallaudet University, for reading the final proof and making some corrections to chapter 5, The American Picture. David and Terry provided me with information from their library. I must also thank the staff of my local library in Terenure for their help, as well as University College, Dublin, for the use of their library.

Magazine and newspaper articles, conference reports, together with published and unpublished books and booklets have been my main source of data. I am particularly indebted to Fr. O'Dowd for his *History of the Catholic Schools for the Deaf, Cabra,* and to Harlan Lane for his *When the Mind Hears* in which I found extensive records of the Milan Congress of the Deaf and utilised them in some rather long passages in order to give a comprehensive account of it and its kinship with the Cabra ethos since 1946. Material not readily available to the general reader is included in the appendixes.

Most of all I thank all the deaf people for their contributions, great and small, without which I would not have had the spirit to go through with it.

Preface

The intention behind this book is to open up free discussion on the subject of deafness in our society, with a view to informing those especially concerned and primarily reponsible for the education of deaf children—their parents or guardians, and those teachers in mainstream schools who teach over two-thirds of all deaf children in Ireland.

I have been involved in it as a parent since 1960 and have built up considerable insights from experience both in Ireland and the United States. I have searched through much of the available literature on the subject and attended many functions. In retrospect, my search for information when I first came to it puts me in mind of rushing across the country to keep an early morning appointment, driving through unfamiliar roads, meeting junctions without a signpost and others with the signposts turned in the wrong direction, while most people who could help appear to be asleep in their cosy beds.

People in my situation have found almost a palpable ignorance among the general public and the professions regarding some of the most basic knowledge of what the deaf really need in education. The ignorance is compounded by the fact that more than 95 per cent of deaf children come from hearing parents, while the deaf have been excluded from positions of the slightest influence in education until the nineteen-eighties. Few parents, at the crucial period, are even acquainted with someone in a similar predicament, and we fall for the assuring voices of authority.

This study looks at the current situation in some detail, with the emphasis on aspects that up to now have received little airing in the public arena, outside circles of deaf activity abroad. The climate of tolerance of minorities since the nineteen-sixties has, however, helped the deaf themselves to reveal their widespread dissatisfaction with the present systems of education.

While the existing Irish institutions have concentrated primarily on religious instruction, speech training, and a watered-down version of the standard curriculum, the deaf community through its organisation, the Irish Deaf Society (IDS), has, since its foundation in 1981, worked on social matters such as their own identity, language, and self-esteem. What they were denied in their homes and schools they set about building up themselves. Those deaf who are finding their feet now display a pride in being deaf, as individuals and as a community.

With the co-operation of Trinity College, Dublin, the Irish Deaf Society in 1996, initiated the first course on Deaf Studies, with the aim of spreading the body of knowledge on deaf culture to third-level students from the perspective of the deaf themselves to counteract the prevailing pathological depiction of deafness.

The common misconception propagated by the oralists (who rarely socialise with the deaf community), that deaf people are unusually lonely, is easily dispelled by spending some leisure time with a deaf signing group. The authority for this is Helen Keller, a famous deaf-blind person who did`nt have the benefit of such experience.

One of the common threads running through the history of education of the deaf is the dedicated promotion of oralism as the ideal means of educating the deaf to "make the deaf child more normal ... integrate ... and fit him to take his place in a hearing world." Another is the subtle use of half-truths, misinformation, and the hostility towards Sign Language by the authorities in the support of this thesis. It can be traced from Periere in France in the mid-1700s to Lew Golan in the United States in 1996 (see chapters 2 and 5, and appendix O).

In order to to put the story in perspective it is necessary to give the whole story of the education of the deaf, from the earliest records. The few bits of written material available on the subject in Ireland have come from the Cabra establishment and tend to be one-sided, and the deaf when they do write do not want to appear "to bite the hand that fed them" by being critical of their alma-mater. As 80 per cent of them leave school with a reading age of eight or nine, it is not surprising that they are a bit shy about expressing themselves in print. This text attempts to be objective in approach as well as redressing the prevailing imbalance in the picture.

The arguments in the book are supported by numerous references and appendixes and by the recent report *Study of the Dublin Schools for the Deaf* by Dr. Ethna Swan. Her report was an unexpected stroke of good fortune, which came out when this work was virtually complete. Her data was collected by questionnaire direct from deaf individuals, thereby bypassing the establishment, and therefore reflected the unadulterated feelings of the deaf. It gives much statistical validity to my hypothesis.

Written text on the subject is not readily available in Ireland, and therefore I have included a lot of it in the appendixes to save the interested reader the bother of searching for it. It is interesting to note that a century has gone by since a contribution of Irish deaf educators to the education of the deaf attracted a comment in publications from outside our shores.

Ireland started with a few small schools early in the 1800s, but it was the

Catholic hierarchy's two schools in Cabra at mid-century that really put it on its feet. By adhering to sign communication, the boys' school won international recognition for teaching English, although they used a mentally restrictive methodical system of signed English that they adapted from one invented by a French priest at a time when the American deaf had gone a long way in developing American Sign Language.

Strict discipline in Cabra and segregation of the sexes kept the children's own natural Sign Language underground and inhibited its development; a boy and girl from the same family could not communicate with each other, or other members of their family; signing was stigmatised in society.

The blanket chaperoning of the activities of deaf people continued after they left school. Nuns or Brothers were their only interpreters for the hospital, the doctor, or the policeman. Without their own newssheet or clubs the tiny deaf communities had a sort of underground existence.

The introduction of oralism to Ireland in the nineteen-forties and fifties was heralded as the panacea to "cure" all the "problems" of the deaf: it would "integrate" them into "normal" society. Oral schools were opened, one each in Dublin, Cork, and Limerick, and new schools were built in the existing establishments to segregate the deaf from the not so deaf. Every effort was made to eradicate signing.

Economic prosperity in the sixties allowed massive expansion and reform of all education services. Mainstreaming started and now accounts for two-thirds of all deaf pupils. The length of the school course was doubled, and the pupil-teacher ratio was more than halved. Teacher training was transferred from Cabra to the rather alien setting of University College, Dublin.

Oralism emphasised the pathological approach to education, concentrating attention on speech training. In addition, the complication of catering for multi-handicapped children led to the neglect of the bulk of the pupils—those with a natural inclination to communicate by signs. The semi-medical term "educational treatment" became the buzz word of the educationalists. The changes were carried out at enormous cost and produced only a small number of pupils who succeeded in getting to Leaving Certificate level and on to third level.

The Cabra oralists are not shy in singing the praises of kudos won by the schools in education in the international stakes (which were earned in the pre-oral days). Those with first-hand knowledge of literacy levels in pre and post-oral eras acknowledge that it was, generally, higher in the signing era, although they had only half the schooling time.

The invaluable resource of the feedback from the deaf community or the opportunity for deaf adults to become teachers of the deaf must be excluded under an oralist regime. The belief that the Catholic church should have the divine task of caring for the weaker elements of society can provide a licence for nuns and Brothers to mollycoddle them and teach them what the psychologists call learned helplessness. The result is evident in their lack of courage to challenge the vested interests in the education establishment.

The leadership in education has been in middle-class hands and consequently appearances have been high in the agenda: speech is more highly valued than signing. It is not surprising that the Dominican nuns opted for oralism before the more humble Brothers.

The public perception of deafness and signing has changed completely in the last decade, and deafness is no longer something to cause embarrassment thanks mainly to the progress made abroad and displayed on our television screens. In fact it is now becoming embarrassing for us hearing people who have not got their language. The spotlight of disability is turning away from the deaf and onto the hearing people without Sign Language who mingle with deaf people.

The deaf are slow to see what the education system has done for them compared with what it could have done and to see that anything they have got, including their education, was owed to them and hard won by their own efforts and that they do not owe anybody never-ending gratitude for it. They now organise their news journal and their leisure and sporting activities, which were in the hands of others. Control of their spawning ground, the education service, is still only a dream.

The task of realising the dream will be of David and Goliath proportions because of the inherited perception of the mass of the population. In the media world they are as orphans. One of those lined up against them, for instance, is a patron of Cabra's National Association for the Deaf, who is chairman of the largest newspaper group in the country. Publications of other organisations for the deaf never mention name of the Irish Deaf Society. If the society is discussed it is referred to as "another organisation"; not alone are achievements of the IDS not acknowledged but one is left with impression by the National Association for the Deaf's magazine *Link* that they do not exist. The latter magazine has declared a number of times that the pages are open to readers' comments, good or bad, but one rarely sees in it criticism of the establishment or articles on the philosophy of the deaf community, except in paternalistic terms.

The nineteen-forties and fifties were years of monumental change for the Irish deaf, but there are little or no records of what was going on in the minds of the deaf at the time, and knowledge is fading fast from living memory. The cultural identity treasures of the folklore of the deaf are disappearing by the day, without a thought or a penny to save it.

The superiority of signing over the oralist method of education was illustrated by the first results over two hundred years ago. This is coming to light again since the nineteen-seventies by research in the United States, Sweden, Denmark, Netherlands and Britain. Oralism has been revealed as an outsider's idealistic and simplistic answer to a sociolinguistic problem: it concentrates only on the child's weakness and neglects the strengths.

Cabra has inherited, it must be admitted, a litany of defects that are engrained in the ethos of the institution and will be difficult to dislodge. Also, in fairness, it would be wrong to even try, because it is unlikely that the majority of parents want to change.

The messages coming from research among the deaf community, however, indicates something that can be achieved only by total disentanglement from the existing influences and structures. Attempts to reform are leading to endless and wasteful infighting and frustration which the deaf are already experiencing, not only in Cabra and Gallaudet but elsewhere.

The deaf need their own space to create their own programmes in their own way. The biggest risk facing the Irish deaf community is that they may co-operate with the establishment, however minimally, and give authenticity to a phoney reform. The example of the response I got from Cabra to my attempt at reconciliation in 1992 (see appendixes P and L) does not inspire much hope of reformation, even if the personnel have changed a little in the meantime.

Reference is made throughout the book to the power of the network of the Cabra establishment and in particular on page 65 to the fact that it is the National Association for the Deaf who are accepted as advisers to Government bodies rather than Irish Deaf Society. The latter (and not the former) are recognised by the World Federation of the Deaf as the official national association of the Deaf in Ireland. The NAD are not recognised by any international body in the deaf world. One can see the outcome of this policy and the struggle the Irish Deaf Society have on their hands in the Department of Health's *Towards an Independent Future,* issued as we go to press. This document has come too late for a detailed comment on it in the book, except to say here, that it confirms and extends control by the Cabra establishment and the non-deaf to a far greater extent than anything we have seen before. The NAD, as official advisers to the Health Boards and all government agencies, shepherd milions of pounds to pet projects of the oralists while the doors are closed on the plans of the authentic representatives of the Deaf.

The presence of the NAD on Government bodies, automatically bars the IDS from admission and funding. Apartheid style inequity would not be tolerated, I believe, in any other sector of our society. it should be dealt with immeadiately by the appropiate authorities. Justice delayed is justice denied

Because of the complexity of the subject and the lack of standardisation of some terms, I felt it would be useful to include a brief glossary in the book. In the text of the book I have implemented a few policies that I hope will not give offence to anybody. "Deaf" is used in preference to "hearing impaired", and I have not felt it necessary to apply the policy of using a capital D for "Deaf" when referring to the culture of deaf people. Capital letters have been used for "Sign Language" to help distinguish this concept from methodical signing. Sign language, especially American Sign Language (and Irish Sign Language etc.,) have seen wide usage only since the 1960's, after Dr. William Stokoe's research proved ASL to be a legimate language.

1
Early History of Education of the Deaf

The education of deaf people has for centuries been bedevilled by the conflict over whether they should be taught by speech language or through some form of signing. As might be expected in matters of unresolved conflict, the core issues are overshadowed by the rhetoric issuing from the leading personalities, while in the mists outside the classrooms of the deaf there exists a perception that great things are being done by the deaf education establishments.

This image has been broadcast for more than a century in an indiscriminate crusade to establish the oral system of teaching the deaf. The Cabra schools for the deaf in Dublin, which serve the Catholic population of the whole of Ireland, alone in the western world resisted the campaign for three-quarters of a century. The fact that Cabra had won an international reputation in education and its lack of finances for an oral school were possibly the main reasons for holding firm for signing as the mode of communication. Mountains have been created out of molehills regarding the benefits of lip-reading and the value of speech for communication between and with deaf people, and Cabra's former fame is assumed to have continued and even increased since oralism was introduced half a century ago.

These myths, put forward by authoritative figures and institutions, have a charm that allures the parents of a deaf child and those interested in the welfare of the deaf into compliance and complacency. Old myths—like the belief that deafness was a punishment for some grave sin of the parents[1]—have given way to more subtle ones. Myths and fallacies have long been the main sources of information in our understanding of deafness and the methods of educating the deaf. The purpose of this book is to examine relevant information on the subject in the hope of unravelling some of its

1. Hodgson, *The Deaf and their Problems*, p. 147.

Breaking the Silence

mysteries; without some grasp of its history it is not possible to fully understand the situation as it stands in Ireland today.

Deafness is a condition that knows no racial, national, cultural or territorial boundaries. Historical accounts go back as far as records go, to the Bible and beyond, to Ancient Greece and Egypt. It seems likely that acquired deafness—the common case where children get it from scarlet fever, jaundice, or meningitis—was more prevalent in the days before antibiotics and the great medical discoveries, while inherited deafness caused by the incidence of recessive genes was common in some areas of tightly knit, self-contained communities up to recent times.

The American experience

The island of Martha's Vineyard off the coast of Massachusetts had ten times the incidence of deafness in the rest of the state, and everyone there knew some Sign Language. Although the deaf population had been falling as the island economy changed from fishing to a haven for the wealthy in the nineteen-seventies, Sign Language was still common in some of the villages. More significantly, the island had never had schools for the deaf. Nora Groce, who interviewed several islanders in the research for her book, quoted one:

> They would come to prayer meetings, most all of them were regular church people, you know. They would come when people offered testimonials, and they would get up in front of the audience and stand there and give a whole lecture in sign. No one translated it to the audience because everyone knew what they were saying. And if there were anyone who missed something, somewhere, somebody sitting near them would be able to tell them about it.[2]

During the Middle Ages, people who were unable to speak as a result of deafness were harshly treated. Church law held that the deaf were not eligible to celebrate Mass, because they were unable to speak the words of the Eucharist required for transubstantiation to take place.[3] The lack of speech also precluded men from inheriting property and titles. The deaf bore the brunt of the effect of the premier position given to the value of the spoken word and to learning through hearing. This stemmed mainly from the narrow interpretation of the Bible and Aristotle's much-quoted but faulty assessment of the deaf individually.

The Martha's Vineyard deaf community believe their origin is traceable back to a recessive gene among the Puritan settlers in the early years of the eighteenth century. Very little is still known about genetic deafness or deafness occurring from minor illnesses during pregnancy, mainly because the question does not arise until the child is a year old. It is a field that even in today's medically scrutinised society almost defies research. Deafness was

2. Groce, *Everyone Here Spoke Sign Language*, p. 12.

3. Lane, *When the Mind Hears*, p. 92.

common among families of the nobility, possibly because of intermarriage, and in fact this category provides the first records of the tutoring of the deaf.

Early schooling in Spain

It was the fortunate coincidence of the advanced state of education attained by the Islamic Moors and the high incidence of deafness among some of the Spanish aristocracy, together with the presence of a Benedictine monk, Pedro Ponce de León (1529–1584), that sparked off the earliest efforts in Spain. Ponce is credited with being the first teacher of the deaf, beginning with the five deaf children of the wealthy Valasco family in Valladolid, where he established a school for tutoring deaf children of the nobility. He claimed to have taught the deaf "to speak, read, write, pray, serve at the altar, know Christian doctrine, and confess with a loud voice."[4] Covarrubias, a physician to King Philip IV, quoted Ponce's comment on teaching the deaf through writing: "And thus we begin by speech with those who hear, so do we as well by writing with those whose ears are closed."[5]

The first record of the idea of teaching through writing came in 1528 from Rudolf Agricula (1433–1485), a professor in Heidelberg, who merely mentioned in his writings that he heard of a deaf man who could write.[6] His comment was the inspiration that led Girolama Cardano (1501–1576), an Italian mathematician and physician, to the idea that writing might be a suitable means for teaching the deaf. Cardano, in the year before the birth of Ponce, wrote that he maintained that mental powers are unaffected by the ability to hear, and he promoted the important principle that the deaf can be educated and that instruction can be given by writing.

This principle, described by O'Dowd as "evidently founded on right reason,"[7] in turn influenced Ponce. His method of teaching the deaf received only sporadic attention in the next four centuries, until the American linguist and psychologist Professor Eric Lenneberg argued for its use from the beginning in the process of education of the deaf.[8]

Ponce's success was widely acclaimed, and in a legal document dated 24 August 1578 he testifies:

> I have had for my pupils, who were deaf and dumb from birth, sons of great lords and of notable people who I have taught to speak, read, write, to pray, to assist Mass, to know the doctrines of Christianity, and how to confess themselves by speech. I have taught them all this. Some attained a knowledge of Latin; others taught Latin and Greek, acquired the knowledge of Italian. One who entered the priesthood and undertook a charge and a benefice of the Church, was also able to recite the canonical hours; and several attained to know and to understand natural philosophy and astrology. Another, heir to an estate and a marquisate and led afterwards to

4. O'Dowd, "History of the Catholic Schools for the Deaf", p. 2.

5. Moores, *Educating the Deaf*, p. 42.

6. Lane, *When the Mind Hears*, p. 68.

7. O'Dowd, "History of the Catholic Schools for the Deaf", p. 2.

8. Lenneberg, *Prerequisites for Language Acquisition*.

Breaking the Silence

embrace the military profession, learned, in addition to the knowledge above referred to, every kind of exercise and became a noted horseman. Much more, my pupils studied history, and were able to trace the annals of their own country, and also those of other lands. Better still, they proved by the use they made of them that they were possessed of gifts which Aristotle had denied to them.[9]

Thirty years of inactivity followed Ponce's death in 1584, probably because he neglected to train successors to carry on his work. Apart from the writing methodology, nothing is known of his technique for speech training. Although he produced a written account of his work, no record of it survives.

Some of Ponce's knowledge was relayed to other parts of Europe, however, thanks in part to the dispersal of Spain's non-Christian intellectuals by the Inquisition. Various people in France, Germany, the Netherlands and especially Britain took up the baton and made their contributions over the next two hundred years. The pace was increased by the Enlightenment and the growth of the military and political power of those countries. The British, however, remained rather insular with their work and developed outside the networks that operated elsewhere in Europe and later in America.

The work of most of these pioneers was plagued by the curse of egotism. Plagiarism prevailed; practically all of them wrote about what they did themselves, claiming parentage and sometimes divine intervention for the uniqueness of the method they adopted. Paradoxically, some of the glory-hunters in the field, while leading the pack backwards in detail sometimes brought it forward in general by the publicity given to their efforts.

The first book on teaching the deaf, *The Reduction of Letters and the Art of Teaching the Deaf to Speak*, came in 1620. The author, Juan Pablo Bonet (1579–1629), was a Spanish soldier of fortune. He took complete credit for developing a system, making no mention of Ponce or of Ramírez de Carrión, with whom he probably worked, and both of whose work he obviously copied.[10] Although he presents himself in his book as the inventor of the art of teaching the deaf to speak, he never in fact taught a deaf person.

Bonet advocated the synthetic method of teaching the sounds of individual letters and combinations of letters, as the title of his book indicates. He gave each letter a standard hand-shape and, by extension, its standard sound value. The former has become the almost universal one-hand finger-spelling used around the world (except in Britain). The pronunciation part, where each letter or symbol represents only one sound, suited his own Castilian Spanish as well as German but encounters a stumbling-block in the chaotic spelling of English.[11] Bonet's book attracted the attention of scholars throughout Europe and was the basis for all further efforts to make the deaf speak.[12]

9. Moores, *Educating the Deaf*, p. 41.

10. Moores, *Educating the Deaf*, p. 42.

11. Gerald Parstall in his book *English: a Glorious Mongrel* claims that there are six times more words in the English language than in French and three times more than in German.

12. Lane, *When the Mind Hears*, p. 87.

4

1 Early History of Education of the Deaf

Ramírez de Carrión (1579–?) was the third of the early Spanish educators of the deaf. In 1629 he published a book on the "secrets of nature", in which he discusses his secrets of teaching the deaf to speak. It included such delights as shaving the back of the head and rubbing in nightly an ointment of oils, brandy, and one of the ingredients of gunpowder. His most noted pupils became highly literate and successful figures: Prince Emmanuel of Savoy, the Marqués de Priego, and Don Luís de Valasco. Luís was a grand-nephew of the deaf Valasco brothers who were taught by Ponce de León; he was a brother of the Constable of Spain and a favourite of King Henry IV, who appointed him the first Marqués of Frenzo. Bonet did not disclose background information essential for evaluation of his method, such as the age of onset of deafness of his pupils.

British efforts

The centre of gravity of deaf education moved from Spain to England for some time after 1644, thanks to the pen of Sir Kenelin Digby (1603–1665). Digby was a charmer who cajoled his way into the company of the great philosophers of his day. A contemporary historian described him as a "compleat chevalier".[13] He accompanied the future King Charles I on his marriage-broking visit in 1623 to the Spanish royal family. Spain was then the most powerful and most wealthy country in Europe; it was also the most educationally advanced, still possessing many of the remnants of Islamic civilisation. Some twenty years later, after he was banished from England following the execution of his friend Charles I, Digby published an account of his various experiences and travels in Spain, which included a description of the advances made in the education of the deaf. He reported that the thirteen-year-old Luís de Valasco was

> borne deaf ... if a gun were shot off close to his eare he could not heare it ... The loveliness of his face, and especially the exceeding life and spiritfulness of his eyes, and the comeliness of his person and the whole composure of his body throughout were pregnant signes of a well tempered mind within. And, therefore, all that knew him lamented much the want of means to cultivate and to imbue it with the notions which it seemed capable of ...
>
> At last there was a priest who undertook the teaching him to understand others when they spoke, and to speak himself that others might understand him, for which attempt at first he was laughed at, yet after some years he was looked upon as if he had wrought a miracle. In a word after strange patience, constancie and paines, he brought the young lord to speak as distinctly as any man whatsoever, and to understand so perfectly what others said that he would not lose a word in a whole dayes conversation. Those who have curiosity to see what steps the master proceeds

13. Lane, *When the Mind Hears*, p. 87.

Breaking the Silence

in teaching him may satisfy it by a booke which he himself hath writ in Spanish upon that subject to instruct others how to teach deafe and dumbe persons to speak.[14]

The English philosopher John Bulwer (1614–1684) became interested in deafness through his friendship with two deaf brothers, Sir William and Sir Edward Gostwicke, with whom he communicated by means of alphabet signs.[15] He was greatly influenced by Digby's report, and although he had no experience of teaching the deaf he made a study and wrote several books on what he called the natural language of the hands. He also advocated lip-reading as the salvation of the deaf. He was possibly the first to advocate special schools for the deaf.

John Wallis (1616–1703) was Oxford's and England's leading mathematician. In 1660 he began to teach Daniel Whaley, the 25-year-old son of the mayor of Northampton, who had become deaf at the age of five, and claimed to have trained him to articulate distinctly within a year. He noted that deaf speakers, unable to hear themselves, needed constant correction from somebody else: in other words, their speech deteriorates after tuition.

Wallis's fame spread following a demonstration of the articulation of his protégé to the fledgling Royal Society and was crowned by an audience with the king, Charles II. Admiration for Wallis's breakthrough was not checked by the fact that Whaley already had the bones of the English language before he went deaf and still had some residual hearing. Although Wallis was a founder-member of the Royal Society and keeper of the archives at Oxford, he was, according to a contemporary historian,

a most ill-natured man, an egregious liar and backbiter, a flatterer and a fawner ... a person of real worth [who need not] be beholden to any man for fame, yet so greedy of glory that he steels feathers from others to adorn his own cap ... puts down notions in his notebook, and then prints it without owning the authors.[16]

That there was something suspect about Wallis's reputation is also evident from a comment of the philosopher Thomas Hobbes, his contemporary in Oxford:

He who can make a deaf man hear deserved to be honoured and enriched, he who can make him speak only a few words deserves nothing; but he who brags of this and cannot do it deserves to be whipped.[17]

By the end of his short career in the education of the deaf Wallis stopped his glamorous articulation training altogether and taught his last two pupils through writing.

The English divine William Holder (1616–1698), also a member of the Royal Society, hotly disputed with Wallis the honour of being the inventor of the art of teaching the deaf in letters. A summary of his method was

14. Lane, *When the Mind Hears*, p. 88. One of Digby's books had the impressive title *Two Treatises: in One of Which the Nature of Bodies, in the Other, the Nature of Man's Soul is Looked into: in a Way of Discovery of the Immortality of Reasonable Souls* (1644).

15. Moores, *Educating the Deaf*, p. 45.

16. Lane, *When the Mind Hears*, p. 104.

17. Lane, *When the Mind Hears*, p. 105.

presented to the Royal Society in 1669. As did his Spanish predecessors, he advocated writing as the first step and alphabet signs for speech training. This presentation and the controversy in such exalted company no doubt aroused curiosity and gave valuable publicity to the cause of education of the deaf.

George Dalgarno (1628–1687), a Scot, was headmaster of a private (hearing) school in Oxford. Although he never worked at it, he gave the subject of education of the deaf a lot of thought, publishing a masterful treatise in 1680, *Didascalocophus; or, the Deaf and Dumb Man's Tutor*.[18] He too believed in teaching the deaf through writing. He was the first writer in English to advocate finger-spelling (the British two-hand version); he was far ahead of his time with his advice that all children's schoolbooks should have the signing alphabet printed on the back.

Dalgarno believed that if a child's carer "had as nimble a hand as commonly they have a tongue" they would acquire language as the hearing do. This holds true if the hand-shapes represent ideas rather than letters, and it was an inspiration for devotees of Sign Language in the centuries that followed. Equally importantly, following Cardano a century earlier, Dalgarno was one of the first to proclaim that the deaf had a potential for learning equal to the hearing.

Enlightenment influences

The publication in Amsterdam of *The Speaking Deaf* in 1692 and *A Dissertation on Speech* in 1700 by Johann Konrad Amman (1669–1724), a medical doctor who escaped persecution in his native Switzerland for his religious beliefs, had a profound effect on several generations of educators, especially the Germans, who launched the first oralist education institution of the deaf.[19] The persuasive power of Amman's belief in the divine quality of speech comes out in his books:

> The breath of life resides in the voice, transmitting enlightenment through it. The voice is the interpreter of our hearts and expresses its affections and desires ... The voice is a living emanation of that spirit that God breathed into man when he created him a living soul ... I will state preliminary axioms of indisputable truth, by which it will be shown from the nature of God that creatures formed in God's image ought of necessity to be able to speak and in this respect resemble the Creator ... How inadequate and defective is the language of gesture and signs which the deaf must use. How little do they comprehend, even superficially, those things that concern the health of the body, the improvement of the mind, or their moral duties.[20]

Amman was invited to live with a wealthy Amsterdam businessman to treat

18. Moores, *Educating the Deaf*, p. 46.

19. Moores, *Educating the Deaf*, p. 53.

20. Lane, *When the Mind Hears*, p. 100–101.

his daughter, who was born deaf. When he failed medically he adopted the methods of his contemporaries, which were readily available in Spanish Holland at the time, but he claimed to have developed them independently. However, unlike most educators of the period, he did not hesitate to circulate his ideas widely.

After four years he had six pupils, all from wealthy families. He wrote that

> I have often been amused by those who complain that I ask too great a fee ... whereas they do not know that I am put to immense expense and incredible labour for a year or so in giving instruction to a single deaf mute ... The patience necessary to the practice of my method is all but miraculous.[21]

More profound thinking was going on elsewhere, however, mainly in Paris in the early years of the eighteenth century. The belief that knowledge could be acquired by experience and reason was gaining ground, and every new discovery was scrutinised scientifically. This movement was possibly the agent that brought about the spontaneous birth of education centres for the deaf around the seventeen-sixties in France, Scotland, and Prussia.

The French oral school: Pereire

In France, Jacob-Rodrigues Pereire (1715–1780) took the lead. He was a member of a Jewish family, a casualty of the Spanish Inquisition, that escaped and settled in France in 1741. Like many of their faith, as outcasts in society they were identified as *marranos* (swine) and had to suffer the indignity of lying low, adopting Christian names and making a pretence of conversion to Christianity in order to stay alive. Pereire devoted his life to education of the deaf, starting in his teens with his deaf sister. His charisma and dedication made him a gifted teacher; his attention to sense training influenced educators of the retarded such as Itard, and Seguin a century later.

Pereire's reputation rested on the strength of sensational success with two or three aristocratic pupils and attracted the attention of the nobility, including several European monarchs. The leading philosophers of the day, such as Rousseau, Diderot, and Condillac, were fascinated by the discoveries of Pereire and others in the education of the deaf. He presented his pupils in a number of demonstrations before the two prestigious Royal Academies, of Sciences and of Letters, and before Louis XVI, who was so impressed that he gave him a pension in 1750 to make him financially secure for life.

With the awestruck intelligentsia and the royalty protecting him, Pereire's position as an expert was beyond the questioning of mere mortals. He preserved his prominent public position by surrounding his method with a haze of mystery; his pupils, estimated to total only about a dozen in the

21. Lane, *When the Mind Hears*, p. 101.

forty-four years of his career, were sworn to secrecy: his family and even his best friend failed to find out the elusive secret. But no-one could conceal the fact that his pupils' speech deteriorated when training stopped. It took one of his own, the contemporary oralist Heinicke, to cut through the aura with the comment that Pereire may have picked pupils who were not profoundly deaf and have played down the importance of this information.[22]

Pereire was brought down to earth by the deaf author Pierre Desloges (1749–?), whom he met the year before he died. Pereire was astonished to discover that a deaf man could become so educated without speech, through Sign Language and reading. In a written conversation with Desloges, Pereire was quick-witted enough to acknowledge that

> undoubtedly, signs are essential for instructing not only the deaf but everyone and without them nothing could be taught or learned ... One gesture speaks a thousand times more and better than the most powerful language ... Deschampes believes as I do that signs are appropriate, even essential.[23]

In the last decades of his life Pereire, the world's greatest oralist (until Alexander Graham Bell a century later), saw his dreams come to dust. He had no pupils or school and had to give up teaching speech. Louis XVI withdrew his personal income, and its diversion to Epée's signing school marked the first convincing victory of signing over oralism.

Desloges's comments in his book, which he published in 1779, on his experience of the signing environment gives a flavour of the world of the deaf of Paris in the seventeen-seventies:

> There never was a writer in a situation comparable to mine: a deaf mute from the age of seven, abandoned to myself, without any instruction since that time, knowing only how to read and to write a little, come to Paris at age of 21, taken into apprenticeship against the wishes and advice of my parents, who considered me incapable of learning anything, obliged to seek work for my existence, without aid, without protection, without resources; reduced twice to the poorhouse for lack of employment, obliged to struggle incessantly against poverty, against prejudices, set opinions, insults, scoffings of my parents, friends, neighbours, and companions who called me an animal, an imbecile, a fool pretending to more spirit and reasoning power than they but destined some day to be placed in confinement[24] ... But things are quite different for the deaf in a great city, in Paris for example, which could justly be called the epitome of all the marvels of the universe. In such a theatre our ideas develop and when an isolated deaf man arrives he learns to polish and organise his signing, which was formerly without order and linkage. Dealing with his comrades he quickly learns the supposedly difficult art of portraying all his thoughts, even the more abstract. I ought to be believed, as this is what happened to me.[25]

22. Lane, *When the Mind Hears*, p. 82.

23. Lane, *When the Mind Hears*, p. 95.

24. Lane, *When the Mind Hears*, p. 94–95.

25. Lane, *When the Mind Hears*, p. 10.

The British oral schools: Braidwood

The first school for the deaf in Britain served only those with wealth. It was opened by the scientist Henry Baker (1698–1775), who tutored the three deaf children of a London lawyer in 1723.[26] He required a £100 bond of each pupil not to reveal the secret of his method. His school was short-lived, and although he was a prolific contributor of information of all manner of scientific interest he never disclosed his magical secret of teaching the deaf.[27]

The most influential early British educator of the deaf was the Edinburgh mathematics teacher Thomas Braidwood (1715–1806). He was father of a family dynasty in the field in Scotland and England, building up a chain of small schools for the deaf, run by his sons, sons-in-law, and nephews, which monopolised the speciality for sixty years. Some Americans, still feeling dependent on the mother-country, also sent their children to his schools. As a rule he taught rich hard-of-hearing children. He took his first deaf pupil, a boy who became deaf at three, in Edinburgh when he was in his forties.

Braidwood's fame was driven by compliments from the dignitaries of the day, such as Samuel Johnson and Zachary Macaulay, father of the historian. Macaulay, as editor of the *Christian Observer*, reported that "he had the blessed art of making the dumb to speak and the deaf to hear."[28] Braidwood spread the idea that he had discovered some hidden formula for his task, and, like the other oralists, he knew he could get short-term results provided he had dedicated teachers. The schools used speech with finger-spelling as their means of communication and had little to show in the way of academic advancement. Braidwood had to charge hefty fees, as he could handle only a few pupils at a time and had no other source of income. In his schools the head teacher got the pupils' fees and the assistant teachers received only minuscule salaries out of the charity collected by the school board for the less-well-off pupils.

The first signing school: Epée

It was the accidental encounter of an almost sixty-year-old French priest on his pastoral rounds with two teenage deaf sisters in the slums of Paris that opened the door to education in Sign Language for the deaf. The Abbé Charles-Michel de L'Epée (1712–1789) was the son of a prominent architect. He qualified as a lawyer in 1733, after coming to grief in his study for the priesthood over his refusal to take an oath renouncing Jansenism. He persevered with his first love, however, and with the help of a lenient bishop became a priest at the age of twenty-six. Little is known of his life for the next thirty years.

---

26. O'Dowd, "History of the Catholic Schools for the Deaf", p. 3.

27. Lane, *When the Mind Hears*, p. 431.

28. Lane, *When the Mind Hears*, p. 195.

With no previous experience in teaching the deaf, Epée came to the conclusion that their signs would serve as a means of communication for teaching them the basics of Christianity. Like many of the wealthy philanthropists of the eighteenth and nineteenth century, he discovered that his real vocation was in educating the poor and powerless. He embraced one of the most excluded and destitute classes of society, who had no way of discussing their frustrated desires with a hearing person. He started his school for the deaf in his father's home in the seventeen-sixties[29] with half a dozen pupils, but this figure had grown to seventy-two by 1785. After his death, the National Assembly of the Revolution provided a building and named it the National Institution of the Deaf.

Epée adapted parts of the natural Parisian Sign Language of the twin sisters with additions of his own to synthesise it to make it comprehensible for himself. His signing was artificial, but it was something to get them started. Evidently Sign Language was well established in Paris before that time, according to one of the delegates to the Revolutionary Congress:

> Before the Abbé de L'Epée, the deaf were not such wise theologians but communicated their thoughts easily enough among themselves, and with others close to them ... The deaf mutes that I have known had quite their own sign language grammar long before the Abbé de L'Epée established his school.[30]

Epée was an immediate success, and the news that it was possible to educate the deaf became the talk of Paris and spread rapidly throughout Europe. He produced the evidence by inviting spectators to witness his results in his classroom on two afternoons a week; by 1771 he had to hold the public sessions in a hall that held a hundred people, and demand was so high that spectators were requested not to remain more than two hours. A year later King Louis XVI was so impressed that he withdrew funding from Epée's oralist rival, Pereire, and gave it to Epée's school.

The sessions were attended by leading figures of the Enlightenment, including Condillac, who wrote that he thought Sign Language was far less prone to ambiguity than oral language. The attendance also included the Papal Nuncio, the archbishops of Tours and Bordeaux, the Holy Roman Emperor, Joseph II, and his sister Marie-Antoinette, John Quincy Adams, and the Russian ambassador on behalf of the Empress of Russia, who offered money—which Epée refused, asking for a deaf pupil from Russia instead.[31]

It was not all plain sailing for Epée, however: he was subjected to personal attacks in the early days from the oralists Pereire and Heinicke on the relative value of their methods. Although he was not opposed to speech-training he knew that communication through it was much slower than signing, and he was more concerned with intellectual development than articulation. He

29. Lane, *When the Mind Hears*, p. 423.

30. Lane, *When the Mind Hears*, p. 58.

31. Lane, *When the Mind Hears*, p. 46-48.

invited both his rivals to visit his school and see his method and his pupils at first hand, but they declined. Heinicke also declined his invitation to have the Berlin Academy judge which was the better system in the interests of present and future deaf people.[32]

Epée studied the writings of Amman and learned Spanish so as to study Bonet's book. In his odyssey with the deaf, which lasted for the last fifteen years of his life (the same length as Thomas Gallaudet, his equally successful American counterpart), Epée brought the best opportunity so far for the deaf to come out of the lonely islands that can exist in the hearing community and family life. He wrote several books on the subject, including the first dictionary of his methodical signs.

Thanks to the participation of deaf teachers in his school for the deaf and the pupils' freedom to use their natural language, by 1830 Epée's methodical signs for the spoken language had given way to native sign languages in Europe and America.[33] It is understandable that Epée, in his short and hectic time with the deaf, did not realise that the natural language of his pupils among themselves had all the characteristics of a natural language and was therefore a language in its own right and so held special educational possibilities for them. Deaf educators up to the present day, even with the benefit of the new science of linguistics, have difficulty with the same reality.

The German oral school: Heinicke

The German contribution to deaf education came from a Prussian soldier, Samuel Heinicke (1723–1790). He was the originator of what is generally known as the German method, the official name for oralism.

Heinicke educated himself during his long career in the army, which took him to posts in several German cities. In this itinerary he also picked up the experience of tutoring deaf children.[34] He received royal patronage in opening a small school in Leipzig in 1778 serving the deaf from all levels of society. He was opposed to the use of any methodical signs for teaching, although, like all oralists, he used some form of signs and finger-spelling. He also had the fortuitous advantage of working in a language with a phonetically elegant spelling rather than one with a lot of pronunciation traps such as English.

Heinicke's method was the antithesis of Epée's signing system, then thriving in Paris. In 1782 he wrote to Epée, his great signing rival, in defence of his method:

> No other method can compare ... with that which I have invented and now practise, for mine is built entirely on articulate and vocal language, and on taste which supplies the place of hearing ... The method ... was never known to anyone besides

---

32. Lane, *When the Mind Hears*, p. 430.

33. Lane, *When the Mind Hears*, p. 63.

34. Sister Nicholas Griffey in her book *From Silence to Speech* (p. 71) claims that Heinicke abandoned Sign Language. Epée was his contemporary and was the first to use Sign Language and the only one with a signing school when Heinicke was teaching the deaf. Epée invited him to come to Paris and compare oralism with signing in order to settle the argument of which was the best method of teaching the deaf, but he refused. Like all oralists, Heinicke used some form of signs but certainly not Sign Language.

myself and my son. The invention and arrangement of it cost me incredible labour and pains, and I am not inclined to let others have the benefit of it for nothing.[35]

Heinicke's secret, as revealed in his will, was a form of signing. He disclosed that he used the sense of taste to fix the vowels in the memory: vinegar for *a*, absinthe for *e*, and sugar-water for *o*! With hindsight, it is not surprising to find that his method did not long survive him. The rise of German nationalism, however, brought oralism back to life from the eighteen-thirties onwards, more to serve the Fatherland than to serve the interests of the deaf.

Epée's successors

In 1790, soon after Epée's death and the beginning of the French Revolution, his school came under the direction of the Abbé Roch-Ambroise Sicard (1742–1822). The Revolution provided a new premises and a new title for it: The National Institution for the Deaf. Sicard's life with the deaf could best be summed up by paraphrasing Churchill: never in the history of education of the deaf did anyone collect so much honour and glory by contributing so little. In vain one searches for any advances, only the publicity he drew on himself as a "miracle-worker" in the education of the deaf.

Sicard attained his reputation on the success of a remarkable deaf student, Jean Massieu, in the small school for the deaf set up in Bordeaux in 1786. Massieu, who never spoke, was one of a family of four deaf brothers, and the language he acquired through signing in his home environment no doubt accounts for Sicard's description of the deaf:

> The deaf man is not all that destitute ... He brings a communicative spirit to his teacher's lessons which ... lights up his face ... and gives his gestures all the shapes they require to designate objects ... Direct from his home and without any lessons he is no less eloquent than the hearing child.[36]

Sicard's introduction to the world of the deaf came when his archbishop sent him to Paris for a year to study Epée's method of education so that he could set up a school for the deaf in Bordeaux. There followed his three-year spell in charge of the new school; but as he was also attending to his duties as canon of Bordeaux and vicar-general of Condom, writing a book and articles on the education of the deaf, and presenting exhibitions of the deaf pupils every Sunday, he found little time for actual teaching. According to his head teacher, Sicard gave fewer than thirty lessons to the pupils in the period, and these were on religion.

To say that Sicard was ambitious would be an understatement; and greater fame and fortune beckoned when Epée died. Thanks to his well-publicised "miraculous success" with Massieu and some artful chicanery in the

35. Moores, *Educating the Deaf*, p. 51.

36. Moores, *Educating the Deaf*, p. 23.

arrangement of the examining board (as well as his published hint that the post be limited to abbés), Sicard quickly catapulted himself onto the international stage with one of the top jobs in Paris.[37] The humanitarian nature of his post ensured that Sicard was one of the few clerics to survive with his life in revolutionary Paris during his first decade in office. His monthly exhibitions of performing pupils and metaphysical lectures to the public drew audiences of hundreds as well as such figures as the Pope, archbishops, the Austrian emperor, and dukes and duchesses. These, together with the king of Sweden and the tsar of Russia, lavished on him medals and sashes of honour. Louis XVIII awarded him the Legion of Honour; Napoléon, who saw through his guile and vanity, never went near him or his school, nor did he confer any honours on him.

The annual dawn-to-dusk celebrations of his saint's feast day gave Sicard an opportunity to display his decorations when the deaf and the blind were filed past him, bringing gifts in homage to the great man. The day's programme included parades with bands, Mass, choirs, banquet, speeches, and toasts, ending at nightfall with drum-roll and fireworks display.

When Victor, the "Wild Boy of Aveyron", was captured in the woods of southern France in 1800, one pundit who examined him advised that he be treated by Sicard,

> that philosopher-teacher who has worked such miracles in this kind of education and we may hope that ... he [Victor] will one day become the rival of Massieu.

Realising that he was out of his depth, Sicard took evasive action, which led to the beginning of a fundamental change of direction in the school, away from teaching towards an approach based on medical treatment and oralism.

Sicard appointed the studious young doctor Jean-Marc Itard as medical officer of the school to deal with the project. His own direct involvement with teaching was obviously as slight as it was in the Bordeaux school, considering his extramural activities and periods of imprisonment and exile, including hiding in Paris for two years during the Revolution. As a leading intellectual, Sicard held the post of professor of grammar in the newly created teachers' training college, the Ecole Nationale. He flattered the Republic, which he detested, by calling for a "linguistic revolution" in French spelling "similar to the one that is rocking politics,"[38] and he was given France's highest literary honour by being elected a member of the French Academy. He was also a member of the administration board overseeing all asylums in Paris, a member of several societies, including the Society of Observers of Man, which he co-founded, and editor of the politico-religious newspaper *Religious Annals*, which thumbed its nose at the republic from the sanctuary of the National Institution for the Deaf.

The deaf were Sicard's saviours two years after his appointment to their

37. Moores, *Educating the Deaf*, p. 32.

38. *Chronicle of the French Revolution* (Longman, London, 1989), p. 468.

school. While he was under arrest during the Reign of Terror the voiceless Massieu saved him from certain death by pleading before the Legislative Assembly to have him returned to work with those even more underprivileged than the starving insurgents. Their report stands as a testimony to the value of signing in the education of the deaf as well as giving a flavour of the prevailing ideology:

> He [Massieu] understands all our ideas and can express all his own. He knows all the intricacies of grammar and even metaphysics perfectly. He is thoroughly familiar with the rules of mathematics, celestial mechanics, and geography. He has a knowledge of religion from the beginning of the world to the era of the death of the founder of that religion. He knows the principles of the Constitution and his mind has grasped them with all the more eagerness as it was never corrupted by any of our old beliefs.[39]

A hunter with the hounds and runner with the hare, Sicard threw his principles to the wind by boasting at a later stage of the revolution that

> for me, all authority exercised by the powers that be is by that very fact legitimate. Thus, by the same faith that I was a royalist I am now, since the proclamation of the Republic, a zealous republican.[40]

Sicard never learned French Sign Language, resorting instead to chalk, finger-spelling, and occasionally Epée's methodical signs, which he criticised because of the difficulty of using it for teaching French syntax.

The last five years of Sicard's thirty-two years in control saw the beginning of the decline of the National Institution for the Deaf. The administration was falling apart, with no common textbook or curriculum and every teacher with his own agenda. Oralism was creeping through the cracks, in the person of Jean-Marc Itard, the resident physician. The control of the Institution was bargained over in the next decades by various opportunists, most of whom had no experience of the deaf, including clerics, barons, dukes, and government ministers, inevitably leading to the official banishment of signing in the eighteen-eighties.

Itard, professional analyser

Dr Jean-Marc Itard (1774–1838) had his first experience with the deaf in 1798 when, as a medical student in the Paris military hospital, Val-de-Grâce, he was detailed to give emergency attention to an injured boy in Epée's school a short distance away. Sicard formed a lifelong friendship with Itard after appointing him permanent medical officer of the school two years later, with the primary task of teaching the (non-deaf) teenage "Wild Boy of Aveyron" to speak. This was an important assignment, because of the publicity given to the boy and the high expectation of producing from this supposed *tabula rasa* a

39. Moores, *Educating the Deaf*, p. 24.

40. Lane, *When the Mind Hears*, p. 27.

Breaking the Silence

living model of the ideas enunciated by Condillac and Rousseau. Itard kept him in his bachelor apartment, in isolation from the school and everyone else except his housekeeper, spending the next five years trying (in vain) to train him to speak and to educate him.

Itard maintained a strict professional relationship with his pupils, whom he treated as patients. He never learned to use much signing, nor did he fraternise or empathise with the deaf; nevertheless he pursued his studies and scientific experiments with integrity and arrived at important discoveries. He had done some study under Pinel, the medical director of the asylum for the insane at La Saltpetrière, and read the works of nearly every French thinker of the period. Itard was the first to attempt the instruction of the mentally retarded on a scientific basis by trying to harness the senses of the patient.

On the supposition that deafness is a disease, and with licence from Sicard, Itard embarked on an incredibly brutal series of medical experiments on the school's deaf population, in the belief that he would awaken the sensory faculty of their ears. Instruments of torture used in the Middle Ages to extract confessions from nonconformists would not be much less painful than some of the experiments of Itard on the innocent and powerless deaf: the application of electric shocks, leeches on their necks, hoping local bleeding would help, piercing eardrums (which caused the death of one pupil), and bandaging the ear with a blistering agent. He applied caustic soda behind the ears of thirty pupils and tried to fracture the skulls of a few others with hammer blows behind the ears. With a dozen he applied a white-hot metal button behind the ear. He applied a course of ear drops to the pupils from a secret formula made of herbs and wine he obtained surreptitiously from a fellow-experimenter in Bordeaux. Over a period of a year Itard subjected all but the few he could not subdue of the 140 pupils of the school to head clamping to enable him to probe and syringe their Eustachian tubes. Mercifully he stopped and admitted failure, writing that there is nothing science can do for the deaf.[41] He then resorted to a more humane form of research to test the educational value of oralism.

Itard devised what were the first scientific hearing tests by selecting a handful of pupils with the least hearing loss and who were most likely to profit by the oral method. He had quick success with their speech, for which he got high praise when he showed them off to his fellow-doctors in the Academy of Medicine. Never having learned Sign Language, and believing that it was not a language in its own right, he found to his surprise that although they were speaking French they were learning it as their second language and were translating their thoughts from their primary language into French.

Itard felt that the signing atmosphere of the school inhibited the pupils'

41. Lane, *When the Mind Hears*, p. 132-134.

speech and translation to the syntax of the speech language, and he tried unsuccessfully to get permission to segregate them from the signing environment. He managed to get one boy, Eugène Allibert, established nearby with an exclusively hearing family; his oral pupils meanwhile attended signing classes to obtain explanations in Sign Language of what was being studied but not comprehended in the oral classes. This turned out to be possibly the best form of experiment ever carried out and a rare opportunity, available only in a signing school, to compare the oral and signing methods. It was a simple and foolproof experiment, which obviously cannot be replicated in an oral school, involving one pupil living in a hearing environment and the remainder in the signing environment of the school acting in effect as the control sample. It is interesting to note that trials of a comparable nature were not carried out anywhere again until the nineteen-eighties.

The Academy of Medicine evaluated Allibert and another oral pupil in 1818 and reported:

> One might have thought that the nurture provided by the hearing family would have yielded better results than education by signs in the institution for deaf mutes. The contrary happened: his spoken conversation seemed to be more limited, more narrow than the other child.[42]

Allibert went back to finish his education in the signing classes and became a teacher of the deaf. Some years later he wrote to the Academy that despite the five years of intensive effort Itard lavished on him, despite his own strenuous efforts to speak, which turned his hair grey when only eighteen, and despite residual hearing, he could not be understood orally except by his relatives, and he could not understand an oral address. Five years of this experiment was enough to give Itard the knowledge that speech regresses when training stops and to cause him to state that

> a well-trained teacher and an indefatigable speech therapist were needed nearly full time for just one hard-of-hearing pupil, and even then the process was long and painful, and uncertain of success ... It is absolutely impossible to educate these children exclusively by means of speech.[43]

Itard's modest venture into oralism, by taking only a few from the pick of the pupils in the school, was the most positive contribution ever to the system initiated by Epée, but the all-powerful oralists pulled a veil of silence over this segment of his career. Itard is remembered for his medical and psychiatric discoveries, while his educational experiments on the deaf have been ignored. Edouard Seguin, the internationally renowned educationalist who pioneered modern methods of teaching pupils with learning difficulties, began his career under Itard, taking the entire programme used for the Wild Boy as his model. Maria Montessori in turn got her inspiration from the writings of Itard

42. Lane, *When the Mind Hears*, p. 139.

43. Lane, *When the Mind Hears*, p. 139.

and Seguin for her method of teaching the "free-range" children of the slums of Rome.[44]

Bébian

Roch-Ambroise Bébian (1789–1834) was born in the French colony of Guadeloupe in the Caribbean and educated in the Lycée Charlemagne in Paris from the age of eleven under the patronage of Sicard, his godfather. He lodged with one of the hearing teachers of the deaf (Jean-Baptiste Jeuffret, who later became head of the Tsarina's school in St Petersburg) at the National Institution for the Deaf and wrote that he learned French Sign Language mainly from Laurent Clerc, whose classes he regularly attended at the Institution. A fellow-teacher, Bertier, who was born deaf, stated that Bébian was the only hearing person to master Sign Language.

Bébian became a teacher at the Institution and one of the most important forces in the signing world. In 1817, the year Jamet got his introduction to signing on his visit to the Institute, Bebian wrote in his book *Essai sur les sourds-muets et sur le language narurel: ou Introduction a une classification naturels des idéés avec leurs signes propres* that Sicard had allowed French sign Language to be distorted to conform to French usage that it was sometimes so disfigured as to become intelligible.[45] In the year Sicard died he wrote the first manual on deaf education; but the fractured school board that requested him to produce the manual dithered and shelved it, although they applauded it at first. Internal divisions prevented the adoption of Bébian's manual, while the deaf teachers were being ignored by the leadership. Oralism from Germany was making inroads, and Bébian was lashing out in newsletters at the authorities, which led to his forced resignation.[46]

*

The writings of some of these early notables, though they could be faulted for their extreme and dangerous exaggeration, had the positive effect of motivating many people towards the goal of educating the deaf. Many were fuelled by the quest for knowledge and the ideas of the French Enlightenment on human sensation, liberation, and education. Society in general was waking up to the realisation that the world was made for more than the fittest and that the weaker sections must also be accommodated.

The English Parliament enacted a law against child labour in 1802 and against slavery in 1807. The deaf were among the first to benefit from the new climate of tolerance, as the schools for the deaf incorporated training in the valuable skills then in great demand, and they were forerunners of the technical schools. In addition, the new-rich families of the rapidly expanding

44. Montessori, *The Montessori Method*,

45. Dr. S.J. Supalla. *ASL in Schools*. P.92.

46. Lane, *When the Mind Hears*, p. 119.

middle class brought about by the Industrial Revolution wanted their deaf children to blend into society. They had the means and the influence to force changes and were beginning to demand results. Many of their children became deaf because of local outbreaks of disease. These parents usually knew that their child had at least average intellectual ability and was already able to speak and had acquired the main structure of the parents' language.

Epée's signing school became the model and the spawning-ground for the greatest breakthrough in the education of the deaf. Expansion was assisted by Sicard's bizarre circus acts of self-promotion, which focused widespread attention on the value of the signing system. The ascendancy of Napoléon's imperial power throughout Europe also helped to spread the French system. When Heinicke died in 1790 his oralist ideas were already laid to rest, overwhelmed by the evidence of the numerous case histories of the educational value of signs.

In the sixty years from Epée's standing start, as it were, over fifty signing schools, accommodating two thousand pupils, were established in Austria, Belgium, Italy, Malta, the Netherlands, Poland, Portugal, Russia, Spain, and the United States.[47] (The work done in North America is studied separately in chapter 5.) By the eighteen-twenties the education of the deaf by Sign Language was firmly established and was making rapid strides across two continents.

47. Lane, *When the Mind Hears*, p. 64.

2

The Battle of the Methods in the Nineteenth Century

If I accept another person's language, I have accepted the person ... If I refuse the language I thereby refuse the person, because the language is part of the self.

Shawn Neal Mahshie.

All attempts at resolving the conflict over whether pupils should be taught orally or by signing have so far failed, for a variety of reasons; the confusion over meanings and terminology, the absence of a fair trial and the self-interest of conflicting parties are only some of them.

Two events in the eighteen-eighties that appeared to tackle the issue stand out over all others in the past two centuries: the Milan Congress of September 1880 and the British Royal Commission report of 1889. The former was a teachers' "insider" creation organised by a small group of hearing teachers of the deaf with the sole purpose of eliminating Sign Language from the schools. The latter contained the usual public figures who had only superficial knowledge of the deaf, apart from a couple of clergymen who, as can be seen from their contributions, had valuable knowledge but were isolated from what was seen as the main body. They were, however, allowed to issue an interesting minority report.

The word "insiders" too may be misleading, because the real insiders are of course the deaf themselves. From the deaf perspective the oralist teachers are outsiders, while from the perspective of the general public they are insiders. The self-interests of the two are light years away from each other: the "insiders" are people who have the freedom to choose the field of deaf education as their career and the freedom to get out of it, while the self-interest of the deaf is of their whole being, their birthright and their culture: they have no choice but to live with it.

The terms "oralism" and "signing" each have several meanings, and these meanings overlap each other. Only in very exceptional instances do oralists (even the so-called pure oralists, who use what is called the oral-aural technique) not use some signs in the classroom, as can be seen from the disclosures of Sister Nicholas Griffey, former principal of St Mary's, the school for deaf girls in Cabra: "I must confess that we teachers relied on it occasionally when we wanted to convey a message quickly."[1] In other words, the "pure oral method" is really a fiction. All, even the oralists, use body language and facial expressions, either consciously or unconsciously, enabling them to communicate true meanings spontaneously. In fact one can see some validity in the claim that personal communication is visual for the most part. Tonal variations are the hired hands of speech and also carry valuable messages, even to those with only a little residual hearing. Strictly speaking, only people with their eyes closed can have a pure oral face-to-face conversation with no visual content.

On the other side of the divide there are few signers who will not willingly use whatever bit of speech and hearing they have when the need arises. The deaf have no objection to being trained to speak, provided it is not forced on them beyond the limits of their capabilities.

Although there is less than one deaf child in the world per thousand children, there can be an enormous number of differences between individuals, not counting those with any additional ailments. Nearly every one of them has different educational needs, because they have different types of hearing loss, different age of onset of deafness, different home and family situations, and the usual differences we all have—of intelligence, desires, access to opportunities, and so on. Unlike a hearing school, where a teacher has a class mainly from a single social level, a class of five deaf pupils could span the entire spectrum.

The signing schools in France and America in the early days, though enormously successful academically, neglected to provide speech training for those with the potential for speech. This left the schools open to justifiable criticism, because borderline cases, where a child with a considerable amount of hearing but not enough to keep up in a hearing environment, did not get a chance to develop their voice.

By selecting a few pupils from the myriad available and getting good parental co-operation it was not difficult for a moderately gifted teacher to produce short-term successes with speech. This impressed many parents, desperate for a solution to a problem that had hit them like a bolt of lightning, and secured a supply for the schools. Couple this with a crusading school principal, a generous flow of finance and connections in the leading professions and the authorities, and you have a formidable force and the model of an oralist movement. And the media will be swept off their feet by what they are told, and herald the "good news".[2]

The signing schools, although they are more appropriate for over 80 per cent of deaf children, were simply swept aside in the last decades of the

1. Griffey, "From a Pure Manual Method via the Combined Method to the Oral-Auditory Technique" (see appendix D).

2. *Time*, 29 Jan. 1965, p. 37; *Clare Champion*, 6 Feb. 1987; *Irish Independent*, 16 Dec. 1994; and others too numerous to record.

nineteenth century as a result of these two historical events and the overwhelming influence and manoeuvring of the oralists.[3]

Milan Congress on the Deaf, 1880

Few dates in the history of the deaf world carry more significance than that of the second International Congress for the Deaf in Milan in 1880. The offending matters as far as the deaf are concerned were in these resolutions, which were carried by 159 votes to 5:

    1. The Congress, considering the incontestable superiority of speech over signs, in restoring the deaf-mute to society and in giving him a more perfect knowledge of the language, declares that the oral method ought to be preferred to that of signs for the education and instruction of the deaf and dumb.

    2. Considering that the simultaneous use of signs has the disadvantage of injuring speech, lip-reading and precision of ideas, the Congress declares that the pure oral ought to be preferred.

    3. Considering that a great number of deaf and dumb are not receiving the benefit of instruction, the Congress recommends that Governments should take the necessary steps that all deaf and dumb be educated ...

The five votes against the resolutions were from the Americans, who were the only properly elected delegates and who represented more pupils and teachers than all the other votes put together; they also had the sole deaf delegate at the congress. The British had eight people, picked and led by Benjamin Ackers, who later in the decade played a leading role for the oralists in the Royal Commission. Frenchmen and Italians who organised the congress made up the rest, which amounted to 91 per cent of the total. Because of the recent humiliation of France in war, no invitation was issued to Germany, the cradle of oralism.

Brother Hubert, the school inspector of the Order of St Gabriel, led a delegation of Brothers, many of whom had told Edward Gallaudet (Thomas Gallaudet's son) that they intended to tell the congress that "signs could not be dispensed with in the instruction of deaf-mutes ... Not all deaf-mutes could succeed under the oral method." Hubert, however, got to the podium first and, after thanking the Pereire family for enabling so many of his congregation to get to Milan for the congress, declared himself "today unreservedly in favour of the pure oral method." All eighteen of the Brothers, effectively silenced, voted for the pure oral resolution.

The seeds for the plot were sown in Paris in the eighteen-seventies by Isaac and Eugène Pereire, son and grandson of the oralist Jacob-Rodrigues Pereire. They had become people of influence—financiers, and members of the National Assembly—and had gathered around themselves the directors of

---

3. I am indebted to Dr Lane's book *When the Mind Hears* (1984), chap. 12, and O'Dowd's MA thesis, "The History of the Catholic Schools for the Deaf, Cabra" (1955), p. 207, 219–220, 224, for the material account of these controversial events. Lane, who was visiting professor in the Sorbonne in Paris for five years and head of the department of Deaf Studies in Gallaudet University for many years, left no stone unturned in getting information for his book, making it unnecessary for me to consult originals except in a few instances.

small private oral schools and some others to form the "World Congress for Improving the Welfare of the Deaf". Eugène, in his effort to restore some of his ancestral inheritance, retained the services of Marius Magnat, the director of a small school in Geneva, to research his grandfather's papers. From the research Magnat proudly claimed that his own method was the same as that of the elder Pereire.

There followed a series of public lectures under the newly formed J. R. Pereire Society organised by a new-found friend, Félix Hement, government inspector of schools. Magnat, with the privilege of a government official, was able to kill three birds with one stone—boost his own position, boost that of oralism, and settle a century-old score with Epée for his patron—when he asserted that the "French method" of educating the deaf was not the silent method of Epée but the speaking method of Pereire.[4] Then followed the Pereire School of Paris, with Magnat as director, opened in 1875, and a year later Magnat's book, *Méthode Jacob-Rodrigues Pereire Appliquée ... à l'Enseignement du Premier Âge*.

Two years later, as part of the Universal Exposition held in Paris, Magnat managed at the last minute, with the help of Hement's superiors in the government, to splice in to the International Congress of the Blind the first "international congress" for the deaf. Nevertheless it was expertly planned to achieve their purposes. He rounded up twenty-seven teachers: twenty-three of them from France, one from the Horace Mann oral school in Boston, and the Abbé Don Seraphino Balestra, director of the school in Como, near Milan.

Ernest La Rochelle, a delegate and another of Pereire's biographers, described Balestra as "one of the most passionate apostles of oralism." Balestra harangued the congress with the catch-call of the oralists, "restoring the deaf to society," saying that "everyone recognises the superiority of the oral method over the sign method" and pandering to the nationalism of his hosts: "For the glory of France, choose one of these two doctrines" and "the world is waiting for France ... It will be to your glory, M. le Ministre, to instigate this reform by appointing me to the Paris Institution ... Give me only two months and you will speak to your pupils."[5]

The Pereire clique, however, failed on this occasion to convince their fellow-teachers, though they gave the movement the degree of respectability it needed. The congress agreed that the oral method was unsuitable for some of the deaf: these were pupils, it said, with inadequate intellectual training or capacity. To its credit it also agreed that responsibility for the French schools for the deaf should be moved from the Ministry of Welfare to the Ministry of Public Instruction.

The Pereirites held a national congress in Lyon the following year. They

4. Lane, *When the Mind Hears*, p. 377. The signing system was being a victim of its own success: in America, France and elsewhere at its very peak of prosperity, influential people who earned their laurels in other fields became "experts". They pooh-poohed signs as something for inferiors and produced a success or two orally, sometimes in suspicious circumstances.

5. Lane, *When the Mind Hears*, p. 385.

Breaking the Silence

accepted Balestra's plea to hold the next "international congress" in Milan in 1880 and intensified the campaign for change throughout France and Italy. On the model of the elder Pereire's school, small private schools were opened to serve the wealthy families, thus creating a class division in the deaf world. There was no deaf leadership in Europe equal to the task of defence of their territory. Even influential people who earlier were against oralism or wanted the middle course changed sides, or seemed to in the confusion of terminology.

Adolphe Franck, a distinguished scholar of the French Academy of Sciences, spoke at the congress. Nineteen years earlier he had considered the relative merits of the two methods at the request of the Ministry of Welfare and came out in favour of signing, reporting that

> we cannot prohibit the use of sign, even if feasible, without forcing the pupil to struggle violently with himself, without stopping his intellectual development, disturbing and confusion ... What is taught him under the name of speech is merely a dangerous and useless sham.[6]

Franck spoke to the congress, however, in favour of speech and reported to the Minister of Welfare afterwards:

> As soon as possible we must instruct orally all the pupils of our national institutions and not a select group. Speech training should be the general rule, the absolute rule.[7]

He had probably sensed the harmful polarisation of the deaf world caused by the introduction of oralism, forming two groups now at loggerheads with each other: the small, private oral schools that were restricting entry to those with the potential to speak and the public schools that could not refuse any deaf pupil trying to hold on to signs.

The Pereire crusaders, however, heralded Franck's rather neutral comments on speech training as a recommendation of oralism. Nobody on the side of the signers had an objection to speech training as such, where the pupil had the potential; but it is their preparations and their structuring of the Milan Congress programme that give us an idea of the extent of their hypocrisy and the deception employed as a means to their desired end. Nobody can be faulted for holding the opinion that oralism is the best system; it is when limits are not drawn on the means of reaching their objective that one must object.

For the Milan Congress, Magnat single-handedly drew up a list of topics, which he sent to school principals in Europe and America, together with a request for written opinions on his items. He then wrote a report on their responses, discussing and summarising them, while almost ignoring the virtues of the sign system, and distributed this report to all delegates on their

6. Lane, *When the Mind Hears*, p. 381.

7. Lane, *When the Mind Hears*, p. 396.

arrival.

Balestra, described by a fellow-oralist as "like one of the warrior monks of olden times who threw the Christian armies on the shores of Palestine," whipped up support by launching himself into a crusade to convert the Italian schools—all offsprings of Epée's school and using the sign system when Gallaudet visited them in his European tour of schools in 1867. By 1880 two key schools in Milan had gone completely oral since Gallaudet's visit, and they were used extensively to demonstrate to delegates the "superiority" of oralism. One of these was private, serving rich families, and the other, under the Abbé Tarra, served the rest. Both were observed by the English headmaster Richard Elliott—himself an advocate of oralism—to have screened their admissions according to the pupils' potential for speech and to be exhibiting pupils who had learned to speak. From a statistical report on deafness in Italy distributed during the congress, Elliott calculated that 15 per cent of the deaf in the province and 18 per cent throughout Italy were semi-mute, whereas 63 per cent of one Milan school and 75 per cent of the other were semi-mute. He reported that

> everything had been carefully rehearsed beforehand ... [The pupils] did answer correctly—in fact, they answered too correctly for there were apparently no mistakes made nor was there any deliberation before the answers were given. Indeed, pupils even began answering questions before they were completed.[8]

Elliott's request to have the pupils lip-read while an unknown passage was read to them was refused. A delegate from the New York school thought that the exercises on lip-reading "were very nearly a failure."

While the exhibitions on the "pure oral method" were going on, James Denison, the only deaf delegate and principal of the Columbian Institution (now Gallaudet University), remarked that the pupils awaiting their turn outside,

> noticing the intentness with which I was watching their conversation, abruptly suspended the sign-making part of it ... I enquired in signs whether they ever used gestures. The response was a blank mystified look on each face, then a general shaking of heads. But when I reminded them of what I had just observed, they pleaded guilty, with a propitiatory smile, to having partaken of the forbidden fruit of the tree of knowledge.

Since signs were used so much outside the classroom, Denison concluded that they might not be entirely unknown inside.

The Abbé Tarra was elected president of the congress by acclamation, and his lectures took up the greater part of two sessions and were read again in French by a colleague. Here are a few samples:

> Gesture is not the true language of man which suits the dignity of his nature.

8. Lane, *When the Mind Hears*, p. 389.

> Gesture, instead of addressing the mind, addresses the imagination and the senses. Moreover it is not and will never be the language of society ... Thus it is an absolute necessity for us to prohibit that language and to replace it with living speech, the only instrument of human thought ... The kingdom of speech is a realm whose queen tolerates no rivals. Speech is jealous and wishes to be the absolute mistress. Like the true mother of the child placed in judgement before Solomon, speech wishes it all for her own—instruction, school, deaf mute, without sharing; otherwise, she renounces all ... Let us have no illusions. To teach speech successfully we must have courage and with a resolute blow cut cleanly between speech and sign ... Who would dare say that these disconnected and crude signs that mechanically reproduce objects and actions are the elements of a language? I know that my pupil has only imperfect signs, the rudiments of an edifice that should not exist, a few crumbs of a bread that has no consistency and can never suffice for nourishing his soul, a soul that cries out for a moral and social existence ... Oral speech is the sole power that can rekindle the light God breathed into man when, giving him a soul in a corporeal body, he gave him also a means of understanding, of conceiving, and of expressing himself ... While on the one hand, mimic signs are not sufficient to express the fullness of thought, on the other they enhance and glorify fantasy and all the faculties of the sense of imagination ... The fantastic language of signs exalts the senses and foments the passions, whereas speech elevates the mind much more naturally, with calm, prudence and truth and avoids the danger of exaggerating the sentiment expressed and provoking ... detestable passions ... No shape, no image, no design can reproduce a sign for the soul, faith, hope, charity, justice, virtue, the angels, God. Speech alone, divine itself, is the right way to speak of divine matters. Come to our schools and you will see.[9]

Tarra published his views in a pamphlet that was distributed to the delegates. His impassioned appeal inspired Rev. Thomas Arnold, the British oralist teacher and author of many books on oral methods, to write some time later:

> Those who heard him the day he delivered his speech will remember it as one of the brightest days in their lives. His figure, countenance, eye and voice were to many their ideal as the teacher of the deaf ... His eye and look were as tender as a mother's ... When I heard Tarra describe his conversion to oralism, shape his reasons, recite his practical proofs, in my heart I exclaimed *Il Maestro:* I, too, was justified. Such a time happens only once in life, but like the star that never sets, it shines on through the journey.[10]

Like Tarra's speech, Magnat's long report, which he dedicated to his employer, Eugène Pereire, was merely a litany of assertions based on unverified beliefs and untruths.

The advantages of articulation training, he argues, are that it restores the deaf to

9. Lane, When the Mind Hears, p. 393–394.

10. Lane, When the Mind Hears, p. 393.

society, allows moral and intellectual development, and proves useful in employment. Moreover, it permits communication with the illiterate, facilitates the acquisition and use of ideas, is better for the lungs, has more precision than sign, makes the pupil the equal of his hearing counterpart, allows spontaneous, rapid, sure, and complete expression of thought, and humanises the user. Manually taught children are defiant and corruptible ... It is doubtful that sign can engender thought. It is a dialect you must learn, not universal ... It sets the deaf person apart, it lacks precision. Its syntax is in conflict with the occidental languages and it cannot help in the study of written language. Sign cannot convey number, gender, person, time, nouns, verbs, adverbs and adjectives. The teacher cannot genuinely communicate with his class in sign; it does not allow him to raise the deaf-mute above his sensations. In sign the deaf cannot link secondary ideas with the primary idea. Since signs strike the senses materially they cannot elicit reasoning, reflection, generalisation, and above all abstraction as powerfully as can speech. The sign takes up more space in the eye than the (labial) image of the spoken word and is not always clearly discernible. The deaf-mute does not perceive his own signs. Signs interfere with manual labour ...[11]

Balestra's speech was obviously the highlight of the congress. It inspired Arnold to write:

His gestures, his expressions, his fiery zeal with the vigorous Italian, made us suspect the presence or absence of something that disturbed his mental balance. But we erred. The man was all there but possessed of a soul whose sympathy was with the deaf-mutes. This was his ambition, his mission, and on it he lavished all his genius and affection ...[12]

The Abbé Balestra did not beat around the bush with his convictions or with his advice:

My friends, don't vote if you cannot, but when you go home tell what you have seen here. *The deaf in Italy speak.* We are all children of the one Christ who gave us the example ... The minister of Christ must open the mouth of the deaf ... I will add that for a Catholic priest the mutes must speak, for we have confession and in the countryside the priest would get everything backwards that the deaf-mute tells him in sign ... I beg of you: vote for speech, always speech.[13]

The afternoon sessions of the congress were cancelled and the delegates urged to attend the exhibitions. Personal accounts of the congress show that the speech and lip-reading of the Italian pupils made a great impression on some observers previously uncommitted to oralism; the demonstrations were proudly hailed afterwards as proof of the superiority of the "pure oral method". Denison reported that there was

evidence of a plan to hoodwink the delegates, of long previous preparation, of severe drilling and personal management to produce the most striking effect. There

11. Lane, *When the Mind Hears*, p. 378.

12. Lane, *When the Mind Hears*, p. 392–393.

13. Lane, *When the Mind Hears*, p. 393.

Breaking the Silence

was an apparently studied absence of definite and all-important special information as each case came up for exhibition ... My neighbors, themselves Italian and articulation teachers, informed me that [the best] pupils were not congenitally deaf and had probably mastered speech before entering the institution.[14]

Gallaudet also found the same manoeuvring in the exhibitions, and reported:

I found [that] many of the pupils exhibiting what the "pure oral method" could accomplish with deaf-mutes had in fact learned to speak before losing their hearing ...

Gallaudet advocated the combined system, believing, he said, that speech was important but that no deaf person would change places with a speaking derelict; and he told the delegates:

Thousands of graduates of the signing schools in France and America though not in possession of speech, are living today as educated, intelligent, self-sustaining men and women, happy and prosperous in all the relations of life, useful citizens, grateful for the blessings they have received.[15]

The oralists' rationale was based on assertions of their beliefs, with no proof other than the falsified exhibitions in the Milan schools. The Americans, though no strangers to corrupt politics, were astonished and overwhelmed by what they walked into. Yet ironically it was their attendance that gave the congress the only bit of legitimacy it had. There was nothing "congressional" about the Milan Congress except for the five American delegates, who had been duly elected at a Conference of Principals. And they must have had some forebodings of their future, as in the previous month, August 1880, a meeting of 150 deaf engineers, businessmen and others from twenty-one states had gathered in Cincinnati and formed the National Association of the Deaf.

Tarra expressed the jubilation of the oralists:

All discussions have ceased, serious objections of themselves disappeared, and the long struggle between the systems has ended. Never perhaps has a scientific victory been proclaimed with less opposition.

Within a year nearly all schools had started the changeover. The nuts and bolts of the change to oralism were new rules for the teachers: signing was to be stigmatised, rewards given for a week of not signing, spy-holes installed to detect secret signing. Deaf teachers were phased out over seven years—the length of the school programme. The signing adults were alienated from the new oral school-leavers. Essential feed-back in the knowledge and wisdom of the deaf culture, the dynamic cybernetic nerve system that binds a culture together, was removed. The signing deaf adult was to become persona non grata in his own schools.

14. Lane, *When the Mind Hears*, p. 388.

15. Lane, *When the Mind Hears*, p. 392.

2 The Battle of the Methods in the Nineteenth Century

The French sociologist Bernard Mottez noted: "Milan moved the status of speech from a means of education to the end of education." Schools were transformed into speech clinics. Thirty years after Milan, in 1910, Alfred Binet (1857-1911), director of a clinic for experimental psychology beside Epée's school in Paris and one of the promoters of the Binet-Simon intelligence tests, conducted with Simon the first systematic evaluation of oral education of the deaf by examining graduates of the school.

> We conclude that the deaf-mutes whom we have examined are not able to carry out a conversation with those around them, but they can understand those they know intimately and be understood by them sufficiently for the satisfaction of their immediate wants, by employing a means of communication composed of words, lip-reading, and expressive gestures ... People are mistaken about the practical result of the oral method. It seems to us a luxury education, which boosts morale rather than yielding useful and tangible results. It does not enable deaf-mutes to get jobs; it does not permit them to exchange ideas with strangers; it does not allow them even a consecutive conversation with their intimates; and deaf-mutes who have not learned to speak earn their living just as easily as those who have acquired a semblance of speech.[16]

Further congresses have been held at intervals by the oralist teachers of the deaf. Ireland, the last country to make the change to oralism (completed in 1957), joined the fold in November 1967, being represented for the first time by Sister Nicholas Griffey. By this time the congress was called the International Congress on Oral Education of the Deaf. Griffey's[17] paper was entitled "Speech Methodology at St Mary's School for the Deaf". For the centenary congress, held in Germany in 1980, the name of the congress was made more politically correct by dropping the word "oral", indicating signs of change in the century-long tide of oralism. Griffey's contribution for that congress was entitled "From a Pure Manual Method via the Combined Method to the Oral-Auditory Technique: Educating Profoundly Deaf Children: Experience of Thirty Years Teaching Deaf Children".[18]

The British Royal Commission, 1889

Humanitarian efforts had produced a growth of institutions for the poor and destitute in Britain and Ireland in the early eighteen hundreds. Following the virtual demise of the Braidwood empire in the first quarter, several institutions were established for the deaf, providing instruction exclusively in signs. The first indicators of a revival of teaching by speech appeared in the eighteen-sixties with the arrival of Gerrit van Asch as tutor for the deaf daughter of a wealthy merchant in Manchester. A teacher training school was opened in London in 1872. A well-orchestrated campaign fuelled by a visit of

16. Lane, *When the Mind Hears*, p. 400.

17. Sister Nicholas Griffey is sometimes referred to simply as Sister Nicholas and is listed in some earlier references under the name Nicholas. For convenience and consistency I have employed throughout this book the modern academic convention of using the surname only.

18. See appendix D.

Breaking the Silence

Abbé Balestra and other experts from the Continent, together with criticism of the living conditions in the signing schools, led to a burst of oralist excitement.

An influential member of Parliament, Benjamin St. John Ackers, a barrister and the parent of a deaf daughter, was the torch-bearer of the oral method. He had formed the Society for Training Teachers of the Deaf and Diffusion of the German System (oral method) and opened a private teacher training school in Ealing in 1878.

A conference of headmasters of institutions for the deaf held in London in 1877 resolved that reforms in the methods of education of the deaf were necessary. The Royal Commission on the Education of the Deaf and Dumb, Blind and Imbeciles was established in 1884 and published its four-volume report in 1889. Its membership included St. John Ackers, who had victorious service at the 1880 Milan congress to his credit. Father Thomas McNamara, then rector of the Irish College in Paris, wrote to Cabra warning them of Ackers's crusading activities for oralism and to be prepared for him.

The chairman of the commission could hardly be described as neutral: a few months after it began its investigations he opened a new wing in the school for the deaf in Manchester, declaring that "if only the education of the deaf were begun at an early age 99 out of 100 of the deaf and dumb could be taught to speak by the oral system."

Two junior clergymen on the commission, Owen and Sleigh, were the only members who had any real understanding of the social consequences of oralism and the potential of education for dealing with the social issues of deafness in the real world. Needless to say, there were no deaf people on the commission. What might be called the Cabra establishment, in the person of the chairman of the Catholic Institute for the Deaf, Archbishop Walsh, complained bitterly in well-publicised speeches that there was no Irish person and no Catholic on the commission, although there is no evidence that these constituencies had any special qualification or value for the education of the deaf.[19]

It is evident that the Catholic hierarchy, through the agency of the CID, was paying particular attention to ensuring that the government's noses were kept out of deaf education. A move by the Society of Friends in 1864 to obtain official funds for the education of the deaf was followed up by Brother McDonnell from the boys' school in Cabra but mysteriously fell through. According to O'Dowd, the CID "acted rightly in letting their views be known lest any legislation unacceptable to them should become a precedent in laws to be passed for Ireland."[20]

The deaf had the support of Charlotte Stoker, the mother of Bram Stoker,

19. O'Dowd, "History of the Catholic Schools for the Deaf", p. 124.

20. O'Dowd, "History of the Catholic Schools for the Deaf", p. 93.

2 The Battle of the Methods in the Nineteenth Century

who spoke at a public meeting in Dublin in 1863 supporting the establishment of state schools for the education of the deaf.

An interesting listener was Dr. William Wilde, father of the then 9 year old Oscar and a prominent eye and ear specialist, who had gathered the first statistics on the incidence of deafness in Ireland. Charlotte made an impressive showing, delivering a well-researched and confident speech. She told the audience that such schools for the deaf were available in France, Prussia and the US but not in Great Britain. "England is known to provide so freely for the education of the poor of every class without distinction of creed," she declared; "why should not a privilege be granted to those speechless poor which is so liberally bestowed on all others?"[21]

Despite its shortcomings, the commission carried out a highly professional enquiry, visiting schools in England, Scotland, Wales, Ireland, and the Continent, posing 22,298 questions in questionnaires and examining many witnesses, including the two leading figures in America, Edward Gallaudet and Alexander Graham Bell. A grave criticism of the commission, however, was the omission of a tour of the American schools, where signing had enjoyed half a century of solid success and where many of the schools were still in sign mode. Apart from that deficiency of information and the unbridled pressure from the oralists, the three educational options—sign, oral, and combined—were considered with commendable objectivity.

The commission declared that signing had the following advantages:

1. Sign is the readiest method of acquiring written language; more general knowledge can be taught in a given time by the sign system and it is more economical than any other system.

2. Some dull children can only be reached and intellectually enlightened by signs.

3. Religious knowledge can best be given by the sign system once the pupils know language.

The Americans Gallaudet and Bell were the two key witnesses. The former, who coined the term "combined system", advocating oral for those who could profit from it and sign for the rest, was the most experienced witness. He addressed the commission twice and answered questions for a total of ten hours. He told the members that signs give to the deaf all that speech gives to the hearing.

Dr Alexander Graham Bell had burst onto the scene in the eighteen-eighties with his exciting inventions of the telephone and the gramophone. At a casual glance it might have appeared that his credentials for giving advice on education of the deaf were excellent. Like his father and grandfather, he had made the teaching and study of speech his livelihood. His wife was deaf, and (like Gallaudet's) his mother, although there was no social contact between the deaf community and any of the Bell family. Infatuated like his

21. Barbara Belford, *Bram Stoker* (Weidenfeld and Nicholson, London, 1996), p. 27.

Breaking the Silence

contemporary and fellow countryman, the industrialist, Andrew Carnegie (then the richest man in the world) by the gospel of Herbert Spencer's Social Darwinism, Bell began experiments in animal eugenics, which reinforced his belief that science, not signs, held the solution to deafness. He was an out-and-out oralist. His obsession with speech precluded any compromise on his beliefs in oralism and stirred him to devote much of his wealth to making things difficult for the signing schools.

Bell appeared before the commission on four occasions, urging that all instruction of the deaf be in speech, "as in Germany."[22] The comments of the commission members on what they noted as the disadvantages of the sign system reflect the bigotry of Bell,[23] his ignorance of deaf community life and his hostility towards the embryonic deaf culture growing out of the friendships formed by the deaf pupils at school. The towering influence of Bell's inventive talent, and possibly his wealth, demanded their attention. The commission reported his attitudes:

1. There is no uniform code of signs even in English alone [in fact this is a criticism of the schools rather than the sign system].

2. The custom of using signs leads to inaccurate and ungrammatical use of language.

3. The manual system specially trains the deaf to communicate and associate with the deaf only. Those who communicate by signs live more apart and intermarry more with deaf-mutes than those trained on the oral method. This does not happen so much in Germany and Switzerland where the oral system is in use.

4. The lack of use of the lungs leads to lung diseases and bad circulation.

5. France abandoned the sign system since the Milan congress of 1880.[24]

In contrast to the anecdotal comments and subjective claims made against signs are the seductive claims for oralism. The commission's comments illustrate their ignorance of the realities of deaf community life and the consequent inaccuracies and unfounded beliefs:

1. The oral method restores the deaf more completely to society.

2. The oral method is almost universal in Europe.

3. Parents acquainted with the merits of the two systems have chosen the oral methods. Many private schools in the USA were due to this.

4. Respiratory organs are used naturally and the health of the child is improved.[25]

Further comments of the commission were that the sign system crowds out the oral system, since it is much easier, and therefore the combined method differs little from the pure manual method, and that it was the shortage of good teachers that caused the lack of progress in England compared with the rest of Europe.[26] The former is the common recurring complaint of oralists to this day.

---

22. Lane, *When the Mind Hears*, p. 366.

23. Lane, *When the Mind Hears*, p. 368. A few years earlier, on the instigation of Bell, the American Association to Promote the Teaching of Speech to the Deaf was set up by oralist teachers committed to teaching through speech, and shortly afterwards it elected him president. The name was changed in 1956 to the Alexander Graham Bell Association. Since its inception it has been financed entirely by royalties from Bell's inventions.

24. O'Dowd, "History of the Catholic Schools for the Deaf", p. 215.

2 The Battle of the Methods in the Nineteenth Century

The two clergymen on the commission, Owen and Sleigh, though they signed the general report, issued a minority report in defence of signing:

1. The evidence of missionaries in England who work among the adult deaf and dumb is, that the oral system breaks down after school.

2. From what we ourselves have seen, in visiting the various schools and institutions in the UK, we are bound to assert that with a few notable exceptions and those chiefly semi-mute and semi-deaf, the articulation and lip-reading taught under the oral system is so poor as to be of little value in their intercourse with the general public.

3. They consider that too little importance has been attached to the evidence of Dr. Gallaudet (a non-oralist) considering the high authority from which it emanates.

4. They disbelieve in the "injury to the lung" theory as regards signs, inasmuch as the mutes shout and make all kinds of noise at play.

5. Even in Germany, the home of the oral system, deaf mutes hold conversations and invariably carry on their discussions in gesture.

6. We are of opinion that in the Report an importance has been attached to the Milan Congress which is scarcely warranted by the evidence of Dr. Gallaudet. We refer also to a similar opinion of the Congress expressed by Dr. Elliott, headmaster of the Margate Institution (himself an advocate of the oral system) in the *American Annals of the Deaf* (July 1882).

7. Germany has never given the sign system a fair trial.

8. All children should be, for the first year at least, instructed in the oral system, those who show no potential should then be taught manually ...[27]

The commission's report had an interesting note on the education in the Cabra boy's school—"It is based more on signs and less on the manual alphabet than any school they had visited"—indicating the rare presence of real Sign Language in Ireland or Britain. The members of the commission tested the language attainments of the boys and reported that "the results were very good." An eleven-year-old-boy, asked by a member of the commission to describe an action in writing, wrote: "You are after drawing your nice watch out of your pocket."[28] The commission members described the buildings as

> very economically planned ... well built ... an excellent play shed and play field, a swimming bath and commodious workshops ... a good infirmary separate from the main institution ... Pupils have two and a half hours' instruction in trades daily and all day on Saturday. The boys begin trade schooling at 12 years.[29]

One of the members who signed the minority report, Rev. Charles Owen, afterwards wrote to the Cabra schools praising them for the

> efficiency and excellence of the teaching as well as to the completeness and effectiveness of the industrial training ... considering the institution the best he had

25. O'Dowd, "History of the Catholic Schools for the Deaf", p. 216.
26. O'Dowd, "History of the Catholic Schools for the Deaf", p. 215–216.
27. O'Dowd, "History of the Catholic Schools for the Deaf", p. 218–219.
28. O'Dowd, "History of the Catholic Schools for the Deaf", p. 133.
29. O'Dowd, "History of the Catholic Schools for the Deaf", p. 133.
30. O'Dowd, "History of the Catholic Schools for the Deaf", p. 218–221.

Breaking the Silence

ever visited ... particularly struck with the brightness and happiness manifested in the countenances of the children.[30]

The commission's recommendations for Ireland were:

1. That a grant should be given from the Imperial Exchequer of three fourths of the sum necessary for the education and maintenance and one fourth from the local authorities.

2. That there should be government inspection in all cases where a grant is given.

3. That it should be compulsory on the local authorities, on application of a parent, to contribute to the maintenance of any child of these classes in a suitable institution.

4. That education be denominational.

5. That as soon as properly qualified teachers of the deaf for the purpose can be obtained, pupils who have the remains of hearing or speech should be educated apart from those trained in a pure oral school; and that every child who is deaf should have the opportunity of being educated in the pure oral system.

The first school opened in Britain after the report took the middle ground and adopted Gallaudet's combined system, in spite of the fact that the directors were offered a private gift if it were made "pure oral".[31] Within a few years the authorities had implemented the recommendations on financing in England, Scotland and Wales but found one excuse after another for not doing so in the final thirty-one years of their administration of Ireland.

It would have been better for the deaf if the commission had never come into existence. It must be noted that the Irish Government in its own first thirty-one years of administration also neglected the issue and became involved only when forced to do so by the increasing costs resulting from the introduction of oralism.

*

The Battle of the Methods was conducted over the heads of the deaf, in the form of personal feuds among the teachers of the deaf in Europe and America. In Ireland it was the political campaigning of the Catholic bishops against the British government in their pursuit of control of education, rather than issues concerned with the education of the deaf, that held the stage.[32] Instead of settling the War of the Methods, both sides were given comfort in their trenches to go on fighting.

Except for Ireland, where the issue of the methods never saw the light of day, the outcome of Milan and the Royal Commission led within a decade to the tide going out for the signing deaf in the western world, not to return until it could do so in the aftermath of the civil rights struggles of the nineteen-sixties.

31. Lane, p. 367.

32. O'Dowd, "History of the Catholic Schools for the Deaf", p. 134–146.

3

Early Irish Endeavours

Ireland, being under British rule until 1922, conspicuously failed to benefit from the main developments in the French education system up to the middle of the nineteenth century. The power centres of church and state ensured that few French Enlightenment or republican ideas reached the ears of the masses or disturbed the unwholesome peace in Ireland. One spark of hope was the 1798 rebellion, led largely by the northern Presbyterians to try to gain more rights for Non-Conformists and Catholics. The United Irishmen had French republican assistance and were largely motivated by French and American aspirations for democracy; they were not supported to any significant extent by Catholic Church leaders or the Anglican ascendancy, who generally were terrified by the spectre of the lower classes usurping their positions of power and privilege.

In the specific matter of the education of the deaf it could be argued that the result of that period of political upheaval was a combination of the religious and political establishments that militated against any such new departures; and the defeat of Napoléon and the gradual rise of nationalism in Europe during the nineteenth century turned many countries against French ideas.

Claremont School and provision for minority religions

The Irish National Institution for the Deaf and Dumb, later called Claremont School, was the first school for the deaf in Ireland. It was opened in Dublin in 1816 by Dr Charles Orpen, and the governing body was composed of members of the colonial nobility of church and state. Considering that it had the word "national" in its title and that the British government's policy was to set up non-denominational national schools at the time, we may assume it was non-denominational. Understandably, the Catholic authorities did not take too kindly to it when they found that it encroached on the territory of their beliefs.

Orpen was forced to open his school without a trained teacher. He had naïvely hoped to get one, or permission to send a suitable person for training, from the Braidwood syndicate, which monopolised the schools for the deaf in Britain but was told by one of them that "he would not teach anyone without being well paid and without engagement not to teach anyone else for some years."[1] Some time later agreement was reached with Robert Kinniburg, an evangelist minister and a teacher trained by the Braidwoods whose bond period had expired. Obviously influenced by the Braidwood ethos, Kinniburg's terms were three months' tuition for a fee of £750 and a condition that Orpen's teacher swear never to give instruction to anyone who might set up a rival institution in Scotland.

Enrolment reached well over a hundred but was greatly reduced following the establishment of the school for the deaf in Belfast in 1831, and the Catholic schools in Cabra, which served the whole country. Claremont fell victim to the bitter skirmishing for control of education, and in its later years it catered only for the deaf in the Protestant population, whose numbers were dropping; and the school finally went out of existence in 1971. Today there is no provision for parents who do not want to send their deaf or hard-of-hearing child to one of the Catholic schools except for this option presented by the Department of Education:

> If their parents wish them to attend special schools under Protestant management, arrangements should be made to have Protestant children admitted to suitable schools in Northern Ireland or Britain. Alternatively they can attend Cabra or Stillorgan.[2]

I know a number who took the latter course; and though I never heard them complain, I doubt if they were pleased or that it would be their first choice if a non-denominational school were available. (None of the Protestants appear to have sought to use the courts to correct the anomaly caused by the demise of Claremont.) The present arrangement means that parents in the Dublin area who do not want to send their deaf child to a Catholic school must bear all the costs of sending him or her far from home or even out of the country, and the children must bear the trauma of seeing little of their home and family.

Claremont received no government financial support and was not recognised as a "special" national school. Although O'Dowd found that the school changed to oralism in the late eighteen-eighties,[3] we can only speculate what it had before that, and where the teachers learned their techniques. Was

1. Lane, *When the Mind Hears*, p. 440–441. Braidwood was the man who refused to tutor Thomas Gallaudet, which, as luck would have it, was the cause of diverting him to far better things.

2. Department of Education, *Education of Children who are Handicapped by Impaired Hearing*, p. 122.

3. O'Dowd, "History of the Catholic Schools for the Deaf".

it writing, or perhaps early ASL? The links between the Protestant ascendancies of Ireland and America were strong in those days.

In 1932 Claremont boasted that it was the only oral school in Ireland. It could be argued that oralism was the main cause of its demise, after being worn down by the rapid decline in the Protestant population in the south of Ireland following partition, the failure of oralism to meet the expectations of the parents (as with the Catholic schools at present), political and Government indifference, and the Babel of "Sign Languages" in Ireland.

O'Dowd's history of the Cabra schools

As O'Dowd noted, very little printed material was available on the history of the education of the deaf in Ireland, as few authors have ventured into this field and none of the schools have published their own history. O'Dowd's thesis gives a picture of the schools from the general viewpoint of the Dominicans, and the oralists in particular.

His material was obtained mainly in the archives of the Catholic Institution for the Deaf and directly from the Dominicans' girls' school in Cabra. It is packed with details and is invaluable for any researcher. It reflects and celebrates the Dominicans' belief at that time in the expected triumph of oralism and the demise of Sign Language. Nevertheless he recounts acceptable proof from at least three sources that the pre-oral Cabra schools were superior educationally to any of the British (oral) schools. As if he was bewitched, however, O'Dowd saw nothing illogical in the decision of the nuns to throw out what they acknowledged to be their superior system in preference to an inferior one. On the contrary, he lavishes praise on the oral system and seems convinced that it was the solution to the age-old "problem" of the deaf.

O'Dowd's research seems to have been confined to the archive rooms and the administrators' offices, overlooking the value of personal contacts with those most concerned. It is regrettable that he did not extend his research to the pupils of the day, especially since they were in the transition stage, having notched up some eight or nine years' experience at that time. The new teachers and the sacked deaf teachers likewise were ignored, though they must have had useful comments. And a glorious opportunity of comparing the teachers and pupils in the all-signing boys' school down the road with those of the oral school was, sadly, also missed.

Indeed O'Dowd also gives several gentle nudges to the Christian Brothers to follow the nuns' lead into oralism—which they did, two years later. Commenting on Claremont when it was on its last legs in 1955, with only five pupils, and no doubt echoing the Dominicans' opinion, as he consistently did, O'Dowd seems to display a certain smugness with his remark, "So much for Cabra's old *rivals*" (emphasis added).[4] These sentiments will surprise no-one with a knowledge of Irish society of the time, as illustrated forty years later by Father Des Wilson when he remarked on a radio programme: "This is one of the most clerically dominated places in Europe: in politics, in education ... Sectarianism doesn't come from the people, it comes from the people at the top."[5]

Cork School for the Deaf, 1822

A school for the deaf was opened in Cork in 1822, following a visit by two students from the Claremont school demonstrating their communicating skills.[6] Like Claremont, it was founded by a doctor, Patrick Kehoe, and it was co-educational. It had boarding for 20 pupils. During its twenty-four years of existence 73 pupils were admitted, 51 males and 22 females.

The Cork school has the honour of being one of the pioneers of vocational education, with training in practical skills. Twenty of its pupils were prepared for economic independence by being apprenticed to various trades. It closed for want (or more likely diversion) of funds in the same year that the Dominican school in Cabra opened.

There is no record of what system of communication was used for teaching, but it is not unreasonable to speculate that it was Epée's signing system or ASL. It was almost as easy to get to Paris as to Dublin from Cork in those days; a high proportion of priests in Munster had been educated in the Irish College in Paris,[7] which is only five minutes' walk from Epée's school.

The joint secretary of the school, Rev. T. R. England, had a brother a bishop in Charleston, South Carolina, which raises the possibility of a connection between the Cork school and ASL, then growing on the east coast of America. Large numbers of Irish people had moved to Charleston in the late eighteenth century.

The Cabra schools, 1846

The Cabra schools owe their genesis to the missionary zeal of Thomas McNamara, a member of the Congregation of Missioners (better known as the Vincentians), from his observation of the activities of the Claremont school. He was one of the founders of the Catholic Congregation of the Mission in Ireland in 1833 while he was a staff member of Castleknock College, and founded the Catholic Institution for the Deaf in 1845. He was put in charge of the Irish College in Paris when the Vincentians were given control there in 1858, following a fracas between rivals in the Cullen-MacHale conflict in Ireland.

---

4. O'Dowd, "History of the Catholic Schools for the Deaf", p. 193.

5. "Talk-Back", Radio Ulster, 21 Jan. 1995, 12–1 p.m.

6. O'Dowd, "History of the Catholic Schools for the Deaf", p. 12.

7. Tomás Ó Fiaich, *The Irish Colleges in France* (Veritas, Dublin, 1990), p. 16.

3 Early Irish Endeavours

On the board also was a fellow-Vincentian, Philip Dowley, a former dean and vice-president of St Patrick's College, Maynooth, and later superior of the Irish province of the Vincentian congregation. Since its opening in 1795, a number of émigrés had come to Maynooth from the Irish Colleges of Paris and Bordeaux, no doubt bringing with them knowledge of Epée's work for the deaf. The Vincentians are a French congregation, which McNamara and Dowley were instrumental in bringing to Ireland in the eighteen-thirties.

Some decades later, when his public statements were criticised because of complaints that his emphasis on religious instruction was hindering the education of the deaf, McNamara defended himself in a letter to all four Catholic archbishops by describing the experiences of his early days:

> I resided in the neighbourhood of a Protestant Institution which was carrying on a wholesale proselytism of the souls of our poor Catholic Deaf-mutes. Not content with poisoning their minds by lessons within the institution itself, the teachers took occasion from all things without to fill up their souls with hatred of the religion of their parents; and on a particular occasion when out for recreation, they halted before the church of which I had charge, St. Peter's, Phibsboro, and by fiendish gesticulation sought to impress on the poor creatures by pointing to the doors and then downwards, that all who entered the building should be damned. The occurrence filled my soul with reproach for the Catholic body: "why have we not an Institution for the Catholic Deaf and Dumb?" But what was I to do? I was not one to undertake such work; but at least I could speak of its necessity. I commenced to speak and soon found good and charitable souls.[8]

Ireland, with the Netherlands and Canada, formed part of a general Catholic effort to set up schools for the deaf in the eighteen-forties.[9] This movement saw education as primarily a matter of religious instruction and therefore an ecclesiastical prerogative, and partly as a contest for souls with the Protestants. Life in this world was looked on as a stop-over in preparation for the next. Everyone was a sinner: not even the children were spared.

The Catholic hierarchy, fearing for their flock within the new national primary education plan of 1831, were in the throes of their all-out and eventually successful campaign for denominational schools, under their own control. Thomas Davis, in the tradition of the United Irishmen, had this to say in the *Nation* in 1844 about the dichotomy forming in Irish education:

> The reasons for separate education are reasons for separate life, for mutual animosity, for penal laws, for religious wars ... Let those who insist on unqualified separate education follow out their principles ... Let them prohibit Catholic and Protestant boys from playing or talking or walking together ... Let them rail off each set into a separate quarter.[10]

Davis had a message for the downtrodden Irish of 150 years ago that was

8. O'Dowd, "History of the Catholic Schools for the Deaf", p. 12–13.

9. Hodgson, *The Deaf and Their Problems*, p. 221.

10. Séamus Ó Buachalla, *Education Policy in Twentieth-Century Ireland*, p. 19–48.

Breaking the Silence

taken up only in the nineteen-sixties and that could be the motto for the deaf of the nineteen-nineties: *Educate and be free.*

The Catholic Institution for the Deaf is officially under the patronage of the archbishops and bishops of Ireland. Oddly enough, the bishop of Cork favoured the idea of the central schools in Dublin serving the whole country, at a time when most people depended on horse transport and when a school already existed in Cork.[11] Following a publicity campaign by the CID in the newspapers[12] and a circular to the "nobility and gentry", McNamara reported that "money was coming in a tide." (This was at a time when the huge majority of the Catholic population could not afford to buy food even for their own survival and depended solely on the rarely unfaithful potatoes they grew themselves.) O'Dowd considered that the main objective of the founders was

> the imparting of Religious Knowledge ... Throughout the years there has been no falling off in the standards attained by the pupils in Christian Doctrine as the reports of the Diocesan Examiners show. It is the most important subject on the curriculum in the opinion of the teachers and children and no pains have been spared to make each new generation of deaf pupils closely acquainted with the truths of their faith.[13]

The CID, in keeping with tradition, decided on separate schools for boys and girls. The Dominican nuns willingly took responsibility for the girls' school in the grounds of their new convent girls' school in Cabra. This was a period when the Catholic teaching orders were expanding rapidly at home and abroad, forming networks of schools catering exclusively for Catholics. However, a boarding-school was something new for the Christian Brothers and did not fit into their scheme of things; but after much insistence by the CID and the intervention of Cardinal Cullen they accepted responsibility for the boys. The Female Deaf and Dumb Institution opened in 1846, with 15 pupils in the first year, and the Male Deaf and Dumb Institution was opened in 1857. In the nineteen-sixties the names were changed to St Mary's School for Hearing-Impaired Children[14] and St Joseph's School for Deaf Boys. Note that the new title of the girls' school gives the misleading meaning that it is a co-educational school, especially to people outside Ireland. The invariable use of the masculine pronouns gives it an additional tilt in that direction.

Their approach to the education of the deaf was modelled on a system used at the school for the deaf in the Institut du Bon Sauveur of Caen in France. The Caen school was set up in 1817 by the Abbé Pierre-François Jamet, initially to teach his cousin, a deaf girl. He used a signing method that he picked up on a short visit to Epée's school in Paris; he spent only a matter of hours observing the method practised there and went on from that to invent his own system, described as a "manual pronunciation of words", ignoring Sicard's advice that he should have at least one year of training (in

---

11. O'Dowd, "History of the Catholic Schools for the Deaf", p. 12a.

12. O'Dowd, "History of the Catholic Schools for the Deaf", p. 15.

13. O'Dowd, "History of the Catholic Schools for the Deaf", p. 139–140.

14. The euphemistic title of "hearing-impaired" is now being quietly dropped. Griffey refers to it as St Mary's School for the Deaf in her book.

15. O'Dowd, p.54. Curiously, if the account in the *Encyclopedia Britianica* (1989) is true, Sicard had at that time rejected Sign Language: "Although he long supported teaching the deaf through sign language, he

the signing method) before he could hope to teach successfully.[15]

Considering that the Dominicans had available the ASL that was then flourishing in America, one wonders why they should choose an obscure version of a system based on a foreign language for their means of communication. The answer can be found in the culture of the period, in the influence of the French émigrés in the founding of Maynooth and a mistrust of anything that lacked the singularity of Catholicism and an acceptance of anything that did. The Cabra methodical sign system, from the deaf community's perspective, was an almost entirely foreign invention, in every sense of the word. Its dead, mechanical rules frustrated the internal free human spirit of creation available in the more natural communicating social conditions of signers.

The Christian Brothers' initial first-hand experience with signing was the one they learned in the girls' school. However, they read extensively on the subject and in their first annual report to the CID had the highest praise for the *Course of Instruction* published by the New York Institution. O'Dowd notes: "It seems likely from this that the system of the New York Institute influenced the brothers in their subsequent work."[16]

The Brothers requested finance from the CID to travel for first-hand experience of Sign Language, but they were given the choice only of going to England and France, which they did not accept, and they had to be content with the next-to-impossible task of learning ASL from books. (It is interesting to note that trainee teachers in Northern Ireland are now reduced to a similar fare: they must do their study through correspondence course.) We shall never know why this opportunity was passed up. Perhaps if, in those days of deference and rigid hierarchical control, the boys' school was represented by a priest, as the girls' school was, they would have had more clout in the CID scheme of things; certainly in the listing of members of the board the Brother was at the bottom. Nevertheless the Brothers seem to have had better results educationally than the nuns,[17] contrary to the experience in hearing schools, where female pupils usually outshine the boys.

In fact because of the absence of records of the past pupils from the early nineteenth century one can only speculate on the form of signing used in the boys' school. Stan Foran, however, gives an interesting insight into the boys' school of the nineteen-forties and fifties.[18]

One language for the girls and another for the boys

The adoption of some of the New York signing in the boys' school only is seen as a cause of one of the most extraordinary educational developments in Irish social history, where the boys and girls from the same social group and

turned to the oral method before the end of his career." The *E.B.* account is at odds with Lane's, and like most media accounts, is obviously taken from an oralist source.

16. O'Dowd, "History of the Catholic Schools for the Deaf", p. 65.

17. O'Dowd, "History of the Catholic Schools for the Deaf", p. 65.

18. See appendix H.

19. The linguist and anthropologist Barbara LeMaster of the Medical School of the University of California at Los Angeles made a study of the different vocabularies used by the men and women for her PhD dissertation, "The Maintenance and Loss of Female and Male Signs

sometimes from the same family were taught different languages.[19] Furthermore, parents were not taught either of the Sign Languages, as Griffey tells us in 1967: "In my long experience in the manual school I have never known a hearing parent who was able to communicate manually with a child,"[20] and again in 1994, commenting on the deaf girls after they finished school in the pre-oral era: "It was known from experience that those who returned to the rural areas deteriorated because people were unable to communicate with them."[21]

By 1857 the girls' school had accommodation for 50 boarders, and by 1876 total enrolment of the two schools had reached 423. Numbers dropped to around 320 during the Second World War but came back up to 390 in 1954, though this was partly due to the lowering of the entry age from seven to three on the introduction of oralism in the girls' school.[22]

Because of the recurring political and religious friction between church and state, under both British and Irish rule, it took over a hundred years for the schools to establish formal relations with government departments regarding funding. Professor LeMaster postulates:

> The Department of Education was eager to participate in the schools' administration because the schools had earned an international reputation for the pupils' superb written English proficiency.[23]

In this period the schools survived largely on charity and on the dedication of the nuns and Brothers, who gave their services free, as well as on underpaid lay and deaf teachers. It is interesting to note that when these services came to an end the new qualified teachers had to be paid above the standard national rates to overcome what was described as the "acute staffing difficulties" and "abnormally high turnover of teachers" in the nineteen-sixties.[24]

The religious orders and nineteenth-century Irish society

Training people for leadership has been one of the principal missions of the Christian church since its early days; and when industries and commerce were forcing the pace for increased numbers of educated people for all sorts of tasks, the church in Ireland felt that this too was its domain. It undertook the organisation of education, not because education was good in itself but because it found that it could not do its own missionary work unless its flock had enough learning to read religious tracts. Little consideration was given to the principle of instructing the young in preparation for the needs of ordinary life.

The religious orders set out in the early nineteenth century to seize

---

Sidenotes:

in the Dublin Deaf Community in the late 1980s". See also LeMaster, "When Women and Men Talk Differently", p. 133–134.

20. Griffey, "Speech Methodology at St Mary's School for the Deaf" (see appendix A). Note the use of the inappropriate term "manual" for the signing means of communication, with its derogatory overtones.

21. Griffey, *From Silence to Speech*, p. 50.

22. O'Dowd, "History of the Catholic Schools for the Deaf", p. 78–85.

23. LeMaster, "When Women and Men Talk Differently", p. 134–135.

24. Department of Education, *Education of Children who are Handicapped by Impaired Hearing*, p. 136. See also "Speech Methodology at St Mary's School for the Deaf" (appendix A),

control of education from the government and local authorities of the day, and they acquired the deaf in mid-century. Nobody seems to have questioned the wisdom of literally locking up the female deaf children of the country in one school under the control of single female clerics and likewise the male deaf children of the country in another school under the control of single male clerics—although there were widespread protests at the breaking up of families in the male and female workhouses of the time. O'Dowd's research shows that children were lucky if they got home to their family once a year.

The Dominican nuns, who were given charge of the girls, had a tradition of teaching children on and off for over seven hundred years, while the Congregation of Christian Brothers, which had charge of the boys, was founded only some decades earlier. None of them had any experience in the work they took on; and although special schools for the deaf in a more conventional environment were well established in France, and even better ones in America, their guidance was not sought.

The nuns themselves came generally from families with a strong insular religious bias and were enlisted in their adolescent years. On entering they took vows never again to discuss their feelings and personal problems except with their superiors and not to socialise with the public or enter a family home, not even to attend the funeral of their own parents. They had to set aside their own names, the most crucial aspect of personal identity, in order to repress their past. Personal relationships were forbidden. Movement from convent to convent was by coach or limousine with the curtains drawn. Until 1967 they were not allowed to leave the convent grounds without permission from the bishop. A year later they were allowed to spend up to seven nights a year in their family home.

The nuns' education was more a form of training or indoctrination than a true learning experience. We know they were rarely seen in any "progressive" camp, aside from the crusading work of Griffey to change the deaf education system from signing to oralism, lovingly described in her book, with its evocative title *From Silence to Speech*. When the first Intermediate Examinations were introduced in 1878, the head of the Dominican secondary school in Galway wrote to the bishop complaining that "public examinations are repugnant"; he replied that

> at the outset, I instinctively recoil from the idea of having girls subjected to public examinations ... How is the evil resulting from it to be avoided? ... I would at once say unhesitatingly: have nothing to do with them.[25]

This ban was lifted in 1895, the same year in which Maria Montessori became the first woman doctor in Italy. It is reasonable to speculate that the works of Montessori or those of other educational subversives such as Patrick Pearse,

where Griffey's description of the "ideal opportunities" in her school is in sharp contrast with the situation noted in the 1972 report.

25. Rose O'Neill, *A Rich Inheritance: Galway Dominicans, 1644–1994* p. 115.

John Dewey or Sigmund Freud were not in the nuns' library. In this respect, it is regrettable that Griffey did not include a bibliography in her book to give some idea of the writers who influenced her. There was a bias towards following the traditional pathways, with warnings of the dangers to look out for rather than exploring the excitement of learning by experience.

Nuns reached adulthood without learning the value of everyday experiences or forming the habit of suspending final judgement until they had weighed up all the evidence available, reviewing their opinions whenever more information came along.[26] Many seemed to lack the humble capacity to doubt and to contest all preconceptions. Their consciences operated on judgements that they accepted from their parents and authorities when they were too young to question them: they judged on the basis of their own training, background, and limited experience.

The Dominicans were focused on educating and moulding young girls from the upper layers of society, from "respectable" families, to fit into their "place" as future dutiful wives of the commercial and professional classes. They lived out their lives in a world of their own, isolated from society except for professionally dealing with their strictly disciplined pupils and the occasional visit from a pupil's parent.

Religious beliefs have the potential to drive people to extremes and lose sight of reality. O'Dowd, for instance, found that nothing took precedence over the religious aspect of the nuns' work for the deaf. Indeed, there is a strong trace of a Dominican propagationary spirit right through Cabra's history. But what is good for the Dominicans is not necessarily good for the deaf.

The Christian Brothers, on the other hand, had more modest ambitions. They catered for the bottom layers of society, building their schools in the poorest centres of population. Although they were greatly restrained in their social contact with the public, they could at least see the conditions of people as they walked the streets between the monastary, the school and the hurling field, and occasionally converse with laymen. The Brothers had no boarding-schools until they were prevailed on by Archbishop Cullen of Dublin to accept the boys' school for the deaf. In their educational net they gave children an opportunity that they almost certainly would not otherwise have received.

These religious orders were a legacy of the monasteries of feudal times, mindlessly copied in the nineteenth century as sanctuaries for the surplus members of families wrestling with the consequences of agrarian changes and the Industrial Revolution. Their ethos was developed in the wave of new philanthropic institutions: hospitals, schools, reformatories, and various other houses of refuge or asylums, as they were called. Experience has shown that

26. See Luddy, *Women and Philanthropy in Nineteenth-Century Ireland*, p. 32–54, and Thackeray, *Irish Sketch Book*, p. 71–79.

many of their assumptions, since swept aside by the more enlightened attitudes of the present century, were simplistic and idealistic. Recent research in fact shows that their attempts to "rescue" the weak and destitute often prolonged the agony and hindered political debate and movement, particularly by women.[27] One notable witness at the turn of the century criticised the role of charity:

> But this is not a solution: it is an aggravation of the difficulty. The proper aim is to try and reconstruct society on such a basis that poverty will be impossible. And the altruistic virtues have really prevented the carrying out of this aim. Just as the worst slave-owners were those who were kind to their slaves, and so prevented the horror of the system being realized by those who suffered from it, and understood by those who contemplated it, so, in the present state of things in England, the people who do most harm are the people who try to do most good ... Such charity degrades and demoralizes ... Charity creates a multitude of sins.[28]

*

Both the nuns and the Brothers were captives of that culture and society and were restrained from doing anything about it by their vows of loyalty to the church. It took the demonstrators in the streets of Paris and Selma—people almost from another planet—to break their chains.

One can easily imagine how the Dominican nuns in their socially isolated world were themselves taken in by the propaganda of the oralists. The oralists had the field of education to themselves in America and Europe at the time the Dominicans plunged into their uncharted waters.

---

27. Luddy, *Women and Philanthropy in Nineteenth-Century Ireland*.

28. Oscar Wilde, "The Soul of Man Under Socialism", *Fortnightly Review*, Feb. 1891; *Collected Works* (Collins, London, 1966), p. 1079. Wilde's father, Sir William Wilde, a distinguished Dublin eye and ear specialist, was the medical officer for the Cabra schools and carried out the first survey on the incidence of deafness in Ireland.

4

Recent Developments in Ireland

We burn with a desire to find a solid ground and an ultimate sure foundation whereon to build a tower reaching to the infinite. But our groundwork cracks, and the earth opens to abysses.

Blaise Pascal

Practically all the significant events of the last hundred years in the world of the deaf revolve around the introduction of oralism in the middle of the present century. This change was partly a measure to deal with the social isolation of deaf people resulting from the way the schools were run up to that time. Cabra was the odd one out internationally in deaf education, in that it was the only centre that had not adopted oralism. The conventional wisdom of the period was that "integration" would result if the deaf were trained to speak, and it was believed that the best way to achieve this was to use speech as the means of communication in the schools. Early detection and early intervention—fitting a hearing aid to a child, even at the age of six months, early home training in speech, and an early start at school—were seen as some of the essential conditions for the success of the scheme.

The Cabra establishment

The Cabra schools saw little of the outside world in their first century of existence. Neither did the outside world see or know much about the schools. School business was conducted through its patron institution, the Catholic Institution for the Deaf. There was no direct contact, for instance, between the girls' school and the Department of Education until 1952. Families with a deaf child kept as quiet as possible about it: deviation from the norm was subject to social sanction. Ireland was exceptionally endowed with a culture and institutions that kept this sort of thing out of sight and out of mind.

The advent of oralism of necessity called for massive Government financing. It also called for publicity to sell the scheme. A range of specialist professionals—speech therapists, audiologists, otologists, educators, civil servants, and rehabilitation experts—had to be engaged to play a part in the scheme. It has now grown into a complex network of elements in the form of a self-perpetuating system. Each profession concentrates on its own sphere of expertise, much like the different trades on a building project—but the analogy stops there. On a building site everyone involved has a good idea how the finished product will turn out, and the customer usually knows exactly what they want and has the benefit of statutory regulations and inspectors to look after their interests.

The professionals did not socialise in the deaf community, so they had no first-hand experience of the required result. They were led by the Dominican nuns, who were cut off from the experience of ordinary social life, let alone the social life of the deaf community. The nuns adopted an ideology founded on the assumption that deafness is a medical infirmity and that oralism would integrate the deaf into society. A measure of the influence of its power is that the semi-medical term "educational treatment" became part of the vocabulary of the educators of the deaf.[1] The synthesis of the experts formed what I have called the Cabra establishment; from this was born a whole family of entities, as detailed in the 1972 report of the Department of Education and in Griffey's book, *From Silence to Speech*.

Most doctors involved in the field were ear specialists and invariably attended only to the ears and not the whole person; and, as with the oralists, one seeks in vain for evidence of any ear specialist being involved in the deaf community. Each professional lauds the other's narrowly based expertise in isolation; and opposing opinions, if they ever appear, are seen as unwarranted criticism.[2] One-third of the Department of Education twelve-member Committee on the Education of the Hearing-Impaired of 1972 were doctors, and half were committed oralists, in the form of teachers and parents, including a founder-member of the National Deaf Children's Society (a British parents' oralist movement). It is obvious from the introduction to the committee's report that the department officials involved were there to learn about and to accept oralism.

Fair weather for reform

After a shaky start, oralism struck fair weather following the nineteen-fifties, when the boys' school conformed. The financial floodgates for education opened up in the nineteen-sixties; postwar prosperity allowed the spread of

1. Griffey, "From a Pure Manual Method via the Combined Method to the Oral-Auditory Technique" (see appendix D).

2. When I suggested at a parents' meeting that we should meet deaf past pupils for discussion and obtain their opinions on education, I was met with a stony silence.

Breaking the Silence

education generally and with it the birth of the new career-minded middle class. Parents in that bracket with a deaf child were demanding a better future for their child and were easy targets for the purveyors of high expectations.

Developments in electronics during and immediately after the Second World War yielded precision audio testing instruments and high-fidelity hearing aids. The surge of scientific progress gave oralism a new lease of life when education of the deaf was in the doldrums. The developments aroused the imagination of leading oralists: for instance, Father van Uden of the Institute of the Deaf at Sint-Michielsgestel in the Netherlands had the benefit of the pioneering work of the neighbouring research laboratories of Philips Electrical. Equally active were the Ewings of Manchester University and the oralism promotion organisations such as the Royal National Institution of the Deaf in Britain and the Alexander Graham Bell Association for the Deaf in the United States.

Medical science was also making great strides, and expectations for the deaf were high.[3] The media carried impressive news from these sources of new "breakthroughs" with powerful hearing aids, and the message of the oralists was getting through to the parents of young deaf children: oralism was the solution, and signing was a thing of the past,[4] except for the "dull" and the multi-handicapped. Success was just around the corner.

The chickens, unfortunately, were being counted before the eggs were hatched. The problem with these scientific developments is that they were not scientifically tested: one does not know if an education programme is satisfactory until the person has reached their twenties or thirties.

The Dominicans' fact-finding tour

In 1946, on the occasion of the centenary of the founding of the Dominican school, the nuns, with the approval of the Catholic Institute for the Deaf, went on a tour of twelve oral schools in England and Scotland in an effort to upgrade the education system in the girls' school. Sister Peter Flynn reported:

> In one of the two Catholic Schools there are five Irish children ... These children are fortunately in a Catholic School but there are many Irish Catholic children in the London Protestant Schools. Many parents, especially educated parents, are seeking lip-reading and speech training for their children, and we believe that the time has come when we must offer such a training to Irish Catholic children in their own country ... This is necessary if we are to stop the flow of Irish children to deaf schools in England and Scotland ...[5]

It would appear from this that the decision taken in response to the educated parents who were asking for training in speech and lip-reading was to offer them just that. One wonders if they expected to retain their capacity

---

3. As they are today with the latest "breakthrough", the cochlear implant. The president of the RNID, Lord Ashley, is quoted as wanting it "so that every child born deaf will hear their mother's voice—and learn to speak."

4. Articles in *Time*, 29 Jan. 1965, and *Irish Press*, 26 and 27 Jan. 1969.

5. Griffey, *From Silence to Speech*, p. 155.

6. Griffey, "Speech Methodology at St Mary's School for the Deaf" (see appendix A).

to deliver on general education while this was going on.

In the early days of speech instruction at St. Mary's emphasis was placed on the phonetic aspect. The approach was analytic, and the sounds of speech were taught in a definite order. The practice now is to build speech on the spontaneous efforts of the child.[6]

Perhaps, therefore, teaching was combined with speech training to such an extent that oralism resulted unintentionally, almost by accident. On the vital matter of general education, a prerequisite for human development as well as religious instruction, the girls' signing school in Cabra, from O'Dowd's comment, seemed to be put in the lap of the gods:

Here we must quote the report *verbatim*: "From what we observed in the schools, we are obliged to state, in the interest of truth, that the general educational standard in St. Mary's ... is far superior to any school we have seen."[7]

In fact the report acknowledged that Sign Language is so much easier than lip-reading,[8] and yet it said the introduction of oralism would make it possible for the school to become a leading centre for the education of the deaf. The report also acknowledges that, like their American counterparts in the first half of the last century, the nuns did not give speech training: "We failed to make use of the degree of hearing of the partially deaf."

If they are old enough to use sign language before they learn to lip-read it is very difficult to teach them because Sign Language is so much easier than lip-reading.[9]

This shows that they were aware that their own signing system, with all its faults, was superior educationally to oralism. I found no account of this crucial piece of information until I came across it in my research for this book.

O'Dowd tells us that the nuns got CID approval for carrying out the survey and that they reported their findings to them. The next thing we are told is that it "was decided" to change over to oralism. There is nothing about who did the deciding. The members of the board of the CID in 1946 were: Archbishop McQuaid (presiding); five parish priests; the chaplain, representing the girls' school; the head Brother from the boys' school; a former and a future Taoiseach in the persons of William Cosgrave and his son Liam; and a gentleman from the legal profession. O'Dowd provides no evidence of any public debate on the arguments for and against such a momentous policy change. Indeed there appears to have been no co-ordination in the 150 years of the Cabra schools among any of the partners involved in the education of the deaf in Ireland.[10] The boys' school is only a few minutes' walk from the girls' school; perhaps the CID believed they could eliminate the need for consultation and win over the signing Brothers with a minimum of conflict by the expected success of the oralism option.

7. O'Dowd, "History of the Catholic Schools for the Deaf", p. 228. This report is reproduced by Griffey, *From Silence to Speech*, p. 155–157, but reads somewhat differently from the version given by O'Dowd, who underlines the word *verbatim*.

8. Griffey, *From Silence to Speech*, p. 156.

9. Griffey, *From Silence to Speech*, p. 156.

10. This accounts for the multiplicity of signing systems in Ireland—our home-grown tower of Babel. One unfortunate result is that Catholics and Protestants have different signing systems, although many are now adept in both.

Oralism for the boys' school

When the pressure for oralism was building up from the girls' school in the nineteen-forties, the Brothers carried out their own research in 1948. They toured nineteen oral schools in Britain (in fact all the British schools could be described as oral, though most of them used some signs); and this is what they reported:

> The teachers used no signs and didn't know the sign language alphabet ... In some schools sign language was not allowed ... In a few schools that had special classes for oral failures teachers and pupils using finger-spelling. During recreation they all used sign language ... It is the boast of the oralists that they can make pupils speak like ordinary people ... we got intelligible speech only from those who had hearing or had lost their hearing. The attempt of the congenital deaf to speak was very poor indeed, while their written work was far below Cabra. Some with 4 or 5 years' school could not write "had" or "watch" while boys of 16 could not answer simple questions in writing. The results were better where they had sign language ... Signs seem to be their natural means of giving expression to their ideas.[11]

And so in 1948 they decided to continue with what they were satisfied was the superior system, in a form of combined communication that they had adopted in 1932.[12] Stan Foran, a pupil of the period, has described the pedagogy as a form of bilingualism,[13] a system that is now showing remarkable results in Sweden and Denmark.[14] In contrast to the Dominican nuns, who had very limited contact with society outside the convent grounds, the Brothers' decision was no doubt influenced by their involvement with the education of children from the same social level as working deaf adults; they were more in tune with the relevant facts of the situation. It showed clearly that educating the deaf through oralism had little value for the adult deaf.

Despite all this they changed to oralism in 1957, following an *expressed request* from Archbishop McQuaid of Dublin in 1952.[15] The building of a preparatory boarding and day school for deaf boys up to the age of ten—accommodating fourteen and seventy-eight, respectively—at Beech Park in Stillorgan, Dublin, in the middle fifties at the request of the same archbishop was persuasion they could not resist, as they would have to provide for the boys' continuing education.[16] One commendable feature of the new school was its capacity to serve the south side of Dublin; but why cater only for boys? It certainly did not make it easier for those families with both a deaf boy and a deaf girl.

Audiological clinics

Professor Alexander Ewing, in a lecture at Manchester University, boasted of

---

11. O'Dowd, "History of the Catholic Schools for the Deaf", p. 233.

12. O'Dowd, "History of the Catholic Schools for the Deaf", p. 227.

13. See appendix H.

14. Mahshie, *Educating Deaf Children Bilingually*.

15. O'Dowd, "History of the Catholic Schools for the Deaf", p. 235.

16. O'Dowd, "History of the Catholic Schools for the Deaf", p. 175.

his wife and himself that "on one occasion we saw five hundred [children] in one month."[17] He saw audio testing as the fulfilment of a dream for oralism, a panacea for deafness and the education of the deaf; early detection followed by the fitting of a hearing aid, preferably to the three-month-old child, was expected to do wonders.

An unsavoury feature of the audiological clinics is the hierarchy of categories of deafness given to children. The following are the new audiological terms and decibels for levels of deafness adopted by the British Association of Teachers of the Deaf (1981, amended 1985):

AVERAGE HEARING LOSS	—
PRELINGUAL HEARING LOSS	—
SLIGHTLY HEARING-IMPAIRED	**20 – 30 dB**
MODERATELY HEARING-IMPAIRED	**30 – 60 dB**
SEVERELY HEARING-IMPAIRED	**60 – 85 dB**
PROFOUNDLY HEARING-IMPAIRED	**OVER 90 dB**

The concept of categories has undertones of social status, because it fixes the good speech communicator at the top and the imperfect at the bottom. When people ask me how deaf my son is and I reply that we can speak to each other on the phone when the line is good, they invariably say, "Oh, he's not so bad at all." False and unfounded beliefs were circulated, such as that a deaf child's ability to hear music and to dance to it was held to be an indication of potential for speech.

Detection is not so urgent for children who get the opportunity of Sign Language. A few ordinary commonsense tests by the parents will give a passable result: all one wants to know is whether the child hears ordinary household talk and noise. If not, the child and the family need to consider the alternative of signing, and the child should be tested for a suitable hearing aid so that they can acquire native sign and English at the same time, and as much of both as possible.

Teacher training

The schools for the deaf run by Epée and Gallaudet trained their own teachers and introduced deaf teachers immediately. They were remarkably successful, considering that education of the deaf was in its infancy. Many of the pupils of these schools went on to open up and run their own schools. Training in Sign Language teaching is, according to authorities on the subject, a process that takes several years to reach fluency. Only those immersed in a deaf adult community can become proficient in it. It follows that the nuns, who were insistent on using the methodical signs with those in their care rather than the pupils' natural sign language, could never be fluent

17. Ewing, *Proceedings of Conference,* p. 2.

Breaking the Silence

in Sign Language, while in contrast, from the evidence of the Royal Commission inspection in the eighteen-eighties, the boys' school had gone some distance in the evolution of Sign Language.[18]

Sign Language learning is not a subject that fits into the surroundings of Irish universities, divorced as they are from the natural environment of the deaf. The teacher training in Cabra before the arrival of oralism was, however, very far from ideal, because of the strict segregation of the boys from the girls, both physically and linguistically, and the obsession of the establishment with artificial sign languages.

The first few oralist teachers for the three Dublin schools for the deaf were trained in a one-year course in the Department of Audiology and Education of the Deaf at Manchester University in the nineteen-forties and fifties. This department was run by Ewing and his wife. He had come into the field of deaf education in January 1919 and progressed to the position of head of the department and knighthood for his dedication to the deaf. Like most oralists, he had no first-hand experience of being deaf nor any detailed experience of deaf family or community life—plenty of professional-client nine-to-five experience but none at all of everyday life. The Ewings were foremost in cultivating the oralism culture throughout Britain from the twenties. Their pamphlets were written in an assertive style, promoting the idea of speech training, and were published by the National Deaf Children's Society. Their official magazine gives the clear-cut speech message with its title of *Talk*. The literature was circulated to agencies that had the task of serving the deaf: medical institutions and public health and educational departments of central and local government. The Ewings were pioneers in the development of such services as the peripatetic teachers, parent guidance, pre-school training, and educating the public. They are credited with giving considerable support, guidance and assistance to the Dominican nuns in setting up the course in UCD in the Diploma for Teachers of the Deaf[19]; in fact most of the Dominicans' undertakings for the deaf since the forties follow the British model.

The priests who run the Institute for the Deaf at Sint-Michielsgestel in the Netherlands are also credited with much assistance to Cabra: "many Irish educators and administrators have benefited greatly from visits to this famous Dutch school."[20] Speaking as Emeritus Professor at Manchester University in 1969, Ewing referred to the Dutch school:

> In schools for the deaf that I have known, periods of great achievement have always synchronised with work towards one great objective—teaching the dumb to talk ... I will refer again to Sint-Michielsgestel ... A large stone tablet, near the main entrance there, established the main purpose of the school ... The inscription ... concludes

18. O'Dowd, "History of the Catholic Schools for the Deaf", p. 226.

19. Department of Education, *Education of Children who are Handicapped by Impaired Hearing*, p. 175.

20. Department of Education, *Education of Children who are Handicapped by Impaired Hearing*, p. 175.

with the quotation in Latin from St Mark's Gospel "He maketh both the deaf to hear and the dumb to speak" ... How this is carried out today at Sint-Michielsgestel we heard and saw ... Boys and girls ... relied completely on spoken language ... we did not see a single instance of finger spelling or signing by staff or "normally deaf" pupils ... In all the classes we saw very happy, lively children ... Profoundly deaf children were talking in sentences, often spontaneous ...[21]

The UCD teacher training course was set up and headed by Sister Nicholas Griffey in 1957. On her retirement another former teacher of the deaf from Cabra, Brother McGettrick, was appointed. During my research of their library, in 1995, I found approximately 130 books in the section on education of the deaf. Roughly 98 per cent of the books encouraged oralism. Only graduates from this nursery (which is open only to hearing people) are recognised as qualified teachers or assistant teachers of the deaf by the Department of Education. This service is also being used to train oralist teachers for other countries.[22] It is ironic that UCD and the Department of Education adopted oralism at a time when research by American educationalists was showing up its inherent faults.

The visiting teacher service and mainstreaming

The visiting teacher service was part of the early intervention scheme set up to assist parents in preparing the child for an oral education. It appears that it was introduced in 1961 to support the newly introduced system of mainstreaming, or "integration", as it is called. The visiting teachers have little or no experience in signed English and none at all in Sign Language. The service flies in the face of the philosophy of the deaf community on education of the deaf. (Mainstreaming is examined in more detail in chapter 6.)

Rationale for the changeover to oralism

The following are some of the reasons that have been put forward over the last half century for the changeover to oralism in Cabra.

Precision of thought is only possible where there is speech. This was the principle of Heinicke, the founder of the Prussian oral school in Leipzig. As O'Dowd noted, both Archbishop McQuaid and the nuns were careful to heed what St Paul had said: "So then faith cometh by hearing, and hearing by the word of God" (Romans 10:17); the Dominican nuns reached this conviction later, and it was one of the main arguments that induced them to start oral training.[23] Griffey restated this belief in her lecture to the Second International Catholic Conference on Religious Education of the Hearing-Impaired in Manchester in 1980: "We should never assume that signs and mime convey accurate meanings to them. There is no substitute for verbalisation."[24]

21. Ewing, *Proceedings of the Conference*, p. 6–7.

22. Griffey, *From Silence to Speech*, p. 68–69.

23. O'Dowd, "History of the Catholic Schools for the Deaf", p. 216.

24. *Proceedings of the Second International Catholic Conference on Religious Education of the Hearing-Impaired, Manchester, 1980*, p. 122.

There is plenty of evidence that this judgement may not be true from the experiences in the heyday of deaf education in America in the middle of the last century, when deaf teachers actually set up schools for the deaf, and the argument is coming to the fore again, both in America and Europe, since the rebirth of deaf education through signing in the nineteen-sixties. The expertise in English and in the practice of their religion obtained by those educated through signing in the Cabra boys' school before the imposition of oralism also disproves this belief. The fluency in written English of the editor of *Contact,* Stan Foran, and his brother Chris, is a specific example.

To overcome social isolation. "A manual world is a silent one. It causes social isolation, especially in Ireland where a comparatively small population is spread over a wide geographical area."[25] LeMaster in her field research in Dublin in the late nineteen-eighties found some evidence that the opposite is true in particular instances.

It was clear that the use of sign-language in the schools for the deaf and hearing people de-emphasised the disability aspect of deafness for older members of this population, whereas oralism emphasised disability.[26]

The official magazine of the National Association for the Deaf, reported on a seminar on the "Problems of the Deaf" in 1971, after a generation of oralism, when the oralist professionals had advised the deaf who had jobs not to move to Dublin:

Based on the economics of everyday living this is a sound proposition but the deaf delegates felt that there was a lot more to life ... [They felt] isolated ... in the country ... and cut off and preferred to move to Dublin.[27]

Oralism tends to reinforce the negative aspects of deafness, because the deaf person is not using the natural gifts available to them. In the same way I have often felt deficient in the company of a deaf group because I have no Sign Language. Sign Language, on the other hand, is a positive force that unites the deaf and is bridging the gap with hearing people. Deaf people in a Sign Language environment, with or without hearing people, do not have isolation problems: the problems arise when their own family or the people they associate with have not got or are hostile to Sign Language.

Contradictions seem to be an inherent characteristic of the world of the deaf. For instance, in the signing era not even the families of deaf people knew any sign, yet now in the oral era there are flocks of hearing people all over the country going to signing classes. Like most of the reasons given for adapting oralism, this one was based on an unverified supposition by people whose hearts are in the ideal hearing world.

Parents who were becoming more expressive in their views asked for it.[28] As a parent, I know what it is like to be told that Ireland had the best system of

25. Griffey, "From a Pure Manual Method via the Combined Method to the Oral-Auditory Technique" (see appendix D).

26. LeMaster, "When Women and Men Talk Differently", p. 107.

27. *Link,* summer 1971.

28. Griffey, "From a Pure Manual Method via the Combined Method to the Oral-Auditory Technique" (see appendix D).

education, and, like most other parents, I believed it. Since the forties the oralists have had the field of education to themselves; enquiries to any of the leading national authorities, principally the RNID in England and the Alexander Graham Bell Association for the Deaf in America, drew upon us sanctimonious advice on how to "deal" with our deaf child, the "educational treatment" available, and how to help him to speak and become "normal".

The Dominican nuns also were no doubt influenced by, and willingly accepted, a popular ideology that was promoted by the British aristocracy and that did not threaten their own privileged position. They launched a campaign of "educating" the public on what Cabra were doing for the deaf. Parents and children were given expectations far beyond what was humanly possible to achieve. The Dominicans were in the privileged position of being accountable only to themselves, as acknowledged by Griffey: "Since there was no involvement on the part of the Department of Education we were free to make plans for development of an oral atmosphere in the school,"[29] while the Department of Education footed the bill.

They can communicate more effectively with hearing professionals who work with the deaf ... they know deafness from the inside, as it were.[30] This reason for changing is a logical outcome of the first one and shows the danger of building a proposition on a false premise. More importantly, it is a means of forging an alliance with those deaf who are considered to be the new role models in the deaf world, to fortify and form the front line of defence of the oralist stronghold. It is similar to the idea held and enforced by the Spanish colonisers of America when Carlos II ordered that the "Indians" learn Spanish "because of the benefit it would bring in dealing with those in power." [31]

This policy has produced an unpleasant divide between the deaf who try to make it socially in the hearing world and those who are happier in the company of signing people, be they hearing or deaf. The oralism policy replaced a divide between the sexes caused by their differing signing systems with one of speakers versus signers; worse still, there are some deaf people who sign and speak but cannot make up their minds which side to take.

Speech obviously is convenient for the professionals for communication with pupils on the deafness-hearing borderline; but these account for fewer than 10 per cent of the deaf. One wonders if it means that the feedback from these is valued more than those who cannot speak. But when the chips are down, the teachers fall back on some form of signing,[32] even in the pure oral school. The teachers' own classroom experiences alone are enough to throw this reason overboard. This raises the suspicion that the teachers were not really fluent in Sign Language in the signing era. This is understandable in view of the fact that they insisted on communicating in class by methodical

29. Griffey, *From Silence to Speech*, p. 47.

30. Griffey, "From a Pure Manual Method via the Combined Method to the Oral-Auditory Technique" (see appendix D).

31. Lane, *When the Mind Hears*, p. 284.

32. Examples of oralist teachers using signs are given by Griffey, "From a Pure Manual Method via the Combined Method to the Oral-Auditory Technique" (see appendix D): "I must confess that we teachers relied on it occasionally when we wanted to convey a message quickly," and "When an important message had to be given it was signed and written."

Breaking the Silence

signs: it is unlikely that they used Sign Language with the pupils outside the classroom and methodical signs in the classroom. If that is true the nuns had no chance of learning much Sign Language and therefore are condemning it without giving it a fair trial. Unfortunately the term "sign language" has been used so loosely that we may never know the answer. Griffey's account of her classroom experience would appear to sustain the hypothesis:

> As a young teacher I was expected to sign in conventional English at all times—the order of signs being the same as that of words. I adhered to this—after a long period of preparation—yet, I found that among themselves the children resorted to non-linguistic forms. Their language was pictographic and situation-linked.
>
> This language is purely visual and is richly interspersed with spontaneous dramatisation, mimicry and body language. Some researchers e.g. William Stokoe of Gallaudet College, Washington, claim that this language has structure and grammar. They also claim it exhibits properties common to all languages ... The Americans refer to it as Ameslan (ASL) and I have called the Irish Sign Language Irislan.[33]

It is interesting that Griffey does not seem to have a high opinion of Stokoe or of his assessment of the linguistic quality of Sign Language. Stokoe is a linguist who in 1960 demonstrated that Sign Language has all the qualities of a language. He was the first to make this discovery and as a result is one of the most respected personalities in the deaf world. Anthony van Uden in his book *Sign Languages of Deaf People and Psycholinguists: a Critical Evaluation* (1986) attempted a professional challenge to Sign Language, to which Stokoe replied in his article "Tell Me Where is Grammar Bred?"[34]

The adoption of oralism may have been convenient for the teachers and may have satisfied a tiny fraction of the pupils, but statistics show that 69 per cent of those surveyed by the IDS in 1986 declared that they "lost out in education because of the wholly oral method of communication."[35] From my own enquiries I learned that some teachers in the boys' school who were more tolerant of signing in class used the partial-hearing pupils to communicate their message with deafer pupils through signs. These were judged to be the best teachers in the school.

Deaf adults working in England were having difficulties communicating with their employers who insisted on using speech. LeMaster, from personal communication with Griffey, informs us of this reason for the changeover. The deaf adults asked the schools to provide

> training in speech and lip-reading ... Although the Irish deaf workers' written English was superb (and they often assisted the British deaf with written work), British employers would not speak directly to Irish employees through writing.[36]

Obviously what the deaf adults actually asked for was speech training (not oralism) to be included in the curriculum. Considering the difficulty Irish

33. See Griffey, "From a Pure Manual Method via the Combined Method to the Oral-Auditory Technique" (appendix D) and *From Silence to Speech*, p. 24.

34. William Stokoe, in Gregory and Harley (eds.), *Constructing Deafness*, p. 200–206.

35. See Appendix J.

36. LeMaster, "When Women and Men Talk Differently", p. 133–134.

people with perfect hearing had in those pre-television days in understanding what the English workers were saying, one wonders how convincing this reason is.

The crucial fact about this reason is the claim that it was supported by over 90 per cent of the past pupils, when it appears that it was based on the opinions of only a selection of the past pupils of the girls' school.[37] It is also worth comparing the apparently democratic character of this argument with the fact that democracy is ignored when the figures since 1986 support the opposing argument.[38]

Religious beliefs. A further reason for the change to oralism comes to light in O'Dowd's description of the nuns' 1946 tour of Britain:

> They encountered many Irish Catholic pupils in these schools paying all costs in order to have oralism ... They believed that the time had come to give oralism to Irish Catholic children in their own country.[39]

The trauma for such deaf pupils so far from home was a heart-wrenching matter, not mentioned in the report. The costs were certainly a consideration, as was the loss suffered because of the poor general education achievable in England. Nevertheless there are aspects that lead one to the feeling that this was not a reasoned and intelligent decision but one based purely on religious beliefs, the result of the nineteenth-century Catholic culture still flourishing in Ireland.

Of the six reasons above for the changeover to oralism it would appear that none except the third—that of the parents' express wishes—now holds water. I believe there is a possibility that this too would go if they were given the two sides of the story.

The Department of Education report, 1972

The first official commentary on the education of the deaf is the report of the Committee on the Education of Children who are Hearing-Impaired, issued in February 1972. The Minister for Education, Donogh O'Malley, set up this committee in 1967 but unfortunately did not live to see its completion; considering the productive impact he had on education we can only speculate what he might have done for the deaf. His "free education" scheme, launched in 1965, caught the imagination of the people, opening the way to removing some of the restraints of clerical control; it was this initiative that triggered the huge expansion at all levels of education.

The 1972 report was signed by only nine members of the original twelve-member advisory committee, two having died in the course of the review. If one discounts the doctors and department officials who could only act on the advice of the Dominican professionals we are left with the movers and shakers

37. Griffey, "From a Pure Manual Method via the Combined Method to the Oral-Auditory Technique" (see appendix D).

38. See appendix J.

39. O'Dowd, "History of the Catholic Schools for the Deaf", p. 229, 230, 232.

in the field of education of the deaf in Ireland at the time: Father Gallagher and Brother Wall, Sister Nicholas Griffey and Sister Carmel. The last three were trained in Manchester University, then under the leadership of Ewing, the long-standing authority on education of the deaf in Britain. There was no representation or contribution from deaf past pupils or the deaf community.

I submitted a proposal to the committee on using programmed learning with a Teaching Machine as a means of learning through writing. This device, the forerunner of today's computer learning systems, was popular at the time in armies, public services and large corporations for speed-training new recruits. The Midlands branch of the British National College of Teachers of the Deaf had held a one-day conference on programmed learning and teaching machines for deaf children in Gloucester in May 1969. The paper was presented by W. J. Watts, research fellow of the Reginald M. Phillips Research Unit of the University of Sussex, and published in five consecutive issues of *The Teacher of the Deaf*. Watts told the teachers of an experiment he had arranged for teachers to carry out on seven pupils. The sentence completion test showed gains ranging from 7 to 40 per cent, with a mean gain of 24 per cent. He noted:

> All the children responded to the programmed learning with enthusiasm and the immediate confirmation of correct responses produced a high state of activation and a continuous desire to learn. Each child was able to proceed at his own pace through the programmed material.

In February 1970 I took the principals of the boys' schools of Cabra and Stillorgan to attend a one-day seminar on this method organised by the Institute for Industrial Research and Standards (now part of Forbairt). The proposal, unfortunately, was received in silence. I discovered the reason why in Professor Lenneberg's report only recently. In his lengthly period of research into language acquisition in the Clark School for the Deaf, Northampton, Massachusetts, in the nineteen-sixties, he recommended to some teachers, the reading of books as a means of acquiring English. He found that this casual remark

> elicited a long and serious lecture aimed at elucidating me about the education of the deaf. In essence it amounted to saying that excessive reading of books—"getting lost in reading" as one teacher put it—is harmful to oral education. The child gets too used to reading and afterwards always wants to write instead of using phonics. Books are important, I was reassured, but their use must be supervised and controlled. One way of doing this was to have children make both oral and written reports in class. Periodically, they had the *duty* of reading a book (chosen from a list), and within a week the assignment was due. But aimlessly browsing through the library, so I was told (not that there was much to browse on in this particular

library), curling up in a chair and reading simply to pass the time, that, it was thought, was highly undesirable.[40]

The annual reports for the first decades of both Cabra schools state that they had a well-stocked library, and pupils were encouraged to form a habit of reading. More recent research (1985) shows that the written word surpasses all other means of learning at primary level. Professor Moores, who was involved in the study, states that

> scores on understanding of passives, negatives, and verb tenses suggest that the deaf students tended to process all sentences as simple, active declaratives and to ignore indications of tense, mood, and negation, regardless of the mode of communication. Only when dealing with the printed word did they perform somewhat better.[41]

Fig. 1, based on research carried out by Moores and his associates, shows results for the printed word soaring above the other options, with the oral-auditory method almost marooned in the doldrums.[42] This is a summary of evaluations based on a modification of Cronbach's (1957) interaction model under the following headings: academic achievement, the Illinois Test of Psycholinguistic Abilities, receptive communication, cognitive development, communication patterns, and parental attitudes.

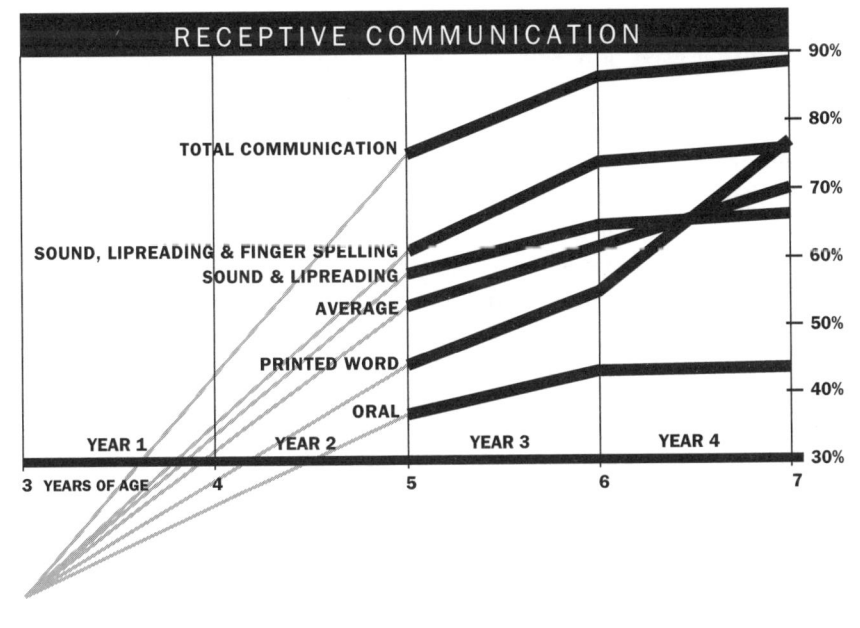

Fig. 1: Receptive communication. Percentage correct for all subjects on receptive communication scale (core items) in second, third and fourth years of testing.

40. Lenneberg, *Prerequisites for Language Acquisition*, p. 1139.

41. Moores, *Educating the Deaf*, p. 236–237.

42. The graph is based on table 10.1 from Moores, *Educating the Deaf*, p. 237.

Breaking the Silence

I attended the one meeting of the committee that was open to the parents' organisations but was so overwhelmed by the concentration of obscure expertise at the top of the table and my own ignorance of the subject of education of the deaf that my mind went blank. It was inevitable that the approving voices from the combination of prestigious (100 per cent non-deaf) doctors, oralist teachers, rehabilitation professionals, crusading oralist hearing parents and others of like mind succeeded in producing such a report. The result was a 50,000-word manifesto of the utopian plans for training the deaf pupil for living with hearing people, in isolation from the deaf community.

The wheres, whats, whos and whys of education were unquestioned, and the how was taken for granted. There is not a single reference to the essential concept of the deaf as a society or a community, as if such a thing was not needed or did not exist.[43] There was not even a glance back to the achievements and the high international standing of Cabra as signing schools.[44] The priorities, repeated on page after page, were the oral method and the grand plan for services that the Government must provide to support it. The list of recommendations for training teachers of the deaf, which included eight specific areas of study in addition to ordinary teacher training, contains nothing about Sign Language.[45] The language of the deaf, even the Cabra classroom variety of it, was to be banned from school and playground and was to be used only as a last resort for the "oral failures", with "crude signs" for the others.[46]

A hopeful item in the report (paragraph 6.34)—"deaf students whose language development and academic achievements are sufficient to enable them to follow higher education should be given every encouragement to do so"—proved to be shallow for our family. We had a long and costly battle to get the Government finance available to a hearing university student from the Department of Education for Brian's education at the only third-level college for the deaf in the world, in Washington. The "every encouragement" consisted of £2,500, the travelling expenses then available to students some distance from the Regional College on a two-year course. The minister described it as "a very exceptional measure".

The report became in effect the official Government endorsement of the policy of oralism. The educational and social issues of value to the deaf, which can be authentically determined only from the perspective of the deaf community, were disregarded. This, for instance, is the vision they had of the way deaf children acquire the means of communication in the world of oralism:

The acquisition of language by a child with a severe hearing impairment is a slow

---

43. In fact a deaf community hardly existed in Ireland before the civil rights movements of the nineteen-sixties, which saw the beginning of the liberation of minorities. Socialisation among the deaf was inhibited by the fact that men used a different language from women, while low incomes and low self-esteem prevented them from procuring suitable meeting-places for leisure activities. Alternate weekly catechetical meetings in rooms in the city centre provided by the church was their lot; in the NAD magazine in 1971 this service was elevated to the more politically correct status

and laborious process and in complete contrast to the seemingly effortless assimilation of the structure of language by his hearing peer.

Through vision, touch and feeling of vibration the deaf child learns that things have names.

By watching faces and lips he gradually learns that he can, to a certain extent, interpret the thoughts and wishes of other people.

However, he cannot lip-read a word or expression until he is familiar with its meaning. He must grope through a maze of words, idioms and grammatical structures, if he is to communicate effectively (in spoken English) and learn to organise his experience verbally.

Finally, by artificial means he has to learn to manipulate teeth, tongue and lips to perform movements that result in speech.[47]

This gives a flavour of the teachers' almost impossible task at the business end of the oralist education system and probably shows why they regularly use the terms "educational training" and "educational treatment" rather than "teaching" to describe it. The fact that through the use of Sign Language a deaf child in a signing environment acquires Sign Language and English with almost the same effortless assimilation as their hearing peer is not mentioned. This is what occurs with the hearing and deaf children in families of deaf parents. The child can almost simultaneously learn their second language—that of the household—in the way, for example, that hearing children in bilingual homes acquire both Irish and English and some reading before they start school. In fact deaf parents have told me that deaf children of deaf parents are usually the most advanced in the class and are often shown off by the teacher as examples of what good work goes on in the oralist classroom, without informing the visitor that it was the home signing environment that made the difference.[48]

The Cabra schools, for the first century, resolutely resisted Government interference in how the schools were run. The Government, I believe, would be right not to interfere as long as it was satisfied that they were doing the best possible job of it. Oralism, because of its extra cost, changed all that, and since 1952 we have split responsibility and an extra layer of bureaucracy to clog up the progress of decision-making. I believe it would be more healthy to have the Department of Education, which is the real employer of the professionals running the schools, keep a strict professional-client relationship with the schools, setting the standards and taking appropriate action in cases of poor performance. To properly and fairly assess performance of schooling for the deaf the department would need people elected by the deaf community, and the inspectors would have to live strictly at arm's length from the schools.

of a "club". The men socialised every second Sunday under the portico of the GPO in the nineteen-fifties. The deaf never had a newsletter of their own until St Vincent's Deaf Club in Rathmines, Dublin, started producing one around 1970, informing members of events, sports results, and religious services. The Irish Deaf Society started its journal in 1987 in a similar vein.

44. O'Dowd, "History of the Catholic Schools for the Deaf", p. 65, 220–226.

45. Department of Education, *Education of Children who are Handicapped by Impaired Hearing*, p. 137. Forty years passed before this matter was addressed. Now, in 1996, trainee teachers' training in methodical signs in UCD and mature teachers'

Breaking the Silence

Forum on the Education of Hearing-Impaired Children, 1991

The Forum on the Education of Hearing-Impaired Children, held in Dublin in November 1991, was the only public meeting on the subject open to all ever held in Ireland. On the surface it offered opportunities never granted before to the adult deaf.

The deaf community were in high spirits, having earlier that month successfully presented the European Festival of Deaf Culture, in the heady days when the Department of Education was working on the White Paper for the first comprehensive Education Act. The main underlying issue of the proposed Act was the political one of the restructuring and democratising of the control of schools, a subject close to the heart of the progressive element of the deaf community. Everyone involved in education—parents, teachers, and school managers—was active with meetings and television debates. The shadow-boxing of the leading participants in the debates was making headlines, but there was no reporting of the efforts of the deaf community.

The forum was organised by the National Association for the Deaf, and their acceptance of the Irish Deaf Society as a partner in the event gave great encouragement to the deaf community. But it was a false hope. As things turned out, it bears comparison with the infamous Milan congress and with the 1972 report of the Department of Education. Doris Nelson, chairperson of the NAD, said in her address that the forum

> was organised by the Review Committee on Education of Hearing-Impaired Children to enable all who are interested in or are dedicated to the education of the deaf to air their views. Today we have the opportunity to pass informed comment which can help structure the education our deaf children will receive in the future.

She told the forum that the 1972 report was to form the basis of the work in hand. But the NAD control and reporting of the forum saw to it that their own "informed comment" was made available, together with a mainly censored version from the deaf.

Everyone was pleased at the large attendance, which I estimated at 220, including 40 deaf adults. The chairperson of the forum was a Supreme Court judge, the late Niall McCarthy.

Judging by the content of the NAD contribution, the real purpose in holding the forum might seem to have been to whip up support for reversing the recent decision of the Department of Education to widen the duties of the visiting teachers by including other disabilities in their scope. While pre-school service is highly desirable, its oralist orientation negates its value for most deaf parents. The deaf parents tried in vain to express their dissatisfaction with the visiting teachers. (The ultimate affront to the deaf

---

Margin notes:

training in the boys' school has begun.

46. Sister Nicholas Griffey, *Link*, autumn 1973. "Oral failures" was the common term for those who couldn't make it in the oral class.

47. Department of Education, *Education of Children who are Handicapped by Impaired Hearing*, p. 5–6.

48. Moores, *Educating the Deaf*, p. 13; Schlesinger, "Headstart in Deafness—Early Home Environment(see appendix F).

parents was that money intended to help the deaf financed the forum.) The visiting teachers have little or no skill in signing. They visit deaf children of deaf parents as well as those with hearing parents, and they are under instructions not to use or recommend signs. The deaf adults tried to express their dissatisfaction and to inform the authorities of these faults in the service but were snubbed.[49]

A number of other aspects of the forum will help in making an assessment of it and of the NAD.

Communication between the NAD and the IDS coming up to the forum was exceptionally tortuous, involving the exchange of telephone messages, because the NAD organiser was not available. The IDS request to set up an information stand at the forum was turned down. The IDS asked for the agenda and were told that there was none but that the programme would be given out on the morning of the forum.

The deaf were allowed to present only one paper, compared with seven by the non-deaf experts. The deaf were told that, because of time constraints, they would have not more than ten minutes for their paper—and it had to be approved by the NAD some days beforehand. The time restriction defeated any hope of making an understandable presentation: it would be an impossible task to present even an outline of the case of the deaf community in anything less than half an hour. The deaf delegate, Fergus Dunne,[50] before he delivered his paper complained to the audience on the point, but to no avail. (In fact he finished his speech two minutes short of his allotted ten minutes; in contrast, at least two of the experts took double their allotted time.) The chairperson also attempted to cut out the scheduled discussion following Dunne's paper (on grounds of time constraints), though a protest by the deaf people put it back on the agenda.

The NAD insisted that the deaf delegate include in his speech a call for the re-establishment of the Review Committee, in effect coercing the deaf delegates to approve the 1972 report in front of the audience.

The interpreters provided by the NAD used methodical signs instead of Sign Language. None of the experts nor the many visiting teachers in the audience used signs.

At the very end of the forum, with no advance notice, the chief executive of the NAD proposed a triple resolution: "That this meeting is deeply concerned at *(a)* any proposal to reduce the Visiting Teacher Service to deaf children or to integrate it with a Visiting Teacher Service for other children with other handicaps, *(b)* the continued suspension of the Special Review Committee on the Education of Hearing-Impaired Children in 1990 by the Minister for Education, and *(c)* the absence of any representative of the

49. See videotape recording of the forum.

50. Fergus Dunne was the Irish Deaf Society representative and the only deaf member of the Review Committee on the Education of Hearing-Impaired Children.

Breaking the Silence

Department of Education at this meeting." The NAD magazine reported that these resolutions were passed unanimously,[51] in spite of the fact that the deaf, who accounted for at least 20 per cent of the audience, were against them.

The NAD turned down an IDS questionnaire[52] about the forum because they did not like one particular question, without informing the IDS in time for them to have a revised one prepared.

The NAD magazine's report of the forum, although it referred to the essence of the deaf delegate's contribution, could not resist a jibe at Dunne's criticism of the educational expertise of the oralists. It all showed a good day's work for the NAD and the visiting teachers, although the Department of Education did not yield an inch on the resolutions. Éamonn Ó Murchú, one of the seven members of the review committee present,[53] in his summary described it as "a unique learning experience and a unique seminar." In fact the forum was a humiliating and soul-destroying experience for the deaf adults present and, by extension, the deaf community.

To these criticisms of the handling of the forum there was no comment from the leading lights of the NAD. The IDS acted in good faith at all times in their dealings with the NAD on the forum and were expecting the same from them. It was a valuable learning experience that will not be forgotten. The event also showed the glaring lack of sophistication in the art of politics and communication on the part of the deaf community, particularly in the company of such articulate people and experts in their field.

The NAD v. the IDS

The National Association for the Deaf was founded in 1962 in the Dominican Convent in Cabra by Sister Nicholas Griffey with a committee composed mainly of prominent figures from the legal and commercial world. Their names feature in Griffey's book,[54] but there is no record of the names of the deaf adults whom she says she consulted on its formation.

Unlike the American NAD, founded a century earlier by deaf people to combat the intrusion of oralist activists led by Alexander Graham Bell into their educational province, the Cabra NAD is "for", not "of", the deaf and in fact was modelled on the oral ideology of the RNID in Britain. The NAD was set up to propagate the Cabra ethos, which means control by an oralist-centred, non-deaf and Catholic institution. An NAD spokesman, in letters to the IDS journal, described the association as

a national umbrella organisation catering for the problem of all hearing-impaired people including born-Deaf, deafened, hard of hearing, Deaf old folks, and Deaf people with other disabilities and their families and supporters ... The NAD is a fully legal and democratic body.[55]

51. *Link,* winter 1991, p. 9.

52. See appendix K.

53. When this committee's turn came to make a presentation at the National Convention on Education in Dublin Castle in 1994, nobody turned up.

54. Griffey, *From Silence to Speech,* p. 85, 183–186.

55. See appendix L.

The NAD is indeed democratic to the extent that its paid-up members have a vote in elections, but the paid-up members are mainly parents following the Cabra line, who outnumber the adult deaf membership; from my enquiries it would seem that relatively few deaf adults are, or want to be, members of the NAD as it is at present constituted.

The Irish deaf community found inspiration from their own achievements while taking part in and organising athletic events in the new field of international sports for the disabled in the nineteen-seventies. This new realisation of their potential raised their self-confidence and gave birth to the Irish Deaf Society in 1981. The IDS, because of its philosophy and composition, is recognised by the 116-member World Federation of the Deaf as the official association of the deaf in Ireland, while the NAD is not. Yet it is the NAD that represents the deaf community on official bodies in Ireland.

The NAD's superior communication skills, networks, media friends and official contacts give ready access to publicity. While they acknowledge that the deaf have a right to develop their own language,[56] they have taken away their means of accomplishing it; in the meantime they promote their methodical signing as the official "sign language" of the whole country. The Irish Deaf Society's report,[57] issued in 1995, on their Irish Sign Language Research Project is an example of the jockeying for position by the vested interests of the Cabra establishment.

The NAD is aware of the basis of the criticisms of it by the IDS. An article in the NAD-sponsored magazine, while offering the following advice to the IDS:

> There are too many organisations ... The IDS should disband and the members join the NAD with its superior numbers ... The majority of deaf people are not interested in the politics of deaf-related issues ... so there is no need for the IDS now ...

went on to admit:

> Some deaf people asked for direct representation on the Board of the NAD, but the response was: "There is no need for that; you can be assured that we know well what you need ... you can trust us." What a pity that this undoubtedly sincere attitude was taken, because otherwise we would not now be contending with such difficulties and tensions that should not be around at all.[58]

The writer then suggested that the NAD should amend its constitution to provide for an equal number of deaf and hearing members on the Board of Directors. The questions the commentator obviously has not considered about the 50-50 marriage he desires is, will the deaf adults carry the same weight as the non-deaf experts across the table?

Faced with the growth of the IDS in the late nineteen-eighties, and because they found the rules of their organisation unworkable, the NAD

---

56. Griffey, *From Silence to Speech*, p. 136. "It [Irish Sign Language] is a rich heritage and I would be the first to treasure it. However, if we wish people such as hearing parents of deaf children and student-teachers to learn sign language, the success rate will be higher if there is a single version for all. Of course, this does not prevent deaf people from using among themselves whatever version they wish." (Note the use of the term "sign language" to mean methodical signs.)

57. See appendix N.

58. *Contact*, Mar.–Apr. 1992.

Breaking the Silence

restructured their organisation in 1987.[59] A non-deaf former Cabra teacher with some methodical signing experience, Niall Keane, was appointed to the newly created position of chief executive. This was the first time that a person with a knowledge of signing was appointed to a senior position in the organisation.[60] The significance of deaf power was beginning to be felt in Cabra, and they did not like it.[61]

The various activities and publications of the NAD give one a window into its ethos from the outside. In the nineteen-nineties they had appointed to the chairmanship a Supreme Court judge, Niall McCarthy, whose knowledge of the deaf was only what the NAD told him. In the official magazine of the NAD, in the report of a function to honour Niall Keane's predecessor, Mr Justice McCarthy said of this obviously very competent official:

> Wherever I went I knew Ted would be there ahead of me and whatever I had to say I knew he had it there for me. All I had to do was add a little colour ... You always knew he was a jump ahead of you, when you thought you had a problem to spring on him he already had thought out a solution or indeed two solutions from which you could pick ... to restrain ... members of the committee to point out to them the dangers ... or some backlash, or some prospective difficulty ... and most frequently to have it all written out in advance ... When Ted was briefing me ... it was there ... the clues were all there to act on.[62]

Appendix M gives examples of how the NAD defence mechanism goes into action when they got what was intended as a little healthy and constructive criticism. We had a visit from an American deaf man, Grover Odenthal, and his fiancée Brenda Marshall, in 1986—friends of my son in Gallaudet University—and we introduced them to the boys' school, to various deaf people, and to the deaf in the pub and deaf club life in Dublin. As they were interested in the progress of the deaf and had already visited several European countries, we discussed how the education and social situation of the deaf in Ireland stood.

They were particularly struck by the paternalist attitude of the Irish people towards the deaf. On enquiring about the extent of interpreter services for the deaf in Ireland at their visit to the boy's school in Cabra they were told by one of the Brothers that there was none. They were appalled to hear him say that there was no need for an independent services because the Nuns and Brothers looked after it for them. They were told that an independent service was not in keeping with the Christian charitable way of doing things in Ireland, and got the feeling that it would not be welcomed here. In disscussion regarding independence for deaf people to run their own affairs he emphasised, as an example, that the NAD (of Cabra) was best

59. *Link*, autumn 1987, p. 14.

60. Griffey, who has signing experience, founded the NAD and therefore cannot properly be described as being appointed to it.

61. Griffey, *From Silence to Speech*, p. 111.

62. *Link*, autumn 1987.

able to function when people of influence (clergy, judges and business leaders) were at the helm.

I considered their observations to be of value to the Irish deaf and suggested he should write to the newspapers about it in the interest of public information on the deaf. On 20 September 1986 Odenthal wrote to the IDS, who then sent it to the three Dublin newspapers and the NAD for publication. It is a remarkable coincidence that none of the newspapers published this quite inoffensive letter, leading one to suspect a nod from the NAD. A hint of this is discernible from the comment in the NAD-sponsored magazine *Contact*, which was the only medium to publish it: "The name of the Irish Deaf was certainly saved from further injury when the daily newspapers refused to print Mr. Odenthal's letter"(see appendix M, p206). *Contact* published it months later in their March–April 1987 issue under the response-provoking heading of "Are we oppressed?" with a request to its readers to reply.

As can be seen, leading the defence by the deaf friends of the NAD is a letter from McCarthy, with a reminder to them of who pays the piper for the magazine. He said he regretted that the visitors should not have got their information from the directors and officials of the NAD.

Initially the NAD saw its function as filling the "major role in the creation of public awareness of the problems and the needs of the deaf"[63] and "better education of the public concerning *the oral way of life* where all types of *hearing-impaired* children receive *treatment* suited to their needs" (emphasis added).[64] They saw oralism as the conclusive solution to the "problems" of the deaf, while signing was the biggest enemy of progress. Because their goal was to get the deaf to speak, to make them "normal", a prejudice against signs was communicated in their propaganda.

The first crack in this policy appeared twenty-five years after its inception when the NAD magazine announced:

> One recommendation that we are able to act on immediately is that we carry the deaf alphabet. Rather than just include this in the magazine we are able, by courtesy of St Joseph's School for Deaf Boys, Cabra to include with each magazine their special card which gives both the single and two handed version … Pass it around … let others learn of the deaf and their problems.[65]

Soon afterwards, the NAD arranged the establishment of "sign language" classes for the public, and they began taking advantage of the rising tide among the hearing public as well as the deaf in favour of signing. The Sign Language Association of Ireland (SLAI) was founded in the nineteen-eighties. Originally an independent body that focused on the development of Irish Sign Language, the SLAI drifted to the NAD following division along the fault line between the personalities and dispositions of the natural Sign Language

63. *Link*, autumn 1987, p. 15.

64. Griffey, "From a Pure Manual Method via the Combined Method to the Oral-Auditory Technique" (sse appendix D).

65. *Link*, summer 1971, p. 2. A news item in *Contact*, Nov.–Dec. 1980, concerning the book *Irish Sign Language* asserts that "in a few years, we will be used to all the signs given in the book. So practice a bit every day." In fact the book is on the Cabra methodical signs for the English language. But perhaps this should be considered the first crack in the oralist shell.

and the methodical signers' camps. Under the umbrella of the NAD and St Patrick's College, Maynooth, the SLAI runs a network of classes on methodical signs throughout the country. This is probably seen by the deaf who co-operate with the establishment as a step forward: some signing is better than no signing. But it is a self-defeating mission that inhibits the natural growth of Irish Sign Language, just at a time when the deaf in the western world are coming to realise the indispensability of their own natural languages. To add to the woes of ISL, Allied Irish Banks recently gave the methodical sign people £25,000 to produce a glossary of methodical signs, and last year the European Union gave funds to start a full-time course for sixteen tutor-trainees.

Another organisation, the Irish Association of Sign Language Interpreters, has since appeared on the scene. Founded in 1994 by the former voluntary Interpreter Group and some graduates of the Horizon One ISL interpreter training course in Bristol University, it is introducing a badly needed awareness of good practice and the ethics of interpreting.[66] Nevertheless, it appears to be going outside the control of the people it serves, and outside its remit, by taking on the task of modifying the vocabulary of ISL, rather than leaving that to evolve naturally in the deaf community. The examples of Carnegie, Sicard and Shaw show that control of languages from above is doomed to fail.

The first interpreter training course in Ireland was set up in 1992 by the Irish Deaf Society in collaboration with Trinity College, Dublin, with the assistance of Dr Jim Kyle, who runs a similar service for British Sign Language at Bristol University. It will take decades to bring this service to a level that satisfies the deaf all over the country.

With the benefit of their natural gift of speech and eloquence in a world dominated by speakers, the NAD leadership have a formidable communication advantage over an organisation run by deaf people. The apparent metamorphosis of the NAD, slowly changing from the oral model of pathological deafness to the deaf identity culture, follows on the coat-tails of the British RNID but with the significant difference that the Irish version has a privileged organisation that also controls one of the Cabra schools. The RNID is a more democratic institution and has not got a school: the British schools for the deaf are independent of the traditional type of control found in the Irish religious model of education.

[66.] *IASLI Newsletter*, no. 1, Oct. 1994.

Attempt by the IDS to reform education, 1991–92

The 1991 forum provided proof for the deaf community that little could be gained and everything might be lost in the education field by any partnership

4 Recent Developments in Ireland

with the NAD and the Cabra establishment. Draft proposals were prepared and presented directly to the Minister for Education, Noel Davern, by the IDS at a meeting a month after the forum, on 4 December 1991. The minister arranged a meeting between his department officials and a delegation from the IDS on 7 February 1992. The IDS delegation included Fergus Dunne, a member of the Review Committee on the Education of Hearing-Impaired Children; Johann Wesemann, director-general of the European Regional Secretariat of the World Federation of the Deaf; Eileen Lemass, a former MEP who had earlier assisted the IDS in its campaign for the official recognition of Irish Sign Language; Patrick McDonnell, a teacher of the deaf; and Brian Crean, an employee of the IDS at the time. The following month the IDS had the distinction of being the only group to be interviewed by the Special Education Review Committee.

The delegation proposed that the Department of Education set about restructuring the education services along lines acceptable to the deaf. The first stage would be for the department to establish a small committee to research the field, study the education programmes abroad that have given the best results, make an inventory of assets, determine the desirable outcomes, and report on their findings. Although this proposal was not ideal, in that the procedures would not be functioning at arm's length from the department, its legitimacy would have official sanction.

The department's response was to put the matter on the shelf. (By this time Davern was no longer Minister for Education.) In the report of the department's Special Education Review Committee a year later the deaf community were sidelined.

> Discussions should take place between the Department of Education and the relevant school authorities with a view to rationalising the structure of the special school provision for pupils with hearing impairment in Dublin ...[67]

A second and even more worrying reason for the lack of progress on the proposal was the lack of commitment by key members of the IDS to the planned campaign to inform the public and win support for the embryo education freedom movement. Additional plans in the IDS education reform campaign that were in train included the establishment of a resource centre in Dublin city centre. This would be a convenient information centre particularly for parents of the infant deaf and a meeting-place that would develop into an enterprise centre for the deaf. It would have had an audio-visual room and a library and bookshop for all those interested in information on the deaf.

Although two seminars on education were held by the deaf at the end of 1992, interest in the IDS project fizzled out. I wrote to the patrons of the NAD

67. Department of Education, *Report of the Special Education Review Committee, 1992*, p. 110.

in April 1992 in an attempt to get them to accept the validity of the IDS case. I was hoping to bring about an arrangement to satisfy all parties and above all to get the NAD behind a movement to bring badly needed unity to the Irish deaf world. The venture drew a belated comment from Griffey (December 1994):

> Requests for *compulsory manualism* were submitted to the Department of Education. Parents were told that all deaf children, once deafness was diagnosed, should become part of the deaf community. *Hearing parents* were frightened because they felt, in the words of one parent, as if they "had given birth to an alien." They were *subjected to discussion [sic]* on sign language of the deaf versus signed English in the education of deaf children. Having seen so many times in the past the panic, grief and even despair of parents, I was shattered to find them subjected to bickering over methods when *they expected deaf adults to be their greatest support* [emphasis added].[68]

The officer in charge of the relevant section in the Department of Education, Matthew Ryan, has told me that he did not know of any such proposal. In view of the fact that the 1986 IDS survey established that only 7 per cent of the adult deaf favoured oralism, the term "alien" seems to be applied to the wrong people. As only one hearing parent made the comment, one is left to wonder what percentage of them hold a similar view.

The chaplaincy of the deaf

The Cabra establishment owes its existence to the missionary element of the Catholic Church. The clergy have always held a central role in the landscape of the deaf community; this was openly and proudly expressed in its early days, although its outline has ebbed and flowed over the years.

Cabra's second chaplain, Father John Bourke, was a gifted educator and is given the credit for formalising the methodical signing system used in the girls' school. He had the co-operation of the two Dominican nuns who were given a period of first-hand experience with Jamet's system in Caen but had run into difficulties in adapting it to English. He produced the standard dictionary of methodical signs for prayers, which are common to men and women.[69] The title of his book, *Practical Application of the Abbé Sicard System of Instruction for Deaf Mutes: an Outline of the System,* would indicate that the girls' school system of signing owes more to Sicard and, by extension, to Epée than to Jamet. Sicard, without shame, had taken the credit for the work of Epée and the deaf teachers of the Paris school.

In the first hundred years of the girls' school the chaplains worked mainly with the pupils in the schools. In the eighteen-eighties the chaplain began attending to the spiritual needs of the deaf men and women of Dublin on alternate Sundays in rooms allocated to him in Marlborough Street. In

---

68. Griffey, *From Silence to Speech,* p. 136.

69. When a bound copy of the original manuscript was presented to Sister Nicholas Griffey in 1994 by the editor of *Contact,* he remarked that he had not known of its existence until fifteen years earlier. This indicates that the force of the new-found popularity of signing among the oralists is uncovering relics of the past and is starting to break down some of their defences.

addition there seem to have been occasional visits to the deaf around the country.

The first sign of improvement in the service for adults was the appointment of a chaplain to Belfast's adult deaf in 1938; he attended to their spiritual needs in the Dominican Convent on the Falls Road. The deaf in Cork got similar facilities in the nineteen-fifties. Irish chaplains were appointed to London (in 1950) and Glasgow (in 1949) to attend to the many Irish deaf in those areas, because of dissatisfaction with the British chaplains.

An expansion drive to improve the service and educate the public on what they perceived as the problems of the deaf was started in the nineteen-seventies following a discussion between Griffey, the chaplain of the deaf in Dublin, Father Dermot Sweeney, and the director of the Sint-Michielsgestel institute in the Netherlands, Father van Eijndhoven. According to Griffey, the discussions

> opened up for me possibilities which had not been dreamt of by myself and my colleagues. We were convinced that the Catholic schools for the deaf had a responsibility to inform the Catholic bishops of the religious needs of the deaf. The People of God needed education concerning the isolation of the deaf within the Church.[70]

A crusade was launched with an international conference in Dublin in 1971. Many other such meetings have been held since. The most recent was in 1994 in the English College in Valladolid, Spain, the home town of the first teacher of the deaf, Ponce de León. The movement was registered in England in November 1986 as the International Catholic Foundation for the Service of Deaf Persons,[71] with Griffey as secretary and Cardinal Pironio, president of the Council for the Laity in Rome, as its patron. Participants selected for the conferences have included bishops, priests, teachers of the deaf, psychologists and social workers from Argentina, Australia, Belgium, Brazil, Britain, Canada, Germany, Ghana, India, Ireland, Kenya, the Netherlands, Tanzania, the United States, and Zimbabwe. A statement and a copy of resolutions passed at the Dublin conference were sent to the Bishops' Conference in each participant's country. The principal thrust of the message to the bishops was the enlargement of the chaplaincy of the deaf to give at least one specially trained priest to each diocese, with one bishop in each country to have responsibility for the spiritual welfare of the deaf.

The remarkable success of this movement, which was led in the main by Griffey, can be judged by the comment made by Father O'Farrell, the retiring chief chaplain (interviewed on RTE television in January 1995), that "the chaplaincy of the deaf is the fastest-growing sector of the Catholic Church." Since the nineteen-forties the chaplains have paved the way and provided the

70. Griffey, *From Silence to Speech*, p. 129.

71. *IDS Journal*, summer 1987, p. 3.

guiding light for the development of many successful sporting and social agencies and organisations.

But a blemish on this success story has been the interlocking of this service with the ideology of oralism as the way to end the isolation of the deaf within the church and, by logical extension, within the hearing world. The status of oralism was copperfastened by the prestige of episcopal authority, virtually putting it beyond public questioning. In fact it could be argued that oralism ran counter to the principal aims of chaplaincy and catechetics, in that it broke an essential rule of missionaries, which is firstly to learn the language and culture of the people they wish to serve. Although the chaplains use signing, it is a mystery how they obey the establishment rule to use the "official" (methodical) signs and yet empathise with the deaf in their own Sign Language. The chaplain is told to interact with parents, teachers and pupils and to follow the establishment policy on oralism: "He should never get caught up in the controversies concerning methods of communication which have plagued the field of education of the deaf for centuries."[72] It is interesting to note that the Protestant clergymen on the British Royal Commission in the eighteen-eighties, going on their field experience visits with the adult deaf, made a strong case against oralism in the schools.[73]

Another unfortunate feature of the chaplaincy is its desire to retain nineteenth-century-style hegemony over all the affairs of the deaf. An example of this is their tactless allembracing claim to be the "National" Chaplaincy for the Deaf in Ireland. Chaplains in other walks of life confine their work to spiritual matters, but not so the Vincentians. A Vincentian historian described one of them being "given charge" of the deaf Catholics in Glasgow and throughout western Scotland.[74] If one reads the brochure produced by the Catholic Institute for the Deaf for the opening of St Vincent's Centre for the Deaf in Drumcondra, Dublin, in 1991 by its president, Archbishop Connell of Dublin, one sees that they have a leading role in almost all areas. The brochure reminds the deaf of the CID's benevolence: "having purchased and renovated the newly acquired St Vincent's Centre [it has] generously provided the Dublin Deaf Association with over 20,000 sq. ft. at a nominal rent." The functions of the premises, according to the brochure, are "offices for the CID, the chaplaincy, a social centre for Dublin Deaf Association and additional space to accommodate future services for the deaf."

It was the concept of priestly mission—to attend to spiritual needs—that for the greater part of five hundred years initiated nearly all attempts to educate the deaf. It was a priest, Father Thomas McNamara, who led the movement that saw the Cabra schools established, principally because he wanted to "rescue" the Catholic deaf children from the Protestant proselytism then rampant in Ireland.

72. Griffey, *Proceedings of the Second International Conference on Religious Education of the Hearing-Impaired*, 1983, p. 119.

73. O'Dowd, "History of the Catholic Schools for the Deaf", p. 218–219.

74. Purcell, *Story of the Vincentians*, p. 210.

With the benefit of hindsight and of the enormous strides made in social and self-knowledge we can stand back and get a better view of the whole picture. We can ponder on the philosophy of the best way to instruct the deaf in religion. Should one follow the traditional way in which it is done with people who can hear? Should one first of all concentrate on providing the deaf child with the very best means of communication and intellectual education around the concrete and moral things of life, in harmony with their biological development, with the religious element given in the same proportion as the hearing child, bearing in mind that a deaf adult or child cannot tune in fully to conventional religious rituals?

I believe that the methodology for this movement must come out of deaf culture itself; I believe it is inappropriate for outsiders to assume that they have the answers to these questions. I believe that the answer is in there, in the deaf, waiting to come out. Who or what is stopping the Irish deaf from being given the opportunity to study these matters intellectually and then going on to study theology and train for chaplaincy?

The relatively cosy moral and social certainties of the eighteen-eighties, when everyone "knew their place," have been put to the test and found wanting in dealing with today's problems. Life nowadays in a democratic community calls for an ever-increasing series of personal choices and judgements that affect individuals and society. New challenges are cropping up as never before. People want to have understanding through dialogue rather than church sermons on issues of morality. Considerations of morality—and most issues have some moral element—are now discussed openly by hearing people on television and radio and in meeting-rooms around the country, where it literally goes over the heads of the deaf. The deaf need the tools and equal opportunity to debate the same issues, and I believe that no-one knows better than themselves where to find them.

Social services for the deaf

The first full-time social services for the deaf at a professional level began in 1970, when two state-financed workers were appointed to work under the direction of the NAD. They were hearing people who had never worked with the deaf before and were mainly involved in research. They noted after their first year

> the loneliness of those living in the country because of the difficulty of making friends in their local community ... It is essential to have regular visits from clergy and social workers ... Regular contacts with their former teachers would be welcomed ... Many deaf people were embarrassed about their deafness ... RTE might be approached with a view to re-introducing religious programmes (using finger-spelling and sign-language as well as speech) for deaf people ...[75]

75. *Link*, summer 1971.

Breaking the Silence

Their report indicated that their roles were defined by the ethos of the establishment, in viewing the needs of the deaf as mainly pathological. They gave priority to the care aspect they thought should be provided for the deaf, as if they were children, rather than what the deaf were capable of doing for themselves.

The most important advice was the feedback from the deaf themselves, but one must go down to the last sentence of the report to find it: "We would like to see more deaf people involved in the activities of the NAD." I saw at first hand at NAD functions I attended in its early days that the only activity of the deaf was making and serving the tea.

Sister Nicholas Griffey turned down a request to carry out a study on the subject of social and emotional development in 1967. As the Dominicans were still strictly isolated from normal social life at that time, her refusal is not perhaps surprising.

> Even though it was suggested to me earlier this year that I speak to you on speech as an important factor in social and emotional development, I felt that I would make a more worthwhile contribution to this conference if I referred to the method of teaching speech which is used in the school in Ireland where I have been working for almost thirty years. You may wonder at my choice![76]

When the deaf established the Irish Deaf Society in 1981 they started at the opposite end. They organised—on a voluntary basis, as they have no state funding—social services that defined the philosophy and priorities of the deaf as viewed from their own perspective. They got permission to teach Irish Sign Language to hearing people in Trinity College and began classes on self-esteem and assertiveness wherever they could find temporary accommodation. These are the very basic values that distinguish a human being from the rest of creation: the language to communicate with one's fellow-humans, development of human dignity and identification. These are skills vital to the human species for mental and physical survival. What they were denied in their homes and schools by oralism they set about building up themselves; those deaf who are finding their feet now display a pride in being deaf, as individuals and as a community.

The terms "deaf pride" and "deaf power" are becoming part of their language, as "black pride" and "black power" are for African-Americans. The public perception of deafness and of signing has changed completely in the last decade, and deafness is no longer something to cause embarrassment, as it was in the bad old days, thanks mainly to the progress made abroad and displayed on our television screens. In fact it is now becoming embarrassing for us hearing people who have not got their language; the spotlight of disability is turning away from the deaf and onto the hearing people without Sign Language who mingle with deaf people. Nevertheless, only a few deaf

76. See Griffey, "Speech Methodology at St Mary's School for the Deaf" (appendix A).

adults have got around to even thinking about this fundamental question.

The deaf of the deaf community consider what the education system has done for them, compared with what it could have done, and they feel that anything they have got, including their education, was owed to them and was hard won by their own efforts and that they do not owe anybody never-ending gratitude for it. They now organise their own news journal and their own leisure and sporting activities, formerly in the hands of the chaplains and the NAD. The first publication of and by the deaf, the quarterly *IDS Journal*, began in the spring of 1987. The two publications *Link* and *Contact*, begun in 1971 and 1979, respectively, are financed by and speak for the Cabra establishment. Although the editor of *Contact* is deaf, it must be said in frankness that he has not got full editorial freedom; he has the unenviable position of having to represent two opposing forces.

In the NAD publications the name of the Irish Deaf Society is never mentioned; if it is discussed in the magazines it is referred to as "another organisation". Not alone are achievements of the IDS not acknowledged but one is left with the impression that any such progress was accomplished by the NAD.[77] *Link* has a number of times declared that the pages are open to readers' comments, good or bad, but one rarely sees there criticism of the establishment.

The deaf community of Dublin had to wait more than a hundred years to get what could be described as a club. Since 1886 the men and women met separately in various meeting-rooms in the city centre on Sundays, primarily for spiritual renewal and no doubt the opportunity of "having a chat" with their own.

The principal club for the deaf, now called the Dublin Deaf Association, began as a men's club in 1945. Like the National Association of the Deaf in the United States, it was founded in the same year that oralism was made official policy for the country. The British Deaf Association was founded under similar circumstances in 1890, a year after the Royal Commission on the education of the deaf issued its report (which had no contribution from deaf people). The fact that the Dublin deaf were at their lowest ebb at the time, having had no premises for the two years before the foundation of the club, was no doubt also a strong incentive and could be food for thought for those who are despondent at present.

Both the National Association of the Deaf in America and the British Deaf Association exerted pressure on the authorities to elevate education and the social status of the deaf, but they were quickly outmanoeuvred by the superior forces of the oralists. The Irish deaf community—unlike their British and American counterparts—had no magazine in which to express their feelings,

77. In her book Griffey never mentions the IDS, its work, or its journal. "A glance at recent issues of *Link* published by NAD and *Contact* published by the Dublin Deaf Association will give an idea of the phenomenal progress that is being made" (p. 137).

Breaking the Silence

so we have no records of their actions. It is unlikely that they made much impression on the authorities in the Dominican convent in Cabra, although they may have had something to do with holding back the introduction of oralism in the boys' school for ten years.

The nineteen-forties and fifties were years of monumental change for the Irish deaf. There is little or no record of what was going on in the minds of the deaf at the time, and knowledge is fading fast from living memory. Even important recent events—such as the celebration of the Irish premiere of the film *Children of a Lesser God*, the transfer of the Deaf Club from Rathmines to Drumcondra, and the Dublin Airport celebration of the return of the deaf community's victorious football team in 1989 as told by the deaf themselves—have not yet seen the light of day. Except for what comes across in the bland monthly television programme *Sign of the Times* and Bob McCullough's column in the *Belfast Telegraph*, not a single news item about the deaf comes from a deaf person in the newspapers, television or radio (through a certified speech interpreter).

Members of the deaf community are already involved in historical research by David Breslin and Christy Foran,[78] but deaf disunity seems to be blocking this potentially fruitful and important field of study. The Irish Deaf Society has the capacity but is hampered by the lack of funds. There must be a lot of data and folklore among the older deaf and their friends and relatives, invaluable for the cultural identity foundations of the deaf community.

*

Events in the deaf world of the last half century must be seen within the perspective of the age in which it lived. We have witnessed the space age, the technological age, and developments that are outpacing our capacity to understand and judge, despite an extraordinary spread of education. But these astronomical steps forward have brought about other problems that are more difficult and more complex than many of the problems they solved.

The world is being run by ever smaller cliques of concept-wise people producing mechanisms that extract the maximum benefit for themselves with the least number of employees and cost; hence the idle hands and despair of the young who cannot make the grade. The deaf too will be numbered among the "also-rans" unless they are allowed to work out their own destiny. The Cabra establishment have made mighty efforts for the education of the deaf since the nineteen-forties, but as we have no before and after reading assessment tests to compare the pre-oral past-pupils with the oral ones, we cannot make an indisputable evaluation of their work.[79] Certainly the recent reading tests show appalling results. In my opinion the record of oralism with

---

78. I did not learn of Christy Foran's death until some time after this was written but I am leaving it stand as an example of what can be done, as I am sure that someone is available to take up the work.

79. See appendix I.

control by the Cabra establishment or non-deaf people or Department of Education officials, provides little hope for the future of deaf people in Ireland. As in other fields, ideology creates an uneasy situation within the establishment for professionals in assessment teams burdened with making choices between loyalty to their team and to their profession. Nevertheless, the study of its history, particularly the mistakes, can provide valuable guidance for the future.

5

The American Picture

You can fool all the people some of the time, and some of the people all the time, but you can not fool all the people all of the time.

Abraham Lincoln

Ireland and America have much in common in the development of education of the deaf. Both went their own way, staying free of the influences of oralism for several decades, both firmly grounded on Epée's sign language method. A profound difference between the two countries, however, was that the Americans, who were developing in a climate wary of European-style religious domination, were able to concentrate on conventional education rather than ideological agendas. Deaf education took off in the country's period of pioneering, not unlike its devlopment in France in the Enlightenment era, under Epée's humble leadership.

It is not surprising, therefore, that the history of deaf education in America is extensively recorded, because of the culture of democracy and the exercise of the freedom of the press but most of all because of the well-educated deaf Americans who were able to take part in much of the debate. This chapter is intended to outline the environment in which it evolved and to use this as a yardstick for measuring developments in Ireland.

The enterprise that had the greatest success and had worldwide influence grew from seeds planted by a few humanely inspired New Englanders in Hartford, Connecticut. It came to fruition with the opening of the first permanent school for the deaf in America in 1817. America was then a young country but growing rapidly, with a population only slightly greater than Ireland's, having only four decades earlier cast off its colonial masters.

Fortified by perhaps the world's most effective liberal constitution, and already possessing some dynamic liberal education institutions, Americans, especially in Connecticut, were already tackling some of the frontiers of social reforms such as universal education, slavery, and child labour. Having removed themselves from the reaches of European autocratic patronage and the charity culture that goes with it, they explored the new world of reason and of democratic government.

The record of the social history of Connecticut, and Hartford in particular, is with good reason the most envied in America. Hartford's principal founder, Thomas Hooker (1586–1647), was a Congregational minister who in 1638 called for government based on the will of the people, and the following year the Connecticut colony put his theories into practice in its state constitution, known as the Fundamental Orders, which served as a model for the United States Constitution 150 years later.

John Higginson, a teacher and minister, founded Connecticut's first school about 1637. A law passed in 1650 required Connecticut towns with more than fifty families to have an elementary school and towns with more than a hundred families to have a secondary school. In 1780 the state sold most of its western land and used the money to finance public education.

The fact-finding tour of Thomas H. Gallaudet, 1816

With this background, it is not surprising that the initiators of schooling for the deaf took an intelligent and realistic approach to setting up their school. The group was headed by the influential Dr Mason Cogswell, president of the Connecticut Medical Society, one of whose five children, Alice, became deaf from scarlet fever in early childhood. The person selected to steer it through was a Yale graduate, Thomas H. Gallaudet (1787–1851), a 28-year old descendant of Huguenot immigrants who had just completed his studies in theology and whose family lived next door to the Cogswells. In 1815 he reluctantly gave up his religious calling to work for the deaf. In the event, he was able to return to his first love, with his mission to the deaf accomplished, after a short fifteen years of industrious effort.

The churches provided statistics on the number of deaf in the state. The state legislature appropriated $5,000, and additional money was collected from private sources. Gallaudet was given the task of researching the best methods available in Europe, and he set off in the spring of 1815, his first port of call being London and the Braidwood academy.

Gallaudet was horrified by the secretiveness and self-centred attitude of the Braidwood family, who rigorously held the monopoly of teaching of the deaf in England and Scotland from the seventeen-seventies to the eighteen-twenties. They put him off for months about arrangements for binding him to a three-year contract of learning by teaching in one of their schools under conditions that he found in the end to be quite unacceptable. They intended him to be an assistant teacher and "to be with the pupils from seven in the morning to eight in the evening and also with the pupils in their hours of recreation." It was revealed later that one of the young Braidwoods was setting up a school in Virginia, which failed, as did another in New York and yet another in Virginia.

Fortunately for Gallaudet, his visit coincided with the Abbé Sicard's promotional tour of London. Sicard, seeking fame and fortune in the one European country still committed to oralism, had his prize protégés, Laurent Clerc and Jean Massieu—both deaf and both teachers of the deaf—to show off as living proof of the success of his school. They gave more than a dozen exhibitions, including one in the House of Commons, and responded to questions from the audience on matters ranging from philosophy to the use of signs to convey abstract ideas.[1]

It is interesting to note in passing that the British turned up their noses at the French system and continued with oralism, and the covert use of their own unique signing, while the rest of Europe (with the exception of Prussia) embraced it. In retrospect, both Gallaudet's and Sicard's visit to London could hardly be worse timed to achieve what they desired. Neither of them was very welcome. England was only recovering from its ineffectual war of 1812 with the United States, and the Battle of Waterloo with Napoléon was only weeks away. Added to Sicard's gloom was the fact that his religion was held in stony suspicion in London: the law still denied membership of the House of Commons to Catholics and was only beginning to allow them education.

Thanks to the presence of Sicard and his deaf teachers in London, Gallaudet was able to compare and evaluate the qualities of both systems at first hand. Nevertheless, he decided that he should spend some months trying to learn about oralism, as he felt it might have some merits. He spent the last five months of 1815 trying fruitlessly to arrange a satisfactory training course in one of the Braidwood schools in London, Birmingham, or Edinburgh.

Gallaudet described his frustration to Zachary Macaulay, who befriended him in London, and Macaulay published a blistering reprimand to the Braidwood clan in the *Christian Observer*, accusing them of a

> niggardly and exclusive spirit ... We should as soon have expected a churlish refusal of vaccine virus to our Trans-Atlantic brethren as a moment's doubt or hesitation of communicating to them the *blessed art of making the dumb to speak and the deaf to hear* ... We are grieved and mortified to find that neither in London or Edinburgh did

[1] Moores, *Educating the Deaf*, p. 59.

Dr. Gallaudet meet with that encouragement which his benevolent purpose merited [emphasis added].

The emphasised part of this quotation shows how effectively the oralists were in deceiving Macaulay, one of the intellectual class, into believing they could perform the impossible. Gallaudet withheld his opinion until he had seen Epée's system in the Paris school.

With a letter of introduction from Macaulay, Gallaudet was received by Sicard with open arms and given the run of the school. For over four months he studied the signing system in use there, taking lessons from Laurent Clerc, who had already learned English so as to perform in the London tour.[2] Gallaudet, convinced that he had found in the Paris school the bones of a workable model that could be used for teaching English, could see his mission crowned if he could persuade Sicard to release Clerc to accompany him back to Hartford. He also wanted an educated deaf person to show the Americans what could be done.

Sicard prized Clerc as his best teacher and tried by every means to stop the move. He was fearful too of the Protestant ethos in America and the risk of Clerc losing his Catholic faith; he saw Gallaudet's evangelist version as the worst form of Protestantism. But, after breaking an earlier promise to release Clerc to run a school in Moscow, he had to accept the inevitable outcome. Gallaudet arrived home in August 1816 with Clerc, eighteen months after setting out.

The first school: Hartford, Connecticut, 1818

Gallaudet's school, in the manner of the times, was originally called the Connecticut Asylum for the Education of Deaf and Dumb Persons. In its first year it had thirty-one pupils, including Alice Cogswell. She was now fourteen, although the average pupil was in the early twenties. A little over half were born deaf, nine lost their hearing before the age of four; 80 per cent had never spoken English to any degree. Nearly all had hearing parents and knew no other deaf outside the family, which increased their isolation—relying on pantomime and home signs. There were a few pupils from the signing community in nearby Martha's Vineyard. The average stay was four years.

Outbreaks of diseases such as scarlet fever were the most common cause of acquired deafness up to recent times. Usually the deaf child had acquired speech and a command of language structure before going deaf. The child's speech usually begins to deteriorate fairly rapidly, depending on the severity of the illness and the amount of exercise of the speech mechanism. This phenomenon of a deaf child with a reasonably good speaking voice and a command of the spoken language may account for much of the success

2. A feature of the early schools in France, as in Cabra, was the holding of performances for the public to demonstrate what the deaf could do- surely a humiliating experience for those concerned. Lane, *When the Mind Hears*, p. 38. O'Dowd ("History of the Catholic Schools for the Deaf", p. 72) refers to "public examinations in the presence of local dignitaries in Clonmel, Drogheda, Dundalk, Carlow, Waterford, Mullingar, Sligo, Galway, and other centres."

claimed by the oralists: reports of oral successes rarely reveal details of the onset of deafness. The fact that Alexander Graham Bell's mother and his wife became hard of hearing about the age of four or five may account for the family being such uncompromising oralists. His wife was surprised when late in life she discovered in old family papers that she was not deafened until the age of five.[3]

Sign Language was not taught in the classroom in Hartford: newcomers picked it up from the older pupils spontaneously and naturally, just by living and playing with each other. In the second year enrolments reached 115, with a staff of three teachers, including Clerc and Gallaudet. One obvious advantage of signing for the deaf is that a signing teacher can communicate to at least as big a class as a speaking one in a hearing school. The school, run jointly by a Protestant and a Catholic, was both non-denominational and co-educational. The pupils stayed in lodgings locally.

The school board arranged for teacher training to start in 1818 to provide teachers for other states that wanted to set up their own schools. After some jousting with an oralist group (which included a grandson of Braidwood, who had dreams of extending the British monopoly to America), the Hartford people spawned a school in New York in 1821, and by the eighteen-sixties this was the largest school for the deaf in the world. A third school was soon opened in Philadelphia, forming a network of three residential schools in America's main centres of population.

As national responsibility for the education of the deaf was falling on the school, the Connecticut General Assembly accepted a request to change the name from the Connecticut Asylum to the American Asylum in 1819. The deaf vigorously objected to the label "asylum", but the board could not accept such a change: appeals for taxpayers' funds could not yet be based on the right of the deaf to education. The offensive term was not dropped until 1895.[4]

By 1830 half the states were sending their state-funded pupils to Hartford; even the distant southern states of Georgia and South Carolina elected to send their children until they established schools of their own. From 1840 to 1860 seventeen new institutions were established, mostly by deaf teachers.[5]

A change was taking place in American society somewhat similar to though more congenial than that of today; unlike today, the demand was for more humane, low-technology skills. The schools for the deaf were at the forefront in training people for new techniques that were being pioneered in America at that time, such as mechanised farming, coach-building, and ship-building. The deaf were then at least on an equal footing with the average hearing worker. Today's new inventions and machines are creating demands

3. Lane, *When the Mind Hears*, p. 450.

4. Hodgson, *The Deaf and Their Problems*, p. 221.

5. Moores, *Educating the Deaf*, p. 63.

only for people with exceptional conceptual skills, so as to make even more sophisticated creations aimed at leaving as many people as possible unemployed. Social Darwinism is ensuring that only the fittest survive; a doorman with a university degree is not a rare sight now.

Edward Miner Gallaudet

The schools for the deaf with the signing system of communication made steady progress, so that by time of the Civil War they catered for the needs of the whole country. At the height of the Civil War the institution that is now Gallaudet University was established in Washington D.C. by Congress and President Lincoln.[6] Edward Miner Gallaudet (1857–1917) and Sophia Gallaudet, son and widow of Thomas H. Gallaudet, were appointed superintendent and matron. Sophia Gallaudet devoted all her efforts to espousing the social cause of the signing deaf and earning for herself the affectionate title of "Mother of the Deaf Community" in Washington D.C. Thomas H. and his eldest son, Thomas were both clergymen, and the latter founded the first church for deaf people in the U.S.

Gallaudet University remains the only liberal arts university of the deaf in the world. In 1988 over 15 per cent of its students were from overseas. These These enjoy the benefit of having half their tuition costs at Uncle Sam's expense while most deaf U.S. citizens get their education paid from the public purse.

The first fifty years of deaf education in the United States is accepted as being the "golden age". However, ominous clouds were appearing by the middle of the nineteenth century. The self-appointed perfectionists led social scientists to think of institutions as the solution for people who did not come up to "normality". Ideally, they believed, these institutions should be established far away from centres of population. Reform carried out on the country's general education system was to sweep the deaf education system along in its wake, into the murky mists of oralism.

Horace Mann, "Father of the Common Schools"

The first schools for the deaf fortunately escaped the influence of these cold-blooded social beliefs, which induced state legislatures to build "asylums" for the disabled. The crusading of Horace Mann (1796–1859), a leader in establishing the elementary school system in the United States, had an important impact on the existing deaf education system. He was motivated by strong moral convictions, becoming a leader in the anti-slavery movement and a strong advocate on a range of social issues, from temperance to the establishment of asylums for the handicapped.

6. The magnificent Lincoln Memorial in Washington is one of the most inspiring monuments in that city, but it has a special meaning for the deaf. In pride of place stands the gigantic white marble statue of Lincoln sitting on an armchair, with the fingers of his hands forming his initials *A* and *L* in the American Hand Alphabet—a simple but fitting mark of recognition to Lincoln and to the language of the deaf.

Mann recognised that schools could be used to mould and homogenise the disparate culture of the immigrants flooding in to the United States; the implementation of his educational policies established a unifying and standardised New England order of behaviour throughout the country. Diversity and deviations from the norm, especially the predominant English language, were discouraged, and the language of the deaf was one of its victims.

Mann gave up his law practice to become secretary of the Massachusetts Board of Education in 1837. He was elected to the US Congress in 1848, shortly after issuing an impressive series of reports of a tour he made of European education systems. Ireland is listed in his itinerary; but it was the system in the German states that impressed him most.

Mann was mute about his lack of sufficient knowledge of German to make the judgements he did on deaf education and about the fact that he had never been inside a school for the deaf before going to Europe. Neither was he aware that in every oral school there are always a few outstanding pupils who can be trotted out to impress the visitors—mostly pupils who are hard of hearing or postlingually deaf: they can speak but are "lip-guessing" most of what is said to them. An example of this situation was seen recently on American television when the interview with the 1994 Miss America by Bryant Gumbel came to an abrupt ending. Miss America, who has fairly good speech, is the first deaf woman to win the trophy. To save embarrassment, Gumbel stopped the interview short when her answer did not square with his question. Only a person fluent in the language would detect her difficulty: a non-English-speaker might be convinced that she had no receptive communication problem.

Based on what Mann saw, he issued a series of reports concerning school buildings, books, apparatus, curriculum, classification, and teacher training; elementary, normal and reform schools; homes for juvenile offenders and poor children; orphanages; prisons; and hospitals for the insane and general hospitals. A tiny fraction of his reporting dealt with the deaf, but it was enough to start a century-long cycle of decline that sapped the foundations of their education system. As with the story of oralism in Ireland in the present half-century, the gullible media were willing collaborators, and the rest followed.

Mann in that flurry of report-writing was probably tricked on the subject of the education of the deaf by his ambitious friend Samuel Howe, who accompanied him on his European tour. Howe was a doctor who had a name for running a most successful Institute for the Blind in Boston. Though he had no part in the education of the deaf, he was an ardent advocate of oralism, and his object was to take the Hartford duties under his belt in Boston and perform miracles for the deaf with the new "discovery" made in Germany. The section of Mann's report dealing with deaf education would appear to have been dictated

5   *The American Picture*

by Howe:

> I have seen no Institutions for the Blind equal to that under the care of Dr. Howe in South Boston, but in regard to the instruction of the Deaf and Dumb, I am constrained to express a very different opinion. The schools for this class, in Prussia, Saxony and Holland, seem to me to be decidedly superior to any in this country. The point of difference is fundamental. With us the deaf and dumb are taught to converse by signs made with the fingers. There, incredible as it may seem, they are taught to speak with the lips and tongue. That a person utterly deprived of the organs of hearing—who never knew of the existence of voice or sound—should be able to talk, seems almost beyond the limits of possibility ... I have had the proof.[7]

Oralism was then enjoying a revival in the German states in the aftermath of the nationalist spirit that was slowly spreading in Europe after the collapse of Napoléon's empire. They harvested every native reserve they had, including the moribund "German method" for the education of the deaf. Mainstreaming—with its "deaf bench" in the corner of the village school—anticipating the present "breakthrough" in Ireland by 150 years, was introduced to over a hundred schools.

Meanwhile, signing continued covertly in class and, naturally, outside the classroom. Nevertheless, although Mann's report has been shown to be a consummate distortion of the facts regarding the value of oralism,[8] his otherwise excellent reputation in education was enough to bring public opinion with him.

Mann's report on oralism caused a sensation in the United States,[9] and Sign Language came to be seen as the cause of the "problem" of the deaf. The tide of oralism in America slowly began to flow; the long-term effect can be seen graphically in fig. 2.

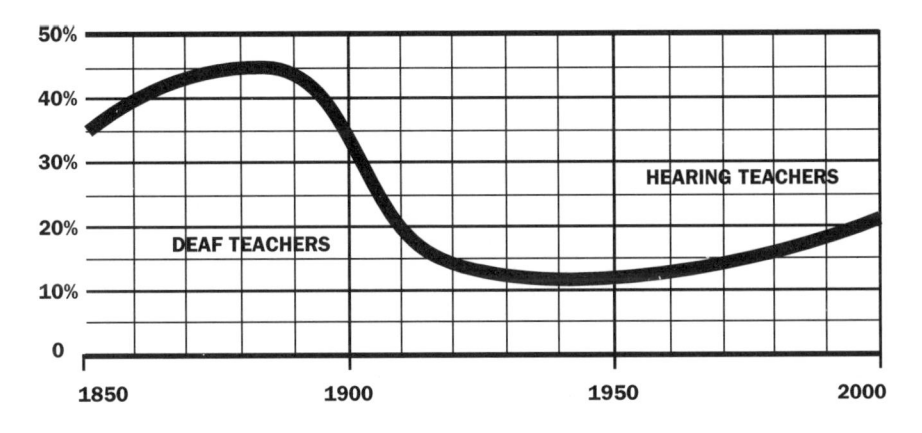

7. Lane, *When the Mind Hears*, p. 298.

8. Lane, *When the Mind Hears*, p. 302–305.

9. Moores, *Educating the Deaf*, p. 65–66.

85

Breaking the Silence

By the eighteen-eighties over 40 per cent of teachers were deaf. The ratio dropped rapidly and levelled off at 10 per cent in the late nineteen-forties, when it started to recover. Although the diagram does not show the restrictions oralism placed on the deaf teachers—they were not allowed to teach the pre-school and elementary classes, because of the exclusive emphasis on speech in this age group[10]—it is a fairly reliable indicator of academic achievements of the deaf. The fact that the concept of oralism cannot tolerate deaf teachers of the deaf is exemplified by the building of special residential oral schools where signing is strictly forbidden during the pupils' waking hours.

Alexander Graham Bell: friend of the deaf?

Howe in his last years passed the baton to younger and even more determined and vigorous allies: to Gardiner Hubbard and, especially, to the man who would emerge as the greatest champion of oralism for all time, Hubbard's son-in-law Alexander Graham Bell. Hubbard, a wealthy Massachusetts senator, had a young daughter, Mabel, deafened by scarlet fever at the age of four-and-a-half. He would have done anything to enable her to live like a hearing person and take her place in society. With the help of Mann and a gift from the wealthy Boston banker John Clarke he set up the Clarke School for the Deaf in 1867, the first oral school to survive in the United States. In keeping with Mann's ideals for the handicapped, it is situated in the backwoods of Massachusetts, in the small town of Northampton, much closer to its rival in Hartford than to the state's main centre of population in Boston. In the same year the Lexington oral school was set up to serve New York. Both of these schools catered only for children with partial hearing.

The publicity given to the Clarke School strengthened the hand of the advocates of oralism generally, and only two years later Boston decided to have its own oral day school. It was named after Horace Mann and was under the direction of Sarah Fuller. Its most famous pupil was Helen Keller, who came there after her initial teaching from Anne Sullivan. This was the age of new discoveries and inventions in America: gold mines, oil wells, steel-making, telegraph communication, the phonograph, the telephone, the coast-to-coast railway, and oralism for the deaf. Signing seemed to belong to the Stone Age!

In 1867 there were 26 institutions for the education of the deaf, and Sign Language was the language of communication in all of them. By 1904 there were 139 schools for the deaf, and signing was allowed in none. The oral method was to remain dominant until the nineteen-seventies. Secondary pupils were kept apart from younger children; deaf teachers were not employed with younger children, for fear they might be exposed to signing.

10. Lane, *When the Mind Hears*, p. 371.

5 The American Picture

The situation was not helped by the fact that the signing schools neglected to include speech training in their curriculum for pupils who had sufficient hearing to benefit from it. Hartford hired its first articulation teacher in 1857 in the first tentative move towards the middle ground of the "combined method"; but it was too little and too late, and it could not stand up to the coming storm.

When Bell arrived in America with his father in 1870 at the age of twenty-three, penniless and suffering from TB, few would have expected him to have much impact on the education of the deaf. But anyone with any sort of a name in speech training was in demand. His father had written textbooks on "correct" speech and had a reputation for teaching the deaf to speak; his father and grandfather already had a reputation for teaching elocution and "Visible Speech" in Scotland and later in London.

Bell was immediately given his first job at the Horace Mann school, teaching Visible Speech. He was a very energetic person and had an extremely inventive mind. He had a winning way and soon had a series of victories to prove it. Within ten years he was restored to health, had invented the telephone, become a professor at Boston University, given private tuition to two deaf teenagers, established a school of vocal physiology, married one of his deaf pupils, and moved to Washington, where he received an honorary Doctor of Humane Letters Degree from Gallaudet College.

The public came to assume that Bell was the authoritative voice of the deaf, and oralism prospered under him through the combination of his wealth, his international fame, his reputation for infallibility through winning a series of court claims, including a smashing defeat of the giant Western Union Telegraph Company, and his dedication to training deaf people to live as individuals in the hearing world. Towards the end of his life he said that he would rather be remembered as a teacher of the deaf than as the inventor of the telephone.

Bell was at odds with the concept of the deaf socialising with each other and of intermarriage. He maintained that the American system of education of the deaf had the effect of isolating deaf people from society. Bell placed assimilation into the hearing world above intellectual development and professional education of the deaf. Nevertheless, like many oralists, he had an ambivalent personality which allowed the accommodation of two opposing concepts at the same time. He could devote most of his energies to "helping" the deaf through oralism while maintaining that "if we have the mental condition of the child alone in view, without reference to language, no language will reach the mind like the language of signs."[11]

Like the authorities on oralism in Ireland, Bell was aware that signing was

11. Lane, *When the Mind Hears*, p. 342. Bell had the dubious honour of setting up the first lip-reading school in the United States, in 1857; his wife wrote a book on *The Subtle Art of Lip-Reading* (1895), which was translated into twelve languages.

Breaking the Silence

the favourite means of communication for the deaf and therefore the most fruitful, but prejudice towards it prevailed over his intelligence. Both his mother and his wife were deaf but never acknowledged it socially. He was, and still is, seen as something of an ogre by the deaf in America. In his lifetime he was described by them as "the most to be feared enemy of the American Deaf."[12]

In 1890 Bell founded and financed the American Association to Promote the Teaching of Speech to the Deaf, later renamed the Alexander Graham Bell Association for the Deaf, with Bell as president and Hubbard as vice-president. The organisation's title belies its real function, which was to lobby, publish and generally promote oralism. Royalties from his invention of the gramophone are to this day financing an unstoppable worldwide promotion campaign for oralism. For the past half century it has been the main source of information on matters of the deaf, and the effect can be seen in the pro-oralism slant on the deaf in the media and in almost every reference book in general circulation in English. It and its fraternal organisations, such as the NAD in Dublin and the RNID in London, grandly retail every latest "breakthrough" to the media.

The deaf education establishment had a leader in Edward Gallaudet who was more than a match intellectually for the oralism ideology lobby led by Bell, but the conflict between them grew into a personal feud. Unfortunately the public perception of the attractiveness of the speaking deaf set the fashion and appealed to the heart. The reality of solid evidence of the superiority of signing from fifty years of experience pioneered by the Gallaudets, father and son, was overshadowed by the romantic outpourings from Bell's oralism headquarters in Washington; and it suited the ethos of outward protective piety and inward indifference towards the real problems of handicapped people at the time. It is Professor Moores's opinion that

> the split between Gallaudet and Bell precipitated an educational "dark age" that lasted well past the middle of the twentieth century ... The spirit of excitement and involvement that had prevailed throughout most of the nineteenth century disappeared, as the field became increasingly isolated from general education and lost its capacity for growth.[13]

Gallaudet was one of the last defenders of the combined oral-manual system in an educational world that was being turned upside-down by the ferocity and inflexibility of the advocates of the oral-only system. The oralist teachers were acutely aware of their pupils' instinctive preference for signs. When signing is allowed to take root it grows rapidly in the many areas where it leaves talk in the shade as a means of communication. The oralists rightly identify signing in class as their last line of defence: yield on that and the

12. Comment by G. Veditz. president of the NAD, 1910.

13. Moores, *Educating the Deaf*, p. 80.

empire disintegrates.

Gallaudet's death in 1917 left the field to the oralists, who now reigned supreme. The policies in education demonstrated by Dewey and Montessori adopted in America went unheeded by the oralists. The empowering quality of progressive education was recognised as a threat by the oralists, whose outlook luxuriated in the security of the traditionalist groves.

The return of the professionals

Oralism, however, never achieved the same hegemony in the United States as it did in Europe, where direct efforts were made to incorporate the recommendations of the 1880 Milan congress into the schools. The new and more humane environment created by the civil rights movements of the nineteen-sixties has provided the first opportunity to mount a viable challenge.

The revival of the progress we see today is largely due to professionals from the academic world: the linguists, psychologists and others who, in their quest for the deeper meaning and understanding of language, turned their attention to the people with language problems: the deaf. It was a repetition of what happened during the French Enlightenment period. The philosophers were then searching for the meaning of life. They had studied Epée's discovery and how he was liberating the deaf from their isolation. Their counterparts in the twentieth century are the philosophers Chomsky, Lane, Lenneberg, Miller, Sacks, and Wittgenstein. They may not have spent a lot of time at it, but what they said gave heart to the deaf. Others who deserve equal or perhaps more credit because of their dedicated work among the deaf are Dr. Boyce R. Williams (a deaf man), Bellugi, Conrad, McCay Vernon, Meadow, Moores, Padden, Stokoe, and Stuckless.[14]

A particular example is Eric Lenneberg, professor of psychology at the University of Michigan, who in the introduction to his lecture to the International Congress for the Oral Education of the Deaf in the Clarke School in 1967 said:

> For the past ten years I have been working with the deaf—not to educate them, but to learn from them ... to substitute empirical knowledge for common-sense reasoning.

Lenneberg displayed the moral awareness and intelligent principles for the advancement of education that bring results. The committed oralists scarcely mix with the deaf communities, in effect throwing a barrier across their own learning pathway, the admission of the existence of the deaf community being tantamount to an admission of the failure of oralism.

The new blood is questioning the assumptions, anecdotal observations

14. See Jack Gannon's book *Deaf Heritage: A Narrative History of Deaf America* for an extensive coverage.

Breaking the Silence

and authoritative assertions of the oralists, while the oralists are reluctant to give time to the basic research and objective analysis of the truth-seekers and philosophers of education. The natural sign language, American Sign Language, was authenticated by the professionals as a language in its own right and is coming back in the schools, taking the place of the methodical "sign language" or signed English favoured teachers of deaf children.

In the late nineteen-sixties a series of studies by Meadow, by Stuckless and Birch and by Vernon and Koh reported that the deaf children of deaf parents who were exposed to signing were superior to deaf children of hearing parents in English, academic achievement, writing, reading, and social maturity.[15] This was in spite of the fact that the hearing families were from a much higher and more motivated social class. It gave rise to the movement towards total communication since 1975. Growth, however, is gradual and erratic, because of the use of methodical signs and signed English rather than the more natural ASL. Its full value will not be evident until the arrival of teachers with fluency in ASL.

The 1975 annual survey of deaf children and youth by the Center for Assessment and Demographic Studies indicates that two-thirds were taught in total communication and one-third in oral-aural classes.[16] More than three out of four secondary pupils are taught through total communication. Moores feels that this reflects a greater emphasis on academic content at the secondary level, which suggests that some younger children might be more appropriately instructed through total communication. It appears, however, that where total communication is applied the great majority of teachers use methodical signs rather than ASL. In a random survey of 1,760 teachers of the deaf, Woodward, Allen and Schildroth found that 32 per cent used oral-only means of instruction, 0.2 per cent used cued speech, 0.3 per cent used ASL, and 67 per cent used an English-based signing system, usually in conjunction with speech.[17] Teachers, even some who use total communication, are reluctant to acknowledge the value of it. To add to the problem some are running total communication down and rejecting it before it has been properly tried. It is interesting to read the negative comments of the oralists, but what they are really criticising is fake total communication, because total communication with methodical signs is only a sham.

ASL is forming a bridge between the deaf and hearing worlds, as can be seen in the numbers learning it in night classes throughout the United States and socialising with the deaf in their activities. Dr Oliver Sacks describes the town of Fremont, California:

> Beside its exemplary school ... it offers unrivalled work opportunities for deaf people, as well as a rare degree of public awareness and respect. The existence of

15. Moores, *Educating the Deaf*, p. 11.

16. Moores, *Educating the Deaf*, p. 11–12.

17. Moores, *Educating the Deaf*, p. 13.

thousands of deaf people in one area of Fremont has given rise to a fascinating bilingual and bicultural situation, whereby speech and sign are used equally ... There is not only interface – and a friendly one between deaf and hearing but – a considerable fusion or diffusion of the two cultures, so that numbers of the hearing (especially children) have started to acquire Sign Language, usually quite unconsciously, by picking it up rather than deliberately learning it. Thus even here, in a bustling Silicon Valley town in the nineteen-eighties (and there is a similar situation in Rochester, New York), we see that the benign Martha's Vineyard situation can emerge.[18]

A significant factor in awakening the deaf from their apathy was the civil rights movement of the nineteen-sixties. Started by African-Americans and taken up by women's organisations, it sent bubbles of ferment coursing from the stronger centres to the fringes of society. The ethics of traditional norms were being questioned, and public opinion was forcing changes.

Demands by the students of Gallaudet University that the board elect a deaf president came to a head in March 1988, when the chairperson remarked that "the Deaf are not ready to function in the hearing world." This was like a spark to a drum of explosives for the deaf students in the college. They erupted in silent rage, flooding into the streets of Washington and shutting down classes for a week. There were calls for a new board, with a majority of deaf members, to replace the existing body, which had only four deaf members.[19] Sacks came down from New York to take part in the marches and wrote in his book *Seeing Voices*:

> It is a sudden manifestation of a latent order, like the sudden crystallisation of a super-saturated solution ... a qualitative transformation, from passivity to activity, and in the moral no less than the political sense, it is a revolution.

Deaf schools throughout the country were closed by protesting students. Every politician in Washington wanted to be counted on the side of the deaf students, including the 1988 presidential contenders. But it was the warning of a cut in finance by Congress that brought the Gallaudet board to their senses. By the end of the week the chairperson had gone from the arrogant "I am in charge here" to the mannerly language of submission and acceptance, based, she said, on the "groundswell of concern for the civil rights of deaf persons."[20]

*

This historic event raised the status of the deaf across the nation; many have been appointed to positions of power, and to policy making groups and school boards; some to the chair of these boards. New groupings of deaf educators are organising workshops, conferences and courses of deaf studies

18. Sacks, *Seeing Voices*, p. 33n.

19. *Time*, Mar. 1988.

20. *Time*, Mar. 1988.

Breaking the Silence

and continuing education.[21] But they are finding that old habits die slowly, and the ingrained structures of oralist oppression will not go away in a week, a year or a decade. In March 1996 Dr. Bruce A. White, a teacher of English at Gallaudet University, noted[22] that his president, vice-presidents, deans, faculty senate chair and nearly all the teaching staff speak while they sign. However, all Gallaudet faculty and staff persons sign at all times, regardless of what form of signing they may use.

The non-deaf culture is too institutionalised in all schools for the deaf to allow the philosophy of the deaf to flourish as it should. A form of Uncle Tomism still reigns in America's schools, as it did for the blacks for decades after their emancipation from slavery. Oralist jobs, power centres, human feelings such as pride are at stake and must form part of their equation for progress.

The dignified and successful siege of Gallaudet is an example of what can be achieved by peaceful means; but one swallow does not make a summer. Gallaudet, however, now has to deal with a virtually unseen and insidious enemy in the form of mainstream schooling, which was created without any grand plan, paradoxically, by the civil rights movement in the sixties. It resulted in a dramatic switch-over from residential and special schools to mainstream schooling at primary level. It strikes at the very heart of the deaf world, because children are shepherded away from the warmth of their natural social environment from the cradle. In addition, students now have the facility of note-takers and interpreters in mainstream universities, allowing more to opt for their local college. Mainstreaming is the dream of the oralists but the nightmare of the deaf community.

Only one-third of all deaf children now have the opportunity of education through Sign Language, and this, coupled with the haphazard attempts since the sixties at Total Communication by teachers of the deaf, is having a profound effect on Gallaudet University. Gallaudet Undergraduate enrolments, too, are dropping, partly as a result of leveling out following the "rubella bulge" and partly due to mainstreaming; but their Graduate enrollment has grown signficantly, and this trend is expected to continue. Also significant is that they have many more brilliant scholars and the number of high-scoring scholars keeps growing each year. Like most universities many entrants are weak in literacy, and as such have attracted the attention of the oralists. One wonders if the recent bellicose lecture delivered in the university by Lew Golan is the first salvo of a new offensive against ASL and the deaf community?

Golan's lecture was published in the influential *Washington Post* under the insensitive headline of "Dialogue of the Deaf: What Gallaudet Won't Teach."[23]

21. See Bienvenu, "Deaf Studies in the Year 2000" (appendix G) for an example of some activities in the deaf studies field.

22. *Washington Post,* March 1996.

23. See appendix O.

It was relayed around the world by Bell's propaganda mill, *Volta Voices*—a copy of which I received from Seamus Clandillon, the new head of the Cabra boys' school. And one also wonders if the castigating of the deaf community by the Royal National Institute of the Deaf on this side of the Atlantic because of their opposition to cochlear implants for deaf children is related.

Golan is a successful deaf 55-year old American businessman who has had the enviable advantage over most deaf people of possessing fluency in English before he became deaf. He published a book in 1995 that had a sub-title that left little to the imagination about his message: *A Totally Deaf Man Makes it in the Mainstream*. His article is quite remarkable in its subtle use of half-truths, misinformation, and hostility towards ASL and the deaf community.

Successful businessmen do not usually use the form of language in public as he did in his article, or the insulting wording of the title, especially in the *Washington Post*, even if they have very firm grounds for it. His terminology of *conspiracy, dishonesty, ASL activists, ASL militants, unqualified adulation of ASL, intolerance, clannishness, narrow-minded arrogance, repeated bashings they get from the "culturally Deaf"* and:

> the militants [who are] part of a minority of deaf people who base their identity on the use of American Sign Language, who view themselves as having their own culture, and who capitalize the D in deaf to distinguish themselves from the 90per cent of deaf people who are not "culturally Deaf"

is reminiscent of the worst outbursts in the Milan Congress. It seems so unfair and irresponsible to try to set up the New Gallaudet and those he calls the "culturally deaf" as scapegoats for the poor literacy now in the university, when the blame lies with the people responsible at the primary level of education. Students are not ready to attempt calculus until they have first mastered arithmetic, algebra, and geometry. If his outburst against ASL in Gallaudet University is anything to guide us, there will be stormy weather ahead within the college.

A beneficial lesson of the history of the American deaf for the Irish deaf is that they made the greatest strides when the deaf themselves were, and are, taking the lead. Deaf professionals founded 24 schools for the deaf in the United States in the last century, and by 1870 42.5 per cent of the teaching staff at schools for the deaf were deaf. Ireland's deaf, by design, have from the beginning been overshadowed and smothered by the patronage of dignitaries from the religious, medical and legal worlds and have yet to taste the freedom the American deaf had in the second and third quarters of the last century.

6

Philosophical Approach to the Education of the Deaf

My philosophy is not easily held today when we are told that every deaf child must be exposed to the language of the deaf and the deaf culture so that he/she will become a happy, well adjusted and educated adult. I do not accept this. Neither do I believe that the reduced literacy levels can be attributed to oralism in the schools for the Deaf. It looks as if we are now going to make a mistake similar to that made by teachers of the deaf in Milan in 1880.

Sister Nicholas Griffey [1]

The philosophical study of any subject demands that we throw aside our prejudices, as far as is humanly possible, and lay open every aspect of the matter to question. Our judgement will nevertheless tend to be influenced by the perspective from which we view it and from the way it affects us.

I am endeavouring to see the education services for the deaf through the eyes of the deaf community. They are the deaf in the deaf community with whom I am familiar and from whom I obtained approval for the opinion expressed in this study. I must plead guilty to not learning Sign Language myself: this is mainly because the deaf member of my family is only partially deaf and has no difficulty communicating with a non-signing person on a one-to-one basis. Also, he went to the Stillorgan and Cabra boys' schools when they were strictly oral. It should not be necessary to repeat that people in the oralist establishment see deafness from an entirely different perspective.

Philosophy is the pursuit of wisdom through open-ended enquiry about everything in a subject. It gives a person a unified view of the world in which he or she lives. It is no longer the function of philosophy either to propound vast systems of thought, after the manner of Aristotle or Hegel, or to tell people how to behave, but to analyse statements and propositions to discover the causes of ambiguities and the foundations of meaning in language. Wittgenstein said that the task of philosophy is

> to clarify the meaning of language ... The object of philosophy is the logical

1. See appendix E.

clarification of thoughts so that the result of philosophy is not a number of philosophical propositions, but to make propositions clear.[2]

When all the fine shrubbery and the weeds surrounding deafness are removed, one is left with the individual deaf adult going through life in a predominantly hearing environment designed only for hearing people. We experience an embarrassing and difficult language barrier between us. Statistics show that the average deaf person's education (but not necessarily wisdom) is behind that of the average hearing person. The intelligences are equal, and the deaf person has spent considerably more time at school, at primary and second level, and has probably tried harder. Statistics, including longitudinal case studies, also show that the deaf have found greater intellectual progress in the signing schools. There is plenty of evidence for this, especially from the early years of the nineteenth century, and more is becoming available. Dr Yerker Andersson, president of the World Federation of the Deaf, in his address to the Second Congress of the Irish Deaf Society in 1993 said:

> Let me tell you about my experience in Sweden, the first country to introduce bilingualism to deaf children. A couple of years ago I spent a sabbatical year in Sweden. There I met deaf children every day. I was amazed by their communication. I remember when I was at their age I had no communication at all. I was forced to produce sounds to make words. It was not easy! I learned almost nothing. Today these deaf children aged seven could tell everything. They could discuss the complexity of science. They could explain some science concepts. Their knowledge was enormous—much greater than mine at their age ... Swedish research showed that you had to master your native language before you could learn other languages ... So the deaf child would have to acquire the natural language, that is, Sign Language, before learning other languages.

Another example is to be found in the description by Father Peter McDonough (a priest from the Manchester area, born deaf in 1955) of his own life. Although he was educated in an oral school, his mastery of language so as to advance to the priesthood is probably due to the signing environment of the home of his deaf parents, which research has shown to be superior to a speech environment.

> Both my parents were deaf ... I used sign language. I have two sisters, one deaf and one hearing ... I went to a Partial Hearing Unit, then to a hearing school, and in fact to several different schools or classes. Eventually I was sent to St. John's School for the Deaf, Boston Spa, Yorks ... I immediately liked it there, and for the first time in my life, I felt I was learning something; I made friends and was no longer bored or lonely as I used to be in the other schools. I spent eight years there and I learned and acquired a spoken language which was a long, slow and laborious process.[3]

2. Stumph, *Socrates to Sartre*, p. 447.

3. In Contact, Mar.–Apr. 1988, p. 15.

Breaking the Silence

Communication seems to be the core issue in the education of the deaf. Communication opens up the world to the deaf and the deaf to the world. If we have communication we have the means of getting to the final social goal: integration. This is especially important to the hearing parents: integration is out on its own, at the top of the list of priorities.

The quest for integration

Deaf people, on the other hand—as can be seen from the many disclosures of the oral teachers—want to communicate and integrate through Sign Language; in fact the deaf's natural fondness for signing is seen as the biggest obstacle to progress through the oral method. And the popularity of signing classes for hearing adults shows that there are many people in the hearing world willing to cross that one-way bridge of signing to integrate with the deaf. Integration, unfortunately, is like a biological one-way street, as much so as the flow of the blood in our bodies; but what is wrong with a one-way street when the circumstances demand it? As we have seen from the Martha's Vineyard experience and Sacks's comments on the deaf community in California, the one-way street works well; in fact it speeds up the traffic by turning disorder into order. Integration comes easily in the signing environment.

It must also be said that there are many deaf people who are quite happy living in the non-signing world, and others in the methodical signing world, and who do not want to change. The trouble is that it is very hard to change after adolescence, and we get only one chance at life.

But there is evidence that the prejudices against signing in the oral schools, the traditional strongholds of oralism, are breaking down. Many deaf people want to be on the winning side and believe that the status quo will continue. They are reluctant to break away from the comforting false security of the oralist establishment. The Sign Language segment of the deaf world obviously need the confidence-building "fix" one gets from a few important victories over the oral establishment to turn the tide in their favour.

The oralist method

The oralists, essentially, aim to prepare the deaf child for integration into the hearing world by training him or her to talk. The Cabra Dominicans claim to have established the method for performing this task,[4] but it is slowly becoming clearer from the evidence that they are not coming through in results. It is hardly a good sign that their enrolment figures have dropped by two-thirds in the last twenty-five years.

We must therefore examine the method or at least some of the things we

4. Griffey in the booklet *Irislan* (NAD, Dublin, 1979), introduction.

know about it. In fact, as noted in the earlier chapters, we know very little about the method, because it is such a well-kept secret. But, like the secret of gravity, we can examine it by its effects and its results.

First of all we must define the term "method". I like this definition from the Canadian theologian and philosopher Bernard Lonergan (1904–1984): "A method is a normative pattern of recurrent and related operations yielding cumulative and progressive results." Lonergan, a Jesuit priest, made a comprehensive study of the elements of a universal methodology in his search for a method for the study of theology and eventually came up with a formula that is useful for tackling any task.[5] Not only is his definition meaningful but each word in it is loaded with precise meaning: for instance, being progressive means it is dynamic and subject to continuous modification. This model method, which Lonergan calls the transcendental method, is built on the not-too-difficult everyday human rules of behaviour: be attentive, be intelligent, be reasonable, and be responsible. Anyone who uses what could be described as a lethal weapon, a motor car, will be well used to it and subconsciously aware of the feelings this formula can evoke.

The pattern of recurrent and related operations of the model method consists of four levels of consciousness or of knowing: experiencing, understanding, judging, and deciding.

> Progress proceeds from originating value, from subjects being their true selves by observing the transcendental precepts [of the method]: Be attentive, Be intelligent, Be reasonable, Be responsible. Being attentive includes attention to human affairs. Being intelligent includes a grasp of hitherto unnoticed or unrealised possibilities. Being reasonable includes rejection of what probably would not work but also acknowledgement of what probably would. Being responsible includes basing one's decisions and choices on an unbiased evaluation of short-term and long-term costs and benefits to oneself, to one's group, to other groups.[6]

A spirit of observation, enquiry and discovery is then nurtured by the model, because it has a pattern of operations wedded to cumulative and progressive results. Where other methods aim at serving the ideology of a particular field, such as in politics, profit-making, or oralism, by exploiting opportunities in the immediate culture, the model method can be aimed philosophically at exploiting the power of the human mind and spirit, which lie at the very heart of education. Intelligent, reasonable and responsible decisions then are more likely to follow from the knowledge of real experience, understanding and judgement of any situation.

It is not necessary to go into detail to show that the oralist method, by Lonergan's standards, appears to fall down, or that its concept would not stand up to critical scrutiny. The surveys on the reading ability of deaf pupils

5. Lonergan, *Method in Theology*, p. 1–55.

6. Lonergan, *Method in Theology*, p. 53.

Breaking the Silence

give an idea of the disadvantage they are toiling under in the critical adolescence stage compared with their hearing counterparts.[7] This is the period in which they are coming to realise that the dreams of retaining childhood friendships with those in the hearing world are beginning to fall apart and the change to the deaf world has not yet occurred. The whole pace of growing up has gone up a gear. Identity and boundary issues of a special kind are piled on top of all the other troublesome questions. This is the period when most of them cast off their inhibition about being seen signing and begin identifying with the deaf community.

The values of the deaf seen from their own world are not things one sees or hears every day in the media: they are only recently coming through the monthly half-hour television programme "Sign of the Times", and I have probably seen more blue moons than items about the deaf of an intellectual or political nature in the daily newspapers. The spiritual stimulation, or Jack Charlton effect, that a person or a group gets from the regular public airing of what they identify with, be it their country, county, hobby, or sport, is a morale boost that the deaf hardly ever experience. To make matters worse, when it occurs the honour has usually gone to the non-deaf, and the deaf are relegated to the position of grateful recipients of an act of charity.

Oralism, by inculcating this culture of dependence, whether intended or not, strikes at the roots of the deaf as a distinct society in formation; and, in addition, the educational expectations were pathetically low.

> [The nuns] are content if their pupils can lip-read people in their environment whom they know well, such as members of their own household and close associates of theirs in their employment.[8]

As a result, the deaf from oral or mainstream schools rarely have the confidence or a sufficient command of English to express adequately their views in print or in public.

Some observations on language

The study of linguistics—the science of language, its origins and structures—has grown rapidly in the twentieth century, especially in the latter half of it, thankfully bringing the language of the deaf under the microscope of professional linguists, psychologists, and philosophers. Much has been written on the subject and on the unique place language occupies in our very being. We are not usually aware of its existence until we come up against another one. Language is prior even to our humanity: without language we would not be human; and we are all born, whether we are deaf or not, with the capacity to create language, provided our fellow-beings will be sociable with us.

The capacity of young children, irrespective of their intelligence, to learn

---

7. James, O'Neill, and Smyth, "Reading achievements tests on 358 Irish deaf pupils, 1991" (see appendix I).

8. O'Dowd, "History of the Catholic Schools for the Deaf", p. 253.

the rules of language is extraordinary: by the age of five they understand the meaning of about two thousand words and by about six have learned virtually all the basic rules of grammar—even before starting school.[9]

Language, among other things, is the mechanism that enables us to function as human beings and learn all the things human beings learn, as no other beings can. Education systems work because of language. Our cradle or primary language is the unique framework on which we build and participate in the education system. The deaf, 90 per cent of whom spend their formative years in a hearing environment, are a stage removed from learning the dominant language of the people, because they cannot hear it. But with their natural talent they will learn Sign Language as effortlessly as a hearing child learns its speech language if they get the chance, as the children of deaf parents do. Once the deaf have their primary language they will learn other languages in the same way that hearing people do, as shown by the example of Laurent Clerc and his contemporaries two hundred years ago; and then the wide field of education is open to them. In the classroom they could have natural Sign Language (not methodical "sign language") rather than speech for communication, as hearing pupils have, and be able to translate the signs into the dominant language for their written work. This is precisely the education system that was operating in Epée's school in Paris all those years ago and that was working in Cabra until the nineteen-fifties.[10]

Speech, rather than the child's natural mode of communication, became the gateway for "education" in the oralists' view of life, as revealed in Griffey's paper at the congress in Germany to commemorate the 1880 Milan congress:

> Speech and lip-reading were adopted in order to give hearing-impaired pupils a better opportunity in a hearing society. *Education came to be considered within the limits and requirements of their future lives.* A manual world is a silent one [emphasis added].[11]

The thought that the Irish deaf might have the capacity to rise to the level of running the schools themselves, as Clerc and his colleagues did more than 150 years ago in America—training their own teachers and even establishing a third-level college—seems never to have entered the minds of the oralists. Cabra is slow to break away from the mediaeval tradition that made all education a training for a particular place in the hierarchy of society. This policy reinforces the feeling among the deaf that they are somehow inferior and that their "place" in the education system is absolute, predestined, and unchangeable.

There are many other qualities of life that this tunnel vision obscures, such as providing a means of communication between the deaf child and the hearing parents and other family members and between one deaf child and another in the class and the school playground or in the family home. We are

9. Kagan and Segal, *Psychology*, p. 232.

10. See appendix H.

11. Griffey, "From a Pure Manual Method via the Combined Method to the Oral-Auditory Technique" (see appendix D).

Breaking the Silence

all born with the framework for psychological, social and physical development, and most of us come, thankfully, into a natural environment in which to grow and mature.

Children acquire basic language as easily as they learn to walk, irrespective of whether they have hearing or not, provided they have the environment. The gift of language is the outcome of that which is inside us that makes us different from all other forms of life. It is what gives us our greatest powers—for good and evil. It is so common, like the air we breathe, that we are unaware of its existence most of the time; but we notice when it is missing, and improvise. The children in the Cabra girls' school, for example, were seen to be re-inventing the wheel: developing their own sign language after signing was prohibited.[12]

There is no thought for psychological development, for dealing with the child's curiosity and potential frustrations. In their journey through their tunnel the oralists never seem to have room for sitting down and really thinking about what they are doing. They close their ears and their eyes to facts of history and to opinions that run counter to their own, and the fundamental question of the deaf child's natural means of communication is ignored.

Curriculum for the deaf

The Cabra girls' school introduced secondary education in the nineteen-fifties with a watered-down version of the mainstream curriculum, and the boys followed in the sixties, after much parental persuasion, producing their first success in the Leaving Certificate examination in 1980. The traditional trade subjects were gradually dropped, ironically at a time when they were being introduced in secondary schools. Some of the deaf began to share in the abundance of education and the bonanza of white-collar jobs coming on offer. Enlightenment-led laws in the meantime were opening the doors for the employment of the disabled in Ireland and raising their horizons.

The other side of the coin shows the job market becoming flooded with people more educated than the educated deaf. The deaf were also beginning to suffer age discrimination, because they qualified much later than their hearing counterparts. The result is that unemployment among the deaf is about double the national average. One wonders which they would choose if given the options of the soul-destroying effect of unemployment and the trades of the old curriculum. This is not to say that either is the best one, or that one could have foreseen the problems; but I feel that if the deaf had the selection of the curriculum they would pick the best from both options and marry them into one that suits their inherent culture.

12. Griffey, "From a Pure Manual Method via the Combined Method to the Oral-Auditory Technique" (see appendix D).

I know also from communication with the deaf that they would wish to have a basic knowledge of Irish. Apart from giving them a broad cultural foundation it would save them from embarrassment when someone greets them in Irish or uses the occasional expression and expects the usual instant recognition. The absence of Irish from the Cabra curriculum is evidence of the low expectation of the educational capabilities of the deaf. Teachers who know the history of the deaf will be aware that pupils in Paris, in the first signing school, learned additional languages two hundred years ago. As the deaf are already deep in two languages, I believe the additional one would help in understanding the basic two, and they might pick up Irish more easily than hearing children do if they got the right type of teaching.

The employment scene has changed dramatically since 1972, when expectations for the deaf were high in the Department of Education:

> It is generally recognised that in the past the average deaf child leaving school was some years behind his hearing peers in educational attainments. We envisage that in the future that gap will be reduced ...[13]

Indeed it is generally acknowledged that the deaf are further behind now. The pool of hearing competition is now far bigger, and hearing trainees have easier access to the educational opportunities now given to school-leavers and to the unemployed. The competition is getting keener for the deaf in the work-place. The few deaf who have, with great difficulty, earned a single third-level qualification must compete for jobs with hearing job-seekers who often have two or three degrees.

Perhaps the stage has been reached where the whole system of education should be investigated. The deaf are bound to make better headway operating in the secure base of their own educational and vocational leagues, provided they have the freedom to expand into the hearing world where they can. There must be a better way than following the relatively new (200-year-old) rigid Industrial Age education system of the hearing world, which is now found not to be working satisfactorily for society in general. The examination and academic points system for entry to third-level education suits the bureaucrats but does not make a lot of sense to the student. It is hardly the most suitable method of selecting the best candidates for physical education. An independent college for the deaf would no doubt bring about an entirely different curriculum from the established one in Cabra.

We must remember that such a college does not yet exist anywhere, although the Americans came near it for a while in the eighteen-sixties. The Irish deaf never got the chance of exploring their own repertoire, so we do not know what will come out of experimenting: the weakening or loss of one of one's senses usually brings a benefit in some of the other senses.

13. Department of Education, *The Education of Children who are Handicapped by Impaired Hearing*, p. 81.

Breaking the Silence

The deaf are now shackled into a structure in which they have no power and that was designed by people who believe they know more about the deaf than the deaf themselves. It is similar to the colonial model of society, which we Irish know only too well. The whole culture of Cabra and oralism in the education of the deaf runs counter to the philosophy of deaf culture. It encourages dependence, sentimentality, helplessness, and the more distasteful aspects of charity. An objectionable aspect of oralism is that it was authoritatively presented and comprehensively accepted as the conclusive solution for the deaf. Had it been the first experiment ever in oralism and pursued in the spirit of experimentation and learning it would have some credibility.

I believe that the curriculum is at the very heart of education of the deaf and unless the resources of deaf culture are tapped for clues to it their education will suffer. Non-deaf educators and anyone not immersed in the deaf culture and community are simply looking through the wrong end of the telescope in trying to find it. With the present concentration of oralist ideology, one wonders how these influences can be entirely excluded from the process of formulating a new curriculum.

Teachers' experience

The oralists claim to have more experience than anybody else and to be the fountain of truth in the field of education of the deaf.

> The education of ... the deaf ... is difficult but we know the techniques ... The methods are established.[14]

Outsiders and researchers are scoffed at.

> There is no substitute for first hand experience in our field ... Professionals in the periphery express great dissatisfaction ... Is it due to lack of experience in the education field? ... I have the advantage of having spent the greater part of my life in a school for the deaf.[15]

The oralists disregard the peripherality of their own position. Sadly for everyone concerned, they do not understand that they lack the most important experience: the experience of being deaf as a baby, in childhood, in adolescence, in adulthood, in old age, in the deaf family and community life, in the hearing world and in an oral classroom. In place of the experience of deafness they construct their own model and try to force their pupils into it by a process of "educational treatment".

The unique teaching experience the oralists possess must be examined. We must discriminate between experiences that are worth while educationally and those that are not. Is it the experience of implementing a fixed method of training to a fixed set of rules as a functionary in a rigid regime, or is it the

14. Griffey, *Irislan*.

15. Griffey, *Irislan*. See also "Oralism versus Signing" (appendix C).

experience that leads to greater understanding of what is going on educationally? The former is concerned only with understanding and perfecting the *method*, ignoring everything else. The oralists do not heed the progressive educational messages and information coming from the pupils: that signing is the easy road to education for the deaf.

> I must confess that we teachers relied on it [signing] when we wanted to convey a message quickly ... Deaf children ordinarily learn to communicate fluently by manual means [i.e. signing] before they acquire competence in English ... When an important message had to be given it was signed and written ... Manual communication is more static [*sic*], more attractive and in some cases has inbuilt concepts so that it is more suitable than the fleeting speech ...[16]

The value of learning from experience has been emphasised by many philosophers and educationalists, particularly John Dewey (1859–1952) and Bernard Lonergan. They showed that because the mind is fundamentally a problem-solving instrument, experiencing and experimenting are the important aspects of the process of coming to the level of understanding. But experience must be stored and critically examined, to save what is useful and to put aside what is not, while learning from both. An educator will, if they have rapport with the pupil, develop strategies more appropriate to the child (and potential adult) than one who must work to some externally preconceived method. But the first step on the ladder to success is experience, coupled with attentiveness, intelligence, responsibility, and reason.

> Every experience is a moving force ... The greater maturity of experience which should belong to the adult as educator puts him in a position to evaluate each experience of the young in a way in which the one having the less mature experience cannot do. There is no point in being more mature if, instead of using his greater insight to help organise the conditions of the experience of the immature, he throws away his insight. Failure to take the moving force of an experience into account so as to judge and direct ... means disloyalty to the principle of experience itself. The disloyalty operates in two directions. The educator is false to the understanding that he should have obtained from his own past experience. He is also unfaithful to the fact that all human experience is ultimately social: that it involves contact and communication. The mature person, to put it *in moral terms, has no right to withhold from the young ... whatever capacity for sympathetic understanding his own experience has given him* [emphasis added].[17]

In the oralist system there is no space for the deaf educator, because deaf people have not got the necessary speaking voice for that sort of communication. The ideas of the deaf are cut off, breaking the feedback loop essential for growth.

16. Griffey, *Iríslan*. See also "From a Pure Manual Method via the Combined Method to the Oral-Auditory Technique" (appendix D).

17. Dewey, *Experience and Education*, p. 38.

A process of decline

What is worse about the ideological method is that what Lonergan called a cumulative process of decline sets in. Discussions based on reason tend to unsettle and threaten some people, activating their defensive system. Decisions become dominated by the need to defend previous bad decisions. Words and terms are remoulded and distorted and given unclear meanings. Orwell suggested that the slovenliness of our language makes it easier for us to have foolish thoughts.

What I call lip-guessing is called "lip-reading"; language is called "speech", implying that Sign Language is not language; what should be called speech clinics are called "schools for the deaf"; methodical signs are called "sign language"; oral mainstreaming is called "integration"; and the negative euphemism "hearing-impaired" is used instead of deaf.[18] The language of the deaf is denigrated, which in turn leads to deaf culture being denigrated. All sign language that evolves outside the oral schools gets the disparaging title of "low-version" sign language, while the school system of signed English is given the more confidence-inspiring title of "high-version" sign language.[19] The stigmatic term "manual" deaf is applied to the deaf community. "Educational treatment" replaces teaching. Deaf pupils and adults are referred to in metaphor: "They can communicate more effectively with hearing professionals who work with the deaf. They know deafness from the inside *as it were* so that much can be gained from their experiences."

The message that oralism was destined to be the ultimate solution for deafness, followed by the phasing out of signing, except for a few individuals, was carried to people in high positions. The proposition was expertly presented (by the non-deaf) to create a feeling of compliance, complacency, and contentment, that we have here people on whom we can depend and who are doing first-class work in difficult circumstances. Below the surface, however, is a maze of subtleties and uncertainties. Statements that appear clear and unambiguous often carry hidden meanings that resonate and bring comfort and satisfaction to audiences with vested interests.

The Dominicans systematically promoted their policies to politicians, bishops, media people and education professionals at all levels. The message is in turn relayed down the line to influence the minds of the public.[20] What is described as the "education" of the public was the first priority of the National Association for the Deaf when it was set up in 1962. The result is that no matter where one goes for information on the deaf, outside the Irish Deaf Society, one is bombarded with the oralist version of things, or meets with a blank face if one's question is a little too deep.

It is well to recall that today's deaf educational institutions, though they

---

18. The positive attitude of the deaf is demonstrated by the expression I heard from one of them recently: "Sign Language was developed not because deaf people *can't* hear but because they *can* see."

19. Griffey, "From a Pure Manual Method via the Combined Method to the Oral-Auditory Technique" (see appendix D).

20. O'Dowd, "History of the Catholic Schools for the Deaf", p. 235, and numerous newspaper articles. The oralist propaganda has recently swept Épée's name out of *Encyclopaedia Britannica*, except as a minor figure in Sicard's world. Sicard gets an entry to himself, and

have become strongholds of oralism, owe their existence to the network of signing systems initiated by Epée and Gallaudet. Oralism was grafted onto the healthy root system of those schools. I believe that the concept of oralism does not possess the seeds to bring forth such fruit on its own and that we have oralism today because the public were not aware of the inside story.

The deaf obviously will not succeed unless they have the authority of the state to clear the decks for them. That, I believe, is the philosophical approach to this seemingly intractable problem. From my experience with deaf people I have no doubt that they are capable of going it alone, provided there is absolutely no-one outside the international fraternity of deaf communities overshadowing them. They must be free to select and employ outside professionals as needs arise.

The latest example of decline, paradoxically, is the resumption of signing in the Cabra schools, in that they are having their teachers taught methodical sign language (rather than Irish Sign Language). They are in effect going back to the barren system used in the era that gave birth to oralism and continuing the downward spiral. Perhaps in another fifty years we can expect a new crop of oralists growing out of dissatisfaction at the progress of this artificial system introduced by today's experts.

Apathy among the deaf community

Possibly the most profound of all the changes has been the change of environment experienced by the young pupil starting in the oral school in Cabra. In the pre-oral days a child came out of a non-communicating hearing family at the age of seven or eight and into, for the first time in their life, a habitat where they could freely discuss their feelings and socialise with children who shared an inborn linguistic identity.

A gaping hole in the oral proposition and culture is the lack of consideration for a means of conversation among deaf people. The emphasis is on getting the deaf person to communicate with the hearing person. The voice and the ears are almost useless instruments of communication among the deaf. A survey of adult deaf in 1988 showed that 68 per cent stopped using hearing aids when they left school, and 83 per cent said they used Sign Language among themselves in school.[21] This fact and its consequences have never been addressed by the oralists. Dr Phoenix told the first congress of the Irish Deaf society in 1988:

> In 1982, I found intelligent young people sitting all over Northern Ireland ... understimulated, mostly frustrated ... unable to communicate with their parents, and longing for some further education and training. Their parents were often bitter and resentful that they were misinformed about the prospects for their deaf

Heinicke, the oralist, an even longer one.

21. Phoenix, Interim Report on a Pilot Survey, p. 19. All had been pupils of oral or mainstream schools, and 20 per cent went to the Cabra schools. The survey also showed that less than half of them understood their teacher.

teenagers. When I recently visited those young people I found that their social and psychological lives had deteriorated in 5 years.[22]

Deaf children need an environment in keeping with their potential socialising strengths that will nurture their inherent identity of deafness. Oralism, on the other hand, tries to deny and hide their nature, concentrating on their weaknesses. Concentrating on the weaknesses diminishes the valuation of their untouched resources. The detrimental impact of this on the child's confidence is cumulative and tends to encourage dependence. Evidence of this can be seen in their unwillingness to challenge the status quo in the education system, which created this apathy. An example of this can be found in the deaf interviewers in the survey carried out in Northern Ireland in 1988 by the psychologist, Susan Phoenix, who

> were themselves shocked that deaf people were accepting things that they did not like in their everyday lives without question ... Many seemed puzzled that their ideas were being sought ... [This] illustrates exactly how passive and neglected the deaf adult population in N.I. have been for many years. Perhaps the expression killing with kindness is relevant here ... "Integration" is definitely not happening except for a small minority of deaf adults.[23]

The Dominicans tried to insulate the girls from life's buffeting to the point where it created a deep, destructive dependence. In 1860 the chaplain noted signs of this when he advised the nuns on the advantage the boys had over the girls: "In fact, this is precisely what requires correction; too much has been done for the girls and they have been made do little or nothing for themselves."[24] On leaving school their environment would change overnight from a seven-year-long dreary institutional regime in a religious community that was completely isolated from the outside world. The fact that the nuns provided a home at the school for up to a hundred deaf women who were unable to fit into the hearing world also indicates the state of dependence when their schooling was finished.

Oralism, by its very nature, in subjecting pupils for fourteen years to an impossible task, tends to condition the pupils to believe that ordinary tasks are impossible. The cultural conditioning is doubly damaging to the deaf because it includes disparagement of any attempts the pupil makes to employ their own natural language and strips them of any aspiration to believe in their inherent capabilities.

The colonial structure of the establishment stands over the deaf like a living Colossus, frustrating every move they make and mopping up rewards rightly belonging to the deaf themselves, while giving the impression, through media headlines, that everything in the garden is rosy. Like the slaves in America, the deaf have neither the power nor the will to win

22. Proceeding of the First Congress of the IDS, 1988.

23. Phoenix, *Interim Report on Pilot Survey*, p. 36.

24. O'Dowd, "History of the Catholic Schools for the Deaf", p. 75.

without the assistance of friends who are willing to struggle for their human rights. They are totally dependent on some efforts from the hearing world to cut the Gordian knot.

On the question of fighting for control of the education system, the plight of the Irish deaf of today may be compared to that of the Irish nation in 1907, as described by the French sociologist Louis Paul-Dubois, with its

> fatalism, lethargy, moral inertia, and intellectual passivity, the general absence of energy and character, of method and discipline, distracted by denominational struggles, sectarian fanaticism, and the first phases of anticlericalism.[25]

Changes, good and bad

A serious scrutiny of some of the measures that were taken to support the Cabra oralism system, and some of the results of it, might help to clear away the mythology surrounding oralism; it might help us take our minds off the wood for a moment and examine individual trees. A system that is specifically defined is usually more yielding to objective evaluation. A little selective information can cloud the mind; a lot may bring a clearer view.

A number of changes directly unfavourable to the deaf population were introduced because they were found necessary for the oralism method:

• Deaf teachers were no longer employed to teach the deaf. The booklet issued on the centenary of the foundation of the Dominican school in 1946 shows a picture of nine such teachers. Only one deaf teacher has been put on the payroll in the last fifty years.

• Teacher training was moved from the schools to UCD, while the Department of Education, as advised by the Dominicans, laid down standards that made it virtually impossible for a deaf person to qualify as a teacher of the deaf.

• Segregation was introduced in Cabra to keep the deaf sequestered from the not-so-deaf. This divided the deaf community into the two separate cultures that are so evident today. Segregation was carried out at enormous cost, because new premises were constructed and existing ones remodelled for the purpose. Oralism requires small, acoustically treated classrooms for a maximum of seven pupils. The signing school had large, well-aired rooms, one of which held 130 pupils in fourteen classes.[26]

• All children had to start in the oral class, and those who failed were termed "oral failures". Deaf children were categorised into a hierarchy of values, giving the child with the best speech the top position. This must introduce a feeling of inferiority to the very people the schools are employed to serve. More deaf meant more inferior. A child who made good progress with oralism

25. Corish, *Maynooth College*, p. 239.

26. O'Dowd, "History of the Catholic Schools for the Deaf", p. 127.

Breaking the Silence

was the favoured one of the teacher and the role model for the class. These were assumed to have higher intelligence than the rest. This lowers the self-esteem of fellow-pupils who find it impossible to lip-read and speak, and the one who is assumed to be more intelligent may not be so. (This is regularly done by innuendo: "In the case of dull children and others who fail to make progress in the oral method ..."[27]) Professional researchers have found that the failure to establish language through speech is not due to "general lack of intelligence [in deaf children] because it does actually not take much of those skills measured in intelligence tests to come by rather good language ability."[28] Before oralism there was just one word in Cabra for all whose hearing was not good enough for a hearing school: it was simply the word "deaf" (or, too often, the more derogatory term "deaf and dumb"), with no discrimination between the degrees of deafness, as there is now.

• With the change of the Cabra schools' ethos by setting their face against signing came the subtle denigrating remarks about Sign Language. I have heard of the following loaded remark made to pupils by one teacher: "Do you want to belong to the deaf ghetto?" Oralism was upgraded by downgrading signing. The prejudice against signing radiated from the centre, to all teachers and staff, to parents, to friends of the deaf, to church and political authorities, and naturally to most of their young, impressionable pupils. The schools no longer identified themselves with the signing deaf child. There was a frown or a wag of the finger, or worse, for the deaf child expressing himself or herself in the way they found easy and natural. Signers became the Cinderellas of the Cabra household. The teachers were aware of this, but they have ploughed on, like those bumbling British generals of the First World War, as they became locked into the system and culture.

• The dismissal of deaf teachers deprived pupils of role models and cut the school off from the benefits of feedback from valuable opinions of deaf adults and their cultural identity markers. It is ironic to read of van Uden and Griffey using that elegant, all-embracing term "cybernetics" to describe the narrow micro-level relationship between the ears and speech and the assumed value of rhythm to the deaf, while they ignore the far more important macro-level of the social relationship of the deaf child within the deaf community.[29] Oralism logically leads to isolation of the deaf children from their natural culture and the study of its history during their formative years. They are not taught the history of their own deaf culture or anything about the turbulent history of oralism. They are deprived of the opportunity for their community to become involved in school activities in early adolescence, which would give them a more gentle transition into the harsh hearing world.

• The stress caused by depriving the children in pre-school and early

---

27. Department of Education, *The Education of Children who are Handicapped by Impaired Hearing*, p. 174; O'Dowd, "History of the Catholic Schools for the Deaf", p. 253. See also Griffey, "From a Pure Manual Method via the Combined Method to the Oral-Auditory Technique" (appendix D).

28. Lenneberg, "Prerequisites for Language Acquisition", p. 1316.

29. Griffey, "Speech Methodology at St Mary's School for the Deaf" (see appendix A), quoting Anthony van Uden, *Principles and Practices of Cybernetical Approach in the Physical Education of a Prelingually Deaf Child* (see appendix A.

6 Philosophical Approach to the Education of the Deaf

childhood of their natural means of communication with family members has been referred to earlier.

The following are some of the beneficial changes brought in since 1946 to support oralism; who can tell what advances would have flowed from them if they were applied to the signing schools?

- The duration of deaf education was extended from approximately seven to fourteen years, or longer if desired by the pupil. Children are now starting in their third year, whereas they started at seven in the pre-oral days. (This extra time required for teaching by the oralist method is consistent with the advice given to a parent in 1883 who wanted to send a child to a Catholic oral school in England: "More could be done in one year by the sign system than in two years by the oral system."[30])
- There are up to three times more teachers now with oralism than in the pre-oral days.[31] In 1955, according to O'Dowd, the norm was 14 pupils to a teacher; it is now down to 6 or 7.
- Educational guidance courses were set up for parents with pre-school deaf children, which made possible an important partnership between pupils, parents, and teachers.
- A peripatetic teachers' service was established to pay educational visits to families with a pre-school deaf child.
- Pupils were given more time at home, for example at weekends. Children in the Dublin area were no longer forced to board.
- The environment and the teacher-pupil relationship in schools has changed from rigid discipline to a more friendly and flexible child-centred one, from the master-disciple relationship of the nuns and brothers in the pre-oral days to the conventional graduate teachers who generally have children of their own.
- Hearing aids of high quality are issued free to all deaf children. Though they are no help to some, they can make a big improvement to the child if they can take the loss down to the 60 dB range in the middle and higher-frequency levels.
- Teachers of the deaf are now paid more than teachers in hearing schools, whereas in the pre-oral days they were paid less. This is by no means a hint that their pay is too high: it is a statement of fact, a factor of quality in the equation that should not be overlooked. It is also a fact that the teachers of the deaf were also very badly paid in America in their golden age of deaf education, from 1817 to 1880, and in France in Sicard's time. Does this show the intrinsic value of love over money as the fuel for the fire of enthusiasm? The beneficial effect of the change to the school was counteracted by the malaise of oralism, which cooled enthusiasm.

30. O'Dowd, "History of the Catholic Schools for the Deaf", p. 212.

31. O'Dowd ("History of the Catholic Schools for the Deaf", p. 217) incorrectly states that only one-third more teachers are needed for the oral system.

Breaking the Silence

The aural-oral system demands that communication be admitted through the ears rather than the eyes. Pupils who have not had home speech training or a suitable hearing aid are evidently introduced with no means of communication and others with little prospect of learning a suitable one:

> A baby who has been using a hearing aid in the pre-school years and who has had home-training will usually have a few words on admission to school. If not he will be able to babble.[32]

This seems to be an unsocial and entirely unsuitable environment for a developing child. The immobility of body and arms demanded by the aural-oral type of oralism practised in Cabra to get the child focusing only on listening must have a numbing effect. This version as practised in Cabra is no doubt one of the most difficult varieties of oralism.

The atmosphere is typified by the pious hopes—reminiscent of Alexander Graham Bell eighty years earlier—of Brother G. J. McGrath, principal of St Gabriel's School for Deaf Boys in Sydney, Australia:

> We absorb the use of the pattern as developed at St. Joseph's School, St Louis, Missouri ... We have a saying to give daily support to our faith in auditory training: "You are going to hear me, not lip-read me ... Our hope is that it will produce rich fruits. Our belief is it will: if, only if, it is supported by quality teaching. Until the day comes when advances in medicine and genetics will prevent deafness, we will have a task to be done ..."[33]

One could imagine what that would do to a classroom: it is the inverse of that wonderful atmosphere created by Robin Williams in the film *Dead Poets Society*.

Griffey also acknowledges the help she received from the Missouri school after she reverted to signing when it came to preparing her class for First Communion; although oddly enough, unlike their advice to McGrath, they recommended lip-reading for Cabra's oral-aural school:

> I wrote to the Sisters of St Joseph who ran a successful oral school for the deaf in St Louis, Missouri concerning my worries about religious instruction for the deaf through the oral method. The principal of the school, Sister Rose, replied: "Having been a teacher in our school before the transition I can judge both sides. Sister, speech and lip-reading make the deaf child much more normal, facilitates his thinking process, and fit him to take his place in a hearing world."[34]

Griffey is profuse in her thanks for the help and inspiration she received from the leading oral establishments: the Ewings in Manchester University, the Sint-Michielsgestel Institute for the Deaf in the Netherlands, the Clarke School in Northampton, Massachusetts, and Lexington School for the Deaf in New York. Nevertheless, though the impression is given abroad that ideal conditions existed in Cabra,[35] there is evidence that after twenty to twenty-five years of oralism things were fairly chaotic, when it was deemed necessary to

---

32. Griffey, "Speech Methodology at St Mary's School for the Deaf" (3cc appendix A).

33. McGrath, *Proceedings of the International Congress on Education of the Deaf, 1970*, p. 373.

34. Griffey, *From Silence to Speech*, p. 45.

35. Griffey, "Speech Methodology at St Mary's School for the Deaf" (se appendix A). In the same paper Griffey mentions that "we are fortunate in St. Mary's that we have schools for the non-deaf on the campus" of the school for the deaf, obviously to encourage an oral atmosphere. However, my enquiries indicate that hopes of fruit from this asset were never realised. The pupils never mixed.

increase the teaching staff by 40 per cent:

> Acute staffing difficulties ... an abnormally high turnover of teachers ... Over the next five or six years it will be necessary to increase the teaching force by about 40 ... from the present teaching staff of 97.[36]

It would be interesting to know how much Cabra would have improved educationally in the signing era if that amount of assistance was given to the schools. It would not be unreasonable to assume that the assistance was given in the expectation of a proportional increase in educational progress. We look in vain today (apart from the recent successes of a relatively small number at second and third-level education) for the fruits of the following Government expenditure, quite apart from the enormous extra input of energy by the pupils:
—on the capital costs of up to £10 million (in today's money) for new schools built for the oralist system;
—on the annual financing of all the extra teachers, including the travelling costs of the visiting teachers;
—on the university teacher training programme.

What touches to the quick is the fact that the majority of pupils sadly now leave the Cabra schools with a reading age of eight or nine[37] and that

> the profoundly deaf four-year-olds, who used Total Communication in their everyday environment, were capable of more independent thought than the 16-year-olds who had been educated orally until the final years of their education.[38]

The oralists try to charm their friends with anecdotes such as the following one from van Uden. When speaking to an audience of bishops, priests, Catholic social workers, teachers of the deaf and psychologists from fifteen countries, he gave a single example of a three-year-old child to prove his point and make it the basis of a general conclusion:

> Once I heard from a teacher of the deaf, an advocate of manualism, that deaf children never ask "why-questions". This is not true at all![39]

Note the disregard for professionalism and the derogatory use of the term "manualism" for signing; and the worst meaning for this incredible statement is hung on an unnamed advocate of signing.

Van Uden's loaded remark is an example of the common thread connecting all oralists through the ages. Deaf culture is damned by false praise, and anecdotal evidence is used in place of research and professional analysis. Their anecdotes are invariably about young children.[40] One remarkable exception is Griffey's statement that "international studies in language attainment have shown that many deaf children reach standards which are appallingly low,"[41] but the phraseology seems to make it appear that Cabra is not included. Recent research, however, shows that Cabra's standard is equally low.[42]

---

36. Department of Education, *The Education of Children who are Handicapped by Impaired Hearing*, p. 135–136.

37. James, O'Neill, and Smyth, "Reading assessment tests on 358 Irish deaf pupils, 1991" (see appendix I).

38. Susan Phoenix, *Disability Today*, 1990.

39. Anthony van Uden, *Proceedings of the Second International Catholic Conference on Religious Education for the Hearing-Impaired, 1983*, p. 62.

40. See *Sunday Times*, Dec. 1987, for correspondence among oral "experts" citing the progress of young children and some young adults.

41. Griffey, "From a Pure Manual Method via the Combined Method to the Oral-Auditory Technique" (see appendix D).

A number of other changes have also come about, mainly from the more liberal climate in Ireland since the nineteen-sixties. They occurred independently of oralism (although the oralists claim credit for any progress of the deaf) and were enormously beneficial for deaf pupils and all schoolchildren. Parents have become more supportive of their children since becoming conscious of the importance of education, and the presentation and graphics in schoolbooks are a huge improvement on the books of the pre-oral days. And the climate in the able world is slowly becoming more tolerant of minorities and disabled people.

Early intervention

The main part of the oralist early intervention programme is aimed at the identification of children with hearing loss and providing for their language acquisition through speech training. There is no dispute or complaint about the wisdom of providing early intervention to teach the parents how to cope with their new situation. The idea is one of the most praiseworthy undertaken by the Dominicans. The defect in it was the use of oralism to achieve it.

The deaf signing parents of deaf children who know about these defects are its strongest critics. At parents' meetings, as at any meeting of hearing people, the most vocal people dominate, and the deaf are no match for them in making this point. The early intervention is serviced by the visiting teachers, and because of the potential for embarrassment in the relationship between the parent and teacher, parents are slow to criticise. There are therefore few reports of complaints about the service.

Neglected in the early intervention programme was any attempt to educate the public on the dangers to health lurking during pregnancy because of smoking and other causes. In several studies of the aetiology of deafness in the last 150 years, about 30 per cent of cases were shown to arise from unknown causes.[43]

Perhaps the most invidious aspects of the oralist version of early intervention are the attractiveness of the term and the reassuring effect it has on the new parent of a deaf child. Their introduction to it is part of the medical scheme of things; the Cabra Clinic programme assures the parents that help is at hand and there is nothing to fear: we have the answer to your problems. The parents are caught at their lowest ebb and are grateful to leave things to take their course. The doubts may not arise until the child is about seven, after he or she has had a few years' schooling with very little to show for it.

42. James, O'Neill, and Smyth, "Reading assessment tests on 358 Irish deaf pupils, 1991" (see appendix I).

43. Moores, *Educating the Deaf*, p. 90–91.

Mainstreaming and the visiting teacher service

Mainstreaming, or "integration", as it is sometimes called, is a by-product of oralism. It is based on the belief that if speech is a suitable means of communication for a deaf child, then it is logical to educate the child in the local school, where they will have the support of a hearing environment both at school and at home. It is a very attractive proposition, especially if the child's hearing test shows that they have a fairly "flat" curve well below the 70 dB mark[44] and the school principal is willing to take them on.

Mainstreaming hardly existed in Ireland before the oral era, but, for reasons not yet fully explored, it now accounts for more than two-thirds of the deaf pupil population. A clue may be detected in the CID's brochure issued for the opening of the premises for the deaf in Drumcondra, Dublin, in 1991:

> Arrangements were then [1961] made by the Department of Education with the Principal of St. Mary's School for the Deaf for the setting up of classes for hard of hearing pupils in ordinary schools in Dublin and Cork. Through St. Mary's Clinic many hard of hearing children wearing hearing aids were integrated on an individual basis in a number of ordinary schools throughout Ireland. However, the need for special supervision for them was obvious. Following requests to the Department of Education a Visiting Teacher of the Deaf Service was established. For the first two years of its existence the work was supervised by the Principal of St. Mary's School for the Deaf. Today there are twenty seven visiting teachers of the deaf in the Republic of Ireland. They are supervised by an inspector from the Department of Education.

The role of visiting teacher is one that many of the deaf in the local deaf community would willingly carry out in their spare time, at a fraction of the cost. Valuable time is being wasted that could be used to teach Sign Language to the family, to say nothing of the cost of the service. In the heyday of deaf education in America, France and Ireland the children did not start school until they were between seven and nine, and they quickly learned their primary language through socialising and playing with their fellow-pupils. Perhaps it is a sign of a realisation by the Department of Education of its limited utility for the deaf that the visiting teachers' work load was recently extended to include children in the general range of disabilities.

Recent surveys indicate that mainstreaming has no educational advantage over the Cabra schools.[45] We had that opportunity of sending our eleven-year-old, Brian, to a small, first-class boys' school when the time came for him to transfer from the Stillorgan Junior School. After much consideration of the damage it might do to his self-confidence if he did not succeed, we decided that St Joseph's School for Deaf Boys in Cabra was a better option. Looking back on it from the perspective of academic progress and friendships earned, none of us

---

44. Susan Phoenix found that parents are often not told that the profoundly deaf child with some recognisable speech has a "flat" curve at 80 dB, whereas their child may have a curve sloping down in the high frequencies and no speech prospects. In our own case we were not told of the significance of the sloping curve.

45. James, O'Neill, and Smyth, "Reading assessment tests on 358 Irish deaf pupils, 1991" (see appendix I), and Phoenix, *Interim Report on a Pilot Survey*.

have regrets over our decision. He had a two-year mainstreaming stint in a regional technical college after finishing in Cabra but did not derive the benefit he should have got because he had not got an interpreter or note-taker.

The method of mainstreaming that would satisfy the deaf community would include a signing environment in the school, home and social circle of the deaf child. These conditions cannot be produced in the manner of a magician pulling a rabbit out of a hat, but a start could be made at short notice where the conditions are right, and it could be extended gradually. On the contrary, it will probably take several years and changes in social attitudes, but it cannot be done without the inclusion of deaf adults in its execution. In fact it would be seen as radiating outwards from deaf adults in the immediate locality of a deaf child: they would tutor the family and people in the locality of the child in Sign Language. The teacher would have one of the bigger and brighter children monitor the child. Short-term arrangements, such as drafting in remedial or visiting teachers to local schools, as practised now, are enormously expensive and not very effective without a signing ambience.

Formerly it was not uncommon for parents of a deaf child to move their family to the Cabra or Stillorgan area so that the child could live near the school. The philosophy of the deaf would avoid this by the creation of a signing environment around the deaf child's family and school district. This seems to be a more humane and more inexpensive way of dealing with it.

Oralist mainstreaming—which, it is worth repeating, is now catering for more than two-thirds of our deaf children—isolates the child in a sea of hearing people. An invidious aspect of mainstreaming is that it cuts off the lifeblood of the deaf community: few of the deaf who go through that system mingle with the deaf community, and they are often at the mercy of hearing people for friendship. Oralists appear to be unaware of this obvious potential for social isolation and all the heartbreak that goes with it.

The idea of mainstreaming is passionately rejected by the progressive elements of the deaf community, because of the isolation it can bring to the deaf individuals in later life and because it is striking at the roots of the deaf community's potential for growth. It has flourished in the United States since the nineteen-seventies, after Congress started promoting mainstream schooling, to the dismay of the deaf communities.[46] Nevertheless it is an option that both the Department of Education and Cabra believe is workable. There are now "about 50 pupils with severe and profound hearing loss being taught in special facilities in ordinary primary and post-primary schools,"[47] partly because of the failure of the special schools to perform to expectations and partly because of the simplistic notion that oralism is workable and extendable to the mainstream schools.

46. Bienvenu, "Deaf Studies in the Year 2000" (see appendix G).

47. *Report of the Special Education Review Committee*, 1993, section 4.2.6.

I have no first-hand experience and little information on the classroom end of it; but I have heard and can easily understand the teacher's complaint at the 1991 forum about how difficult it is to give time to a deaf child in her class of thirty-nine pupils.

It is unlikely that finance will ever be found for the Dominicans' latest dream solution for education of the deaf: mainstream them in primary school classes, which would have to have a maximum of twenty pupils.[48] I believe it is doubtful if mainstreaming deaf pupils in a 20-pupil class would be much better than the 39-pupil class for the child who can hear little of what is going on and has no Sign Language. Germany's abortive adventure in the world of mainstreaming from the eighteen-thirties to eighteen-sixties should give food for thought to those embarking on this policy in Ireland at the present time.

The multi-handicapped child

It is a long-established policy that the multi-handicapped child, if its deficiencies include poor hearing or speech, is handed over to one of the Cabra schools for education. Little study appears to have been done to determine the merits or suitability of this policy from the point of view of those children whose only handicap is deafness. These schools have become a catch-all service centre, because this appeared to be the commonsense way to deal with the problem. Bureaucratic institutions are protective of their powers and personnel and have not got much incentive to change. It is an attractive one for the medical people and civil service, because it allows them to pass the buck. The educational structures and charities were keeping the seemingly intractable problems out of sight and ensuring the survival of the healthiest. It dovetails into the education ethos of the nineteen-thirties, as can be seen in the report of a Department of Education commission of enquiry:

> It is in every way undesirable that mentally deficient children, even of the higher grade, should be placed with normal children. Such children are a burden to their teachers, a handicap to other children, and being unable to keep up with the class, their condition tends to become worse.[49]

The origins of this policy can be traced back to the establishment of the Cabra girls' school itself. This school was modelled on the Institut du Bon Sauveur, Caen, which at that time (1844) had three times more mental patients than deaf pupils. Mental sickness itself was then a catch-all category. Medical treatment in the psychological field changed little until the nineteen-sixties; the differentiation of human dysfunctions was limited to a few obvious categories such as deafness, blindness, and mental illness.

O'Dowd's history in 1955 makes no mention of the multi-handicapped pupils in the Cabra schools. There are eleven pages in the 1972 report on the

48. Griffey, *From Silence to Speech*, p. 143.

49. *Report of Commission of Enquiry into Reformatory and Industrial Schools in Ireland, 1934–36* (Stationery Office, Dublin, 1936).

Breaking the Silence

subject. The incidence of multi-handicap within one unnamed school for the deaf (which may be assumed to be the Cabra girls' school)[50] is 17 per cent, or 27 per cent if language-disorder children are included.

Aphasia (partial loss of the ability to understand or use words, spoken or written) was discovered in the girls' school for the first time after the introduction of oralism.[51] It would be interesting to know what relationship, if any, there is between aphasia and the teaching method; for instance, does the action of signing conquer the problem? Dr Hughlings Jackson in his studies in the eighteen-sixties found that aphasia affected people most in their speech and less so in writing, with hardly any effect on signing. It did not seem to have much effect on limb movement, such as dancing or finger-spelling and what he called "pantomime" (Sign Language?).[52] This may account for the emphasis placed by oralist teachers on rhythm in the teaching of speech.

> Certain signs are accented by being placed at the beginning of a sentence. This form of thinking militates against the development of rhythmic groups which are so important for the understanding and production of language [speech?][53] ...

The same authority states:

> Children who are taught a musical phrase, or better still to play one, will have a better understanding of the melody and rhythm of a sentence as a unit in speech.[54]

Frank Maguire, the vice-principal of Cabra boys' school, advised that

> in the world of deaf education [speech training?] it is rhythm, stress, intonation and voice quality that really matter ... Put the music, put the melody into the speech of the hearing-impaired child. Expose him to the rhythm, stress and intonation of his language.[55]

There is no reason to doubt that the oral teaching methods for the multi-handicapped are complex and that the teachers possess expertise that no-one else has. In ordinary life if something is complex and requires uncommon expertise, the inventive mind sooner or later comes to the rescue. That is a natural human resource common to us all. Most great innovators, such as Montessori and Shockley, although they had the highest academic qualifications in their fields (Montessori was the first woman to qualify as a medical doctor, and Shockley initiated the great electronics revolution), started attacking problems at the bottom, at the level of underlying principles, rather than reading about "breakthroughs" in the latest literature. They took on problems that had not yet been satisfactorily resolved but that showed a reasonable chance of success. They surrounded themselves with all the available information on what had proved possible as well as what had not. They examined ways that had been found unsatisfactory before and learned the reasons why. If you have not got the facts you cannot eliminate the

---

50. Griffey, "Oralism versus Signing" (see appendix C).

51. Griffey, "Deafness or Language Disorder—Differential Diagnosis" (see appendix B).

52. Jackson, "Aphasia and Kindred Afflictions", p. 58–63.

53. Griffey, "From a Pure Manual Method via the Combined Method to the Oral-Auditory Technique" (see appendix D).

54. Griffey, *Proceedings of the International Congress on the Education of the Deaf*, 1967, p. 642.

55. *St. Joseph's School Year Book*, 1980, p. 13–14.

methods that will not work and you waste time working on what has already been tested. These innovators operated as true professionals and invited criticism from their peers, because they were learning from mistakes.

The great inventions too came from simple beginnings to satisfy needs. They came mostly from "uneducated" people and from unexpected places. Writing, five thousand years ago, and the ubiquitous ballpoint pen, fifty years ago, and many other inventions, such as Bell's telephone, came accidentally by good fortune. When something is not working satisfactorily and is exceptionally complex—whether it is a machine, a marriage, or a method—it itself is screaming out for attention or modification. How often has an insensitive driver come to unexpected hardship because he or she did not detect the signals from dropping pressure in a tyre or in the engine oil?

It is not good enough for the teachers to tell other interested parties that unless they have teaching expertise they cannot make justifiable criticisms and contributions. That is like the attitude of the dog in the manger. The establishment's regular byword to parents is "Listen to the informed comment of the experts," giving the impression that they know all the answers. An expert is only a person with one way of doing something. The prudent seeker of truth goes to at least two independent experts. The number of catastrophes caused in all walks of life because too much confidence was placed in experts hardly bears thinking about.

The emphasis and the educational programmes appear to be formulated to suit only the two minorities within the category of deafness: the deaf whose adult life, it is assumed, will be spent with hearing people, at one end of the spectrum, and the deaf with more than one handicap, at the other. The rest, who account for 73–83 per cent of the deaf pupils (based on Griffey's figures) and who have a spread of IQ comparable to hearing children, are subjected to the "educational treatment" of oralism and deprived of education in their favourite and natural means of communication. The main body of deaf pupils are practically abandoned, to satisfy the needs of those at the margins.

Griffey's advocacy of one teacher for each deaf child[56] possibly springs from her understandable concern for the extreme ends of the spectrum. Her reported comments on deaf education concentrate not on education but on the areas of treatment and speech training. On the surface, the individualist approach seems like a reasonable one for pupils in those categories, but it would need testing on selected pupils and strict professional evaluation. Nevertheless it is clearly as absurd to apply individual teaching to the 73–83 percentile as it would be to apply individual teaching to individual hearing children. The only reference I found to this important section of the deaf school population was a comment made by Griffey in 1975:

56. Griffey, "From a Pure Manual Method via the Combined Method to the Oral-Auditory Technique" (see appendix D).

There is a very real danger today that in our preoccupation with the problem of deaf children with additional handicaps—who are in the minority—we may forget the needs of the average and above average child.[57]

One surprising advantage of the individualist approach for the multi-handicapped would be an overall reduction in the number of teachers required for teaching the deaf, as a signing teacher can teach up to three times more pupils in the signing system than with oralism.

For some time I have been considering the psychological effect on the deaf of bunching multi-handicapped pupils into their educational environment. This is a very sensitive matter, which deserves sensitive investigations. I have tried to imagine myself in a similar situation in the hearing world and found it not very attractive. Whatever about the way we should feel about such things, deep down there are certain things we do not like or do not want to be associated with and other ones with which we positively want association.[58] Children instinctively want to be associated with success and excellence and seek friendship with the best of their own sort. Most children harbour notions of reaching the highest level in their own field. Nature provides them with the desire and curiosity to get to know things and explore themselves through others like themselves. This is an innate mechanism we possess from our genes and, together with healthy psychological and humane growth conditions, is the innate right of every child.

One distressing result of the pathologising method of the Cabra educationalists is the routine use of the term "treatment" rather than "teaching" when discussing the education of the deaf. I believe that every remnant of the idea of "treatment" and training must be banished from the environment of schools for the deaf. For this reason I believe that an education establishment committed to the single discipline of the education of pupils whose sole disability is deafness is the most appropriate objective. The incorporation of the multi-handicapped deaf could be considered in the future when the reformed deaf schools have come of age. This incorporation is occurring now in hearing schools as they become more humane places for minorities with the successful mainstreaming of some categories of handicapped children.

I have no experience with the problems of the multi-handicapped child and cannot comment on how it is handled, except to mention the method used by Montessori when she was a student doctor in Rome in the eighteen-nineties. She studied the literature on the earlier attempts of Itard and Séguin, the failures and successes, and learned from the mentally retarded child in a client-centred situation in a professional approach. I believe it

---

57. Griffey, "Oralism versus Signing" (see appendix C).

58. I know that the deaf community were very annoyed with both the chairperson and the chief executive of the NAD joining forces with the National Parents' Council for Special Schools for Mentally Handicapped Children in the campaign by the Belfield Centre for Training and Development to establish a third-level institution for people with mental handicap, as an integral part of UCD. At a public meeting on 19 Nov. 1991 attended by several TDs, including two who are now members of the Government, the NAD chairperson took the liberty of

demands attention independently of the education of the 73–83 percentile of deaf pupils. Treatment, where it applies to the multi-handicapped, should be done by people with special skills appropriate to the disability. Unlike deaf children, who thrive better in a signing environment than in an oral one, the multi-handicapped may be more satisfactorily accommodated in mainstream schools near their own home; but every one of these complex cases will probably need individual attention.

The lip-reading myth

The myth that the deaf have the ability to know what a person is saying by looking at their lips is only about a hundred years old. Alexander Graham Bell, who has the dubious honour of having started the first classes for its study, can also be given the credit for the myth itself. From regular use, started by the oralists, the term is now part of the vernacular. I have on occasion been told by people, in their innocence, that the deaf have no problem communicating by lip-reading and that they could follow what players on a football field are saying. Examples of the dissemination of this *faux ami* of the deaf come at us from all quarters. The presenter of the "Late Late Show", Gay Byrne, responding to the actress Louise Fletcher, who told of her father who was deaf and was once the winner of a propaganda competition for lip-reading in America, said: "He mustn't have any difficulty whatsoever lip-reading."[59] George Bush's comment "Read my lips" is often quoted and will be remembered for the way he used it to emphasise his principal pre-election pledge, not to bring in new taxes. The word has such currency now that it has the respectability of an authorised term; it would look eccentric to give it the quotation marks treatment—"lip-reading"—that a counterfeit term normally gets.

 None of the authorities warn that they are short-changing their readers; but the lip-readers get only about 25p for their pound. Investigations by objective researchers have shown that good lip-readers in a one-to-one situation understand about 25 per cent of what is spoken. In English, 40–60 per cent of sounds look like some other sound on the lips, and even the best adult lip-readers seldom grasp more than 25 per cent of the words spoken, using their knowledge of the topic and of the language to fill the gaps.[60]

 Lip-reading involves much guesswork and is also very tiring. Understanding lip-reading is very like the experience a hearing person has when trying to follow a language in which they are not fluent. If they do not know the topic and its vocabulary they get lost almost before they start. For this reason hearing people, because of their wider range of language, have been found to be better lip-readers than deaf people: they have a bigger

---

describing herself as speaking for the majority of the deaf community. The NAD hand-out for the occasion listed among other things its belief in mainstreaming —something the deaf community opposes.

59. RTE1, Oct. 1993.

60. G. Gustaston, "The development of a sign system for representing spoken/written language" in *Proceedings of the International Congress on Education of the Deaf*, 1980, p. 283.

reservoir of words to work with. One study in the United States found that trained deaf people could not do as well as completely untrained hearing people. In Ireland, we are told that

> the nuns at St. Mary's feel they have succeeded when the pupil's speech is intelligible in the home, with friends and among fellow workers, likewise they do not expect the average pupil to understand everybody's conversation through lip-reading though exceptionally bright children with a flair for this art will succeed in doing so.[61]

It should be noted that it is physically impossible to lip-read and to follow signs at the same time. Lip-reading therefore belongs to the oralist world and is used by deaf people who were educated in the oral schools. Lip-reading, it must be said, is of value to those who become hard of hearing late in life, when picking up a new language is difficult and they do not want isolation from their friends in the hearing world. This category of deafness, however, is worlds apart from the culture of the deaf community.

The deaf community

The study of the nature of deaf communities and their culture is only a recent activity. It is now becoming a subject, like Black studies and many other minority studies, for third-level students in mainstream universities in the United States under the title of deaf studies, with promotion from the College for Continuing Education in Gallaudet University.[62]

Very little is known or recorded about deaf communities, particularly in Ireland, before the nineteen-seventies. Like all minorities, their activities were restricted by social norms; but they did exist, in small groups. Families with several deaf children created their own sign languages and the embryo of a community. Jean Massieu, Sicard's famous teacher, came from such a family. A fact about deaf children that is hardly ever noted is that they can learn Sign Language socially and learn trade skills to make themselves independent without going to any school. If they do not learn to read or write they would be no different from the 10 per cent of the hearing population who cannot either and many of whom lead lives as normal as those who can.

Deaf people obtain normality in the company of other signing people, whether they are deaf or hearing. Their participation in various organisations such as the communities of deaf social and sports clubs allows individuals to acquire a sense of self-esteem, which it may not be possible to develop in hearing groups or groups of deaf people dominated by hearing people.

The deaf communities, like most other minorities, had an underground type of existence until recently. In fact from the following comment one would wonder whether one actually existed in Ireland in 1974 (note the

61. O'Dowd, "History of the Catholic Schools for the Deaf", p. 253.

62. Bienvenu, "Deaf Studies in the Year 2000" (see appendix G).

quotation marks in the original):

> In areas of high density population it is possible to create "deaf communities". The deaf person trained in manual communication can function very well in such a community. This is not the case in my country, for instance, where a comparatively small population is spread over a wide geographical area ...[63]

At the other extreme—that is, where signing is commonplace, as in Martha's Vineyard, or on the east coast of America in the heyday of signing—we know there were no corporate deaf communities. The deaf in America and Britain did not form their national associations until they were threatened by oralism in the eighteen-eighties.[64] Membership of a deaf community is governed by boundaries that distinguish members from non-members. Some are eligible to belong and some are not. Membership is achieved through *(a)* identification with the philosophy of the deaf community, *(b)* shared experiences that come of being deaf, and *(c)* participation in the community activities. Without all three characteristics one cannot be a member of a deaf community. Deaf communities are linked to each other and to communities internationally by their national association's membership of the World Federation of the Deaf. The national association of the deaf in Ireland is the Irish Deaf Society.

It is ironic that the Cabra schools, the core element of the deaf community, is an environment dominated by hearing educators opposed to the use of Sign Language. The Cabra oral ethos marks out clear boundaries between the signing deaf and the deaf who live solely in the hearing world, and between those who accept the "official" methodical signs and the deaf community's natural Sign Language. Nevertheless, it is not uncommon for them to present themselves before the hearing world as members and friends of the deaf community.

Not all deaf people identify with the deaf community. There is an almost endless variety of deaf people. The identity of someone who loses their hearing after adolescence is already fully established as a hearing person. People who become deaf late in life usually find it difficult to learn Sign Language and to empathise with deaf community culture; recent research in Britain shows that they are as likely to stigmatise members of the deaf community as hearing people did in the past.[65] Paul Higgins's research brought him face to face with deaf people in many different walks of life and with combinations of relationships between deaf individuals in the hearing world and others in deaf communities and others in both. The variety of cases is too numerous to attempt summarising them here.

At the heart of every community is its language, and more particularly its jargon and its own peculiar expressions and favourite subjects for discussion.

63. Griffey, "Oralism versus Signing" (see appendix C).

64. The British Deaf Association was founded in 1890 by Francis Maginn (1861–1918) of Mallow, Co. Cork, the son of a Protestant clergyman.

65. Paul Higgins, in Gregory and Harley (eds.), *Constructing Deafness*, p. 24.

Breaking the Silence

This is part of the social cementing that keep communities together. In the larger community it binds cultures, races and nations together. When individuals in minorities use their own language within the larger community they are expressing pride in their social identity and their birthright. Newcomers who take up the language are welcomed with open arms, and the minority community becomes a little stronger.

The deaf community's unique weakness comes from the smallness of its numbers and the dominance of the speech language. It has a very weak inheritance to build on and has a need more vital than any other community to strengthen its language. Paradoxically, however, as history has shown, the need for the existence of the deaf community itself will wane as more hearing people learn to sign.

*

The following is the first sentence of the quotation at the heading of this chapter but with the words "deaf" and "of the deaf" crossed out to move us out of the narrow field of the deaf to see the wider landscape:

> My philosophy is not easily held today when we are told that every ~~deaf~~ child must be exposed to the language ~~of the deaf~~ and the ~~deaf~~ culture so that he/she will become a happy, well adjusted and educated adult.[66]

I have no doubt that Griffey would not want to deprive any child of such freedom; but the remark reveals the predicament she finds herself in because of the circumstances of her own environment. It results, I believe, from the culture of the Cabra Dominicans, as described in chapter 1. We are all creatures of our culture and conduct ourselves according to its customs.

I believe that the decision in 1846 to hand the Dominicans the task of teaching the deaf girls of Ireland must be accepted as having been unfortunate, at the very least. Measures have been taken since then to modify and improve the situation that in fact have made it more difficult to unravel; but that is all in the past. The task of today is first of all to resolve the conflicts in the world of all the Irish deaf so that they may find the strength in their unity to plan and carry through their own destiny in their own way.

66. The passage is from the Thomas Watson Memorial Lecture at Manchester University, 1988, by Sister Nicholas Griffey (see appendix E).

7

Epilogue: The Swan Report, 1994 and a modest proposal

Happenstance smiled on my work as I had it virtually complete in the form of the report of an extensive professional study on the Dublin schools for the deaf[1] (although it would have made life easier if it had come out before I started). The study was carried out for the trusties of the Catholic Institute for the Deaf by a retired UCD professor of psychology, Dr Ethna Swan. The statistics of the report, from the responses of the deaf adults (two-thirds of whom are past pupils of the schools) and the parents of deaf children at these schools in 1993/94, present a model framework for evaluating my hypothesis, by virtue of the fact that they come from a direct linkage to that unique silent majority in the world of the deaf. The feelings of the grass roots of the world of the deaf were expressed through the anonymity of the secret ballot; the centres of power were almost entirely bypassed, except for the supply of physical data.

Several events and processes contributed to the birth of Dr Swan's study. The Cabra oralist education establishment is being sharply challenged by the recent flow of information from other countries on the progress of minorities in general and the deaf in particular, from British television programmes on the campaigns and achievements of the deaf and other disabled people, books and other literature on research, and conferences organised within the domain of the World Federation of the Deaf.

Events in 1991 and 1992, such as the spurious Forum on the Education of Hearing-Impaired Children and the meetings of the Irish Deaf Society with the Minister for Education and his officials and with the Special Education Review Committee, alerted the establishment to the fact that they could not depend on the deaf delegates to meekly validate their policies.

The Dublin schools also have problems peculiar to themselves, such as the extraordinary drop in enrolments, by 40 per cent in fifteen years: from

1. Swan, "Report of the Study on the Dublin Schools for the Deaf" (1994, unpublished; a copy of the report is available in UCD Library).

Breaking the Silence

764 in 1979 to 460 in 1994. Paralysis in the face of a seemingly all-powerful establishment and the spinelessness of the Department of Education[2] have prevented even an examination of the problems. The majority of teachers up to the nineteen-sixties were clerics, but their total number has fallen to six (two in each school) and is expected to shrink further.[3] These problems, which are largely of their own making, gave rise to the phenomenon of the united action by the schools for the first time in their 150-year history.

The Catholic Institute for the Deaf, together with the principals of their two Cabra schools and McQuaid's Beech Park school in Stillorgan, sensing their common weakness in the face in a moving world, took collective action in January 1993 by calling in an outside professional to help. (In fact all the establishment organisations are interlocked in relationships to maintain their common mission: principals of the schools on the CID board, NAD people on Government agencies and parents' councils, and attached to the CID, and so on. In addition, most of the boards can boast since the late eighties of one or two deaf adults.)

The questions in the researcher's brief are evidence that the whole concept of a religious institution in control of the education of the deaf was opening up for review, even from within the establishment. For example, the terms of reference are phrased defensively and address the future of the establishment rather than the education of the deaf:

(1) The future response of the three religious congregations who have run the schools for many years.

(2) The future role of the Catholic Institute of the Deaf in the education of deaf children.[4]

The Swan report is nevertheless the most professional and extensive research ever carried out on the deaf in Ireland. Opinions were gathered from a sample of 237 deaf adults, together with 372 parents of 483 deaf pupils now at school and 78 of their teachers. Questionnaires were also returned from the United States (42), Britain (6), Canada (5), Switzerland (3), Australia (2), Sweden (2), and Denmark (1), making a total of over 300 questions, many of them multiple-choice, and slightly over 750 individuals responding.

In the perspective of the deaf world this is progress analogous to the giant step made for data-gathering in the weather-forecasting profession from the *Old Moore's Almanac* variety to today's satellite technology, with the possibility of verifiable reality replacing inconclusive assumptions and meaningless theories. It would be impossible to do justice to the valuable service Swan has done by letting in the light, seeing what is in the minds of the people who live with and confront the obstacles, as distinct from those in the nine-to-five periphery and those dictating affairs by remote control.

---

2. The Minister for Education announced in the Dáil recently that she is going to reactivate the Advisory Committee on Education of the Deaf; this will be the third resuscitation attempt in the past six years. The 1972 report's recommendation of a co-educational primary school in Cabra was neglected until a few years ago and the plans are now rejected by the Dept.

3. Swan, "Report of the Study on the Dublin Schools for the Deaf", p. 407.

4. Swan, "Report of the Study on the Dublin Schools for the Deaf", p. 2.

7 Epilogue: the Swan Report, 1994

But the study was in the nature of information-gathering and is really technician-level work—the easy part of a process. It must now be taken up to the next level, to that of interpretation, evaluation, judgement and formulation of policy, approval by the deaf community, and further cycles of review. This will call for skills derived from experience that Swan unfortunately does not possess. She is qualified in her field to carry out this survey, but she informed me that she has no experience of deaf family or community life and no deaf teaching experience. The non-disclosure of this information in her report, as also of the fact that she is a Dominican nun, is a critical lapse in its professionalism. It is important that readers of this type of work be fully informed of the background and allegiances of those who produce it; it is all the more important in the light of the probability that Swan is going to do a follow-up survey.

Swan must be given credit for the otherwise excellent job she has done, and all those who assisted her must also be complimented; they confirm my belief that there is a solid body of support for some radical changes among those who are operating the oralist programme. Her professionalism, aside from the weaknesses noted, will hopefully set an example for the future; but if the leadership of the process is in the wrong hands, wrong outcomes are assured. What is needed now are individuals from the deaf community with the necessary skills, assisted by like-minded hearing professionals who have made common cause with their fellow-travellers, as it were, to continue the process. The mystic of the professionals should be treated with scepticism and not be allowed to dominate the process; no action must be taken without the approval of properly elected deaf officers.

The Swan report underpins one of the principal points of my hypothesis: the vital question of classroom communication. For example, out of the 237 past pupils came the following responses on how deaf children should be taught:

	YES	NO
Sign language	206 *(92%)*	14 *(6%)*
Speech and lip-reading	168 *(79%)*	42 *(20%)*
Sign language, speech, & lip-reading	213 *(94%)*	10 *(4%)*[5]

5. Swan, "Report of the Study on the Dublin Schools for the Deaf", p. 342–343.

Although many of the questions asked were a little sloppy—"Should deaf children be taught sign-language?" etc. (in a signing environment deaf children acquire their first language by social living, just as hearing children do: there is little or no teaching involved or required until the spelling, reading and writing begins at school)—it is reasonable to assume that the respondents took these questions as meaning the method of classroom

Breaking the Silence

communication and not just the subject to be taught. When the responses to other questions are studied—for example the teacher's non-use of Sign Language—the inability to understand what the teacher was *saying* is given as the main reason for not doing well at school.[6] Significantly, a large proportion of the parents (84 per cent) support the deaf adults on the issue of Sign Language in the schools.

It is interesting to note the deceptive property of statistics. In the above sample, in two of the three questions 79 per cent of the deaf asked for speech and lip-reading at the same time as 92 per cent asked for Sign Language. In other words, they want speech and lip-reading, but not as much as they want Sign Language. This response comprehensively overturns the following defence used by Griffey to justify the imposition of oralism:

> [1] In a survey carried out in 1946, it was shown that 95% of the past pupils wanted Irish deaf children to lip-read and speak.[7]
>
> [2] In 1950, I found that 90% of the past pupils of our school in Dublin wanted Irish deaf children to speak and lip-read ... The position has not changed much today.[8]
>
> [3] The past pupils of St. Mary's, Cabra, Dublin, were consulted by me when in 1946 it was decided that an oral/aural approach would be adopted ... At that time 95% of our past pupils wanted Irish deaf children to learn speech and lip-reading.[9]

We are not informed whether the selected past pupils in the latter surveys were asked the same questions that Swan asked; but even if they were one could say then, as one could say today with a degree of truthfulness, that 79 per cent were in favour of speech and lip-reading; but that would not be telling the whole story. Neither are we informed whether they were told that the consequence of their responses was the prohibition of Sign Language in the school and in the homes of the deaf and, hopefully, the death of signing in the whole country. Although these surveys were carried out by hearing people there is no reference to the fact that respondents in these situations often give a different answer to one of their own than to a person from a different or especially from a "superior" culture.

A disturbing piece of information thrown up by the report is the exceptionally high number of broken marriages in the hearing families of deaf children. No doubt a child who cannot communicate and express their feelings can be an innocent source of trouble. Oralists must shoulder some of the blame for this problem. It echoes the conclusions in America by Schlesinger, who found "disproportionately high incidences of psychiatric casualties among deaf children" and laid the blame squarely on the lack of adequate communication (i.e. signing) between parent and child in the earlier, formative years. She recommended encouraging hearing parents to communicate with their deaf children in Sign Language during the early

6. Swan, "Report of the Study on the Dublin Schools for the Deaf", p. 352.

7. Griffey, "From a Pure Manual Method via the Combined Method to the Oral-Auditory Technique" (see appendix D).

8. Griffey, "Oralism versus Signing" (see appendix C).

9. Letter to the author, 14 Apr. 1992.

7 Epilogue: the Swan Report, 1994

years.[10] In 1988 I had a discussion about deafness with Stan Foran, a deaf man, prominent in the Dublin deaf community. He told me he was particularly concerned about the frustration experienced by young deaf children unable to hear or sign and therefore unable to communicate their feelings to their minders except by pointing and body language.

The study did not address the philosophy of the control of the schools by a body other than the CID, for example by the deaf, although the questions in the researcher's brief seemed to allow for it. It was an inept omission, because I feel that if the objective direction of the study was extended to that subject, realisation of its inevitability would follow. In fact the focus of the report is on the future of the establishment in the field of education of the deaf rather than the state of the education system, the reasons for its decline, and the best course of action to remedy the CID's problem.

For instance, an option that could be explored in the light of the apparent surplus of classroom accommodation is the opportunity of handing over one of the schools to the deaf community to allow them to develop their own signing school in their own way. This would give the deaf what they desire and allow the Cabra establishment to continue as they desire, at arm's length from each other but hopefully co-operating where possible. This proposal would be an opportunity for the CID to do their part to heal some of the rifts in the deaf world, through consultation with accredited representatives of the deaf community, in addition to formally conceding to them the rights and property of the deaf community. It would be a chivalrous act from the establishment, echoing the petition from *The Merchant of Venice*:

The quality of mercy is not strained.
… It is twice blest:
It blesseth him that gives, and him that takes.

The priorities of Swan's study are in sharp contrast to those proposed by the Irish Deaf Society to the Department of Education in 1992: firstly, to establish the outcome desired by the deaf; secondly, to establish how this can best be achieved; and finally, to redesign the control structures and existing premises to suit the system. The difference between the two approaches highlights the unbridgeable gap between the two organisations.

The question of mainstreaming, which is second only in importance to the Sign Language issue, is dealt with under the misleading title of "integration", and, regrettably, it was viewed through the eyes of the establishment rather than those of the deaf community. In fact the use of the respected term "integration" is a symbolic antidote to the hated terms "segregation", "alienation", and "isolation". The establishment see mainstreaming as "integration" by helping the deaf to become "normalised"

10. Schlesinger, "Headstart in Deafness" (see appendix F).

Breaking the Silence

through speech, lip-reading, hearing aids, regular attention by visiting teachers, a reduction in class numbers, and so on—a very expensive venture with little or no record, or possibility, of success.

The deaf see their own form of mainstreaming as a simple and inexpensive transformation of the hearing and speech environment rather than the conversion of the deaf, introducing some elementary Sign Language in all primary schools and among the family and friends of the deaf child, leading to a normal and meaningful atmosphere for the deaf in the locality of the local school. These two meanings or views of mainstreaming are as different as chalk and cheese, and Swan's handling of the subject demonstrates her own limitations in the field of education of the deaf.

Some of the answers to questions on mainstreaming are untrustworthy because of the wide range of meanings of the term "integration". However, one question to the deaf adults is very clear: "Should deaf children go to a special school for the deaf?" The response was: yes, 204 (93%), no, 13 (6%).[11] By more than 15 to 1 the deaf are against the oralist version of mainstreaming. How much more support is needed to put an end to this madness? Even the majority of the parents (69 per cent) prefer a special school for the deaf rather than a partial hearing unit for the deaf within the mainstream school (53 per cent) or mainstreaming (18 per cent).[12]

Mainstreaming, which began after the introduction of oralism and is in fact a by-product of it and now accounts for two-thirds of all deaf pupils, is manifestly not what the great majority of the deaf want. It is ironic and to some extent weirdly logical that oralism—whether it is a failure or a success—leads to Cabra's demise: if the present trend of enrolments of the last fifteen years were to continue for the next fifteen years they would have no entrants by 2010!

As parents begin to accept that oralism is a failed ideology they naturally stop sending their children to the oralist special schools. On the other hand, if oralism is ever proved, or even believed, to be a success, parents will want to send them to their local mainstream schools. In either case the deaf would lose the opportunity of meeting other deaf children and of immersion in Sign Language and oral culture at infancy. Mainstreaming destroys the embryo of the deaf community. The Swan report notes:

> Deaf people are happier in the deaf community, only 41 per cent are happier in the hearing community, (Table 289) but 80.1 per cent of deaf people think they should be able to move between both communities (Table 290).[13]

Those responsible for the building of special schools to segregate the oral from the signing zone within the special schools will be interested to know what the deaf think of that bright idea: 92 per cent said that "In boarding

11. Swan, "Report of the Study on the Dublin Schools for the Deaf", p. 346.

12. Swan, "Report of the Study on the Dublin Schools for the Deaf", p. 219.

13. Swan, "Report of the Study on the Dublin Schools for the Deaf", p. 351.

school, children who are hard of hearing, partially deaf and profoundly deaf *should live and play together.*" And for further confirmation, 91 per cent said that "in boarding school, children who are hard of hearing, partially deaf and profoundly deaf *should not live and play separately.*"[14]

Under the heading "From your own experience what changes would you suggest in the education of deaf children?" signing teachers, Sign Language in the classroom and other matters relating to signing make up almost half of the 242 suggestions submitted. Fifteen suggestions called for better sex education, the next-biggest matter on their minds.[15] Some further points of interest in the report are:

- The priorities of the researchers can be detected by the questions asked of the parents: five on the parents' opinion of the quality of religious instruction (with suggestions for improvements sought from those who are dissatisfied), but none on the other curriculum subjects. By contrast, in the suggestions box the deaf adults put English grammar at the top of their shopping list.
- Those who replied are almost evenly divided on the almost unanswerable question whether Sign Language prevents children from learning speech.
- The majority stayed at school to the age of sixteen or over.
- More than half said that school did not prepare them well for work.
- Co-education is approved, especially at primary level. (All schools in the United States, Sweden and Denmark are co-educational and have never been otherwise.)
- Of the 61 foreign schools, 46 responded to the question concerning what is described as the local preference for the means of classroom communication, showing 15 (33 per cent) for total communication, 10 (22 per cent) for bilingualism, 9 (20 per cent) for "all options", 7 (15 per cent) for TC plus bilingualism, 3 (7 per cent) for oral-aural, and 2 (4 per cent) for oral-aural only. The difference between oral-aural and "oral-aural only" is obviously that the first admits to using some signs while the latter does not! In either case it shows an oralist minority of 1 against 9.
- One wonders if the absence of communication between the researchers and such old friends of the establishment as Manchester University, the Clarke School in America, the Sint-Michielsgestel institute in the Netherlands and the Bon Sauveur school in France is evidence of a desire by the establishment to start secretly ditching oralism, their main objective being simply the retention of control of the schools. Griffey acknowledges that it was after the advice she got on her visit to the latter two schools in 1951 that she decided on segregating the girls' school in Cabra; and, as she said,

> since there was no involvement on the part of the Department of Education we were free to make plans for the development of an oral atmosphere in the school.[16]

14. Swan, "Report of the Study on the Dublin Schools for the Deaf", p. 348.

15. Swan, "Report of the Study on the Dublin Schools for the Deaf", p. 357–359.

16. Griffey, *From Silence to Speech*, 47–55.

17. Compare, for instance, the launching of Griffey's book (which is openly hostile towards control of the education system by the deaf and pronounces judgements diametrically opposite to those of the majority of the deaf community), six months after Dr Swan's report, by Dr Tony O'Reilly, chairman of Independent Newspapers Group and patron of the NAD. The launching was extensively

Breaking the Silence

- Conspicuous also is the absence of precise information on those who commissioned and produced the report, or of comment on the report from anyone, particularly by the establishment magazines. There was not even a murmur, and nothing of the usual publicity or triumphalism that has accompanied events of far lesser importance to the deaf.[17] The Irish Deaf Society and the Department of Education were each given a copy, without comment, eleven months after it was printed. (It was printed in July 1994 and given restricted public exposure when a copy reached UCD Library in September 1995.) It would seem that the report is being treated the way an unwanted child was in harsher times, as if it were an embarrassment to the establishment.

*

Taking together the responses of the deaf and the parents on the school language policy and mainstreaming, it is not difficult to recognise the need for radical reform and to see why the deaf see oralism and the control of the schools by the non-deaf as the underlying obstruction to all they stand for.

To finish, I will quote the anonymous and poignant response of a past pupil that Swan cites at the conclusion of her section on the deaf adults.[18] Evidently it is from a woman and a past pupil either of the girls' school or the mainstream. It summarises the disabling effect of oralism on a deaf person and probably says more about those institutions than Dr Swan's report and my study put together:

When I was young, I have very poor speech, I am well lip-reader.

I am very intelligent.

When a teacher asks the questions I know answer and wanted to tell her, but I can't talk as she does not understand if I tell her.

I lost my confident.

It is unfair.

---

reported on 16 Dec. 1994 on two pages of the *Irish Independent*, on radio, and on television. The chief executive of the NAD, Niall Keane, reviewed the book in the NAD magazine *Link* (winter 1994, p. 17), starting with "Deaf people, parents, teachers, professionals, read this book," and finishing with "Sr. Nicholas has managed to write a deaf education studies programme for all encapsulated in the pages of this worthwhile book, my advice is read it and read it well."

18. Swan, "Report of the Study on the Dublin Schools for the Deaf", p. 362.

Appendix A

Speech Methodology at St Mary's School for the Deaf

Address by Sister Nicholas Griffey to the International Congress for Oral Education of the Deaf, Northampton, Massachusetts, 1967*

Even though it was suggested to me earlier this year that I speak to you on speech as an important factor in social and emotional development, I felt that I would make a more worthwhile contribution to this conference if I referred to the method of teaching speech which is used in the school in Ireland where I have been working for almost thirty years. You may wonder at my choice! St. Mary's School for the Deaf in Dublin is unique, I think, in that it adhered unflinchingly to the pure manual method up to 1946 when the oral-auditory technique was introduced. The change-over was, as you can well imagine, fraught with many difficulties but, from the problems encountered there emerged a very definite approach to the teaching of speech.

From the outset I would like to stress that my remarks refer to children who may be classed educationally and psychologically as deaf. To me, such children are those who even with expert training and the continual use of a hearing aid from an early age still fail to learn communication skills mainly through hearing. Their impressions of speech are predominantly visual with what cues are available from slight remnants of hearing or from vibration feeling. Their handicap is acquired pre-lingually so that they will not learn to talk without special training. They cannot perceive and therefore control their speech without the use of a high-powered hearing aid and without special treatment from an early age. These children are the speech teacher's greatest challenge.

Having a long and wide experience of both the oral and the manual methods I am convinced that the oral-auditory technique prepares the deaf person, socially, psychologically and economically for wider and fuller experiences in a hearing world which is becoming daily more complicated. I believe that such a goal cannot be achieved unless the deaf child has had ideal opportunities for the development of speech. It is easier to be an "oral failure" than a manual one. Such a conviction has given rise to the emphasis being placed on the following points in our speech methodology at St. Mary's.

*Proceedings of the International Congress for Oral Education of the Deaf, Clark School for the Deaf, Northampton, Mass., 1967, p. 629–643.

Appendix A

1. Speech is developed in the minds of the children

Oralism is a way of life, it is not just articulation lessons in the classroom. Unless the children are thinking in speech both in and out of school our oral work in the classroom is of surprisingly little avail for language learning. Without an oral atmosphere no system of speech training will produce good results. During the transition from pure manualism to oralism I found to my great dismay that our small children failed to use spontaneous speech because they were thinking in signs and gestures which they had picked up from senior manually-taught pupils in the out-of-school periods. They also tended to learn them from some members of staff who had been using conventional sign language and finger-spelling for so long that they could not refrain from using these means when they wanted to communicate with the children who were being taught orally. I mention this particularly because it has a direct bearing on the speech programme in any School for the Deaf.

Uncontrolled out-of-school manual communication such as we had at St. Mary's some years ago will foster the use of signs and finger-spelling for thought processes, with the result that verbal communication will suffer. This in turn will affect the children's language development, and the child with average or below average intellectual functioning seems to be more adversely affected than the brighter child. Since small deaf children are keen visualisers they are adept in picking up manual communication. Left to themselves they will be as Dr Tervoort[1] has pointed out, develop a private system of communication which since it is based on visual impression deviates considerably from the normal acoustical language-patterns of the environment. The experience I have had in my own school has caused me to question the existence of a combined method.

I have found that once small deaf children become interested in signs they fail to pay attention to the lips, and this is to be expected because of the easier discriminability of the signs. Then there is the problem as to whether it is possible to pay attention visually to two separate events. When speech or manual signs or finger spelling are used simultaneously they rarely synchronise.

Twenty orally taught past pupils who had learned manual communication on leaving school reported that when a speaker accompanies his speech with signs they prefer to lipread. Occasionally when they fail to lipread a word they concentrate momentarily on the signs in order to follow the conversation. A few of them said that the signs were rather a distraction when lipreading. In no case did they concentrate on signs and speech simultaneously.

2. Parent guidance

If deaf children are to be enabled to think in verbal symbols they must receive systematic auditory stimulation from the first year of life. For this reason in our speech programme at St. Mary's we emphasise the need for early ascertainment of deafness. With advances being made in the field of detection in deafness it is now possible to diagnose in the first months of life. In our audiology clinic babies are fitted with hearing aids at as early an age as seven months. All children are fitted with hearing

1. Bernard Th. Tervoort, *Language: Report on the Proceedings of the International Congress on the Education of the Deaf* (Washington D.C. 1963) p. 463.

aids no matter how little the response at the initial testing. The parents are then given guidance in home-training. As many of our children come from rural areas courses for parents have to be residential.

The wearing of an aid itself will not enable the baby to speak; there must be direct teaching. At this stage in the child's life the mother is the best teacher, so that education of a deaf child begins with the education of the parents. The mother-child relationship can be made the basis for language development. The mother's conversation with the normal baby during feeding, bathing and dressing is vitally important for speech development while the constant repetition and correction helps to build up a store of linguistic knowledge which eventually forms the basis for speech. The mother structures the environment of the child when she goes about the house labelling objects and attributes. She is constantly making expansions of the "telegraphic" speech or the noun-plus-noun utterances of the child.[2]

It is well recognised today that the "instinctive method" which the mother uses cannot be surpassed. If a mother is to use this method with a deaf child she must be helped to make the necessary adaptations. She also needs encouragement as well as contact with other parents, who, like herself have to cope with deaf children. Without the help of the parents the teacher can hope for comparatively little in the way of language through speech and the use of slight remnants of hearing. One of the great advantages of the oral approach is that the parents are enabled to communicate with the children. In my long experience in the manual school I have never known a hearing parent who was able to communicate manually with a child.

3. Systematic training in sound perception

We were fortunate at St. Mary's in that the change from manualism to oralism was made after World War II when more powerful and more efficient hearing aids became available. From the beginning of the change-over, sound perception training held an important place on the curriculum. All our children wear hearing aids both in and out of school so that they have continuous experience of sound. We observe a tremendous difference in response in the case of children who have had hearing aids in the first year of life. This is to be expected since perceptual behaviour is so dependent on early sensory stimulation. Besides, the ability to recognise and interpret sounds is learned to a great extent during the first year of life.

In the classrooms we use high powered hearing aids. The teachers give group speech lessons. As well as this the children are taken individually for speech by a specialist teacher. Such a system proves satisfactory when class teachers and specialist teachers share the responsibility for speech instruction. At individual and group speech lessons the children receive training in the discrimination of sentences, words and phonemes—in that order—even though only few acoustic dimensions are present in the typically low frequency residual hearing of the profoundly deaf. It is important to remember that constant listening practice associated with lipreading and reading is essential if the child is to interpret the sounds he can be enabled to hear.

The continuity of experience of sound and vibration builds up an immense store

2. H. Kahane, R. Kahane and S. Saporta: *Development of Verbal Categories in Children's Language.* Bloomington, Indiana: Indiana University Research Centre. Anthropological Folklore Linguistics 1958.

Appendix A

of habits, by virtue of which the children are enabled "to respond to the slightest shreds of signals."[3] For sound-perception training words that have maximum sound-contrasts are chosen—for instance, words containing vowels such as /a/, /u/, /i/, or consonants such as *m* and *k*—are selected so that the child's ability to discriminate is built up by means of a trained awareness of the contrasts of both sound and lipreading patterns.

These auditory discriminations are difficult but they are most valuable since they enable the child not only to produce better speech patterns, but to interpret more easily the speech in his environment because we know that the production of speech is closely linked with its reception. If together with systematic sound perception training in school the deaf child has opportunities for integration with non-deaf children he will be helped to maintain auditory alertness and improve his speech and lipreading. We are fortunate at St. Mary's in that we have schools for non-deaf children on the campus.

4. The spontaneous efforts of the child are used as a foundation for speech
In the early days of speech instruction at St. Mary's emphasis was placed on the phonetic aspect. The approach was analytic, and the sounds of speech were taught in a definite order. The practice now is to build speech on the spontaneous efforts of the child. Sentences, words and syllables are used as the units for the teaching of articulation. This helps toward a coordination of the articulatory organs.

A baby who has been using a hearing aid in the pre-school years and who has had home training will usually have a few words on admission to school. If not then he will be able to babble. The speech teacher listens for vocalisation and in the early lessons she is more interested in voice production than in articulation. She discovers the child's interests and she talks about them. She builds up a vocabulary related to the child's experience because it is impossible to separate language and speech development from one's experience. As soon as possible she uses conversation about those things that engage the child's interest. If we are to educate children successfully by oral methods we must teach language through conversation from the beginning.

Here is highlighted the importance of the out-of-school periods and the need for special training for those who look after the children when they are not receiving direct instruction in the classroom. From whole words the child is made conscious of the phonemes. It is only when he has learned a number of words ending in *t* for instance, that he is made aware of the sound itself and taught to associate it with the written symbol. The child must be able after practice to produce the sound at will and we aim at fixing the speech sounds before the child is seven years.

Sounds are usually practised in words. If at any time an individual sound has to be isolated, it is quickly replaced in the word. As you know a simple consonant can become complex by the very fact of its combination with another consonant or a vowel. If phonemes are taught in isolation the deaf child will never master the synthesis which is characteristic of normal speech.

However, even though we use sound perception training there is always a place for

3. Colin Cherry *"On Human Communication"* (Science Editions 1961). John Wiley & Sons, Inc. New York., p. 278.

articulation lessons. We cannot allow deaf children to use approximate speech patterns if we want them to be understood. The purpose of speech is to enable one individual to communicate with another. Clearly, the production of a pleasant voice, the use of good phrasing and the mastery of rhythmic patterns of themselves do not ensure intelligibility because certain articulatory movements are essential to the formation of vowels and consonants which constitute the words used in spoken language. The rate of utterance is also important. Deaf children speak at a slower rate than the normal child. John[4] has shown that by means of teaching directed at improving time factors in the speech of severely deaf children there was a 56% improvement in word intelligibility.

5. Emphasis on the principle of feedback or the cybernetic approach

In the cybernetic approach used at St. Mary's the aim is to establish a link between speaking, "hearing", breathing, reading and writing. If the child is to speak well he must be helped to establish an ear-to-voice link which is essential for normal speech development. You may argue that this is impossible in the case of profoundly deaf children, but it is my experience that children with no measurable hearing beyond 500 c/s who have been fitted with hearing aids in the first year of life and trained in a cybernetic way are capable of a certain amount of sound discriminations. This is in agreement with the findings of Stritzver[5] who discovered that the frequency distinguishing capacity of 500 c/s is more important for the understanding of speech than 1000 and 2000 c/s.

Furthermore the association of vibration feeling with the movement of the child's own speech organs as well as those of others enriches and enhances sensory experience. In this way too auditory feedback is integrated with kinaesthetic feedback. We encourage the children to speak close to their microphones so that they can be enabled to appreciate their own speech efforts. Parents and teachers are trained to speak so that the microphone is not more than three inches from the mouth. One of the most important lessons given to parents during their course in home-training is the setting of the child's volume control because if auditory feedback is to be established speech must be loud enough for the child especially in the early years.

The principle of feedback is applied to vision as a help towards better speech. The children are trained to observe the movements of their speech organs as well as those of their teacher or parent in a mirror. Early in their school life they are taught to read and write. I have found a correlation between speaking, lipreading, reading and writing. However, when teaching speech I usually give the oral form of word before the written one. As mentioned earlier on, emphasis is placed on conversation about the child's interests because there is a feedback between the speaker and the recipient. Revesz[6] has noted that: "reciprocal communication is the basic condition of all forms of communication."

By the use of musical training as described by van Uden[7] the feedback process is related to movement. The children are made aware of their own sound-producing movements—walking, dancing and playing of such musical instruments as the

4. J. E. J. John & Jean N. Howarth: *"The Effect of Time Distortions on the Intelligibility of Deaf Children's Speech"*. Reprint: University of Manchester, 1966.

5. G. Stritzver. *"Frequency Discrimination of Deaf Children and Its Relation to Their Achievement in Auditory Training"*. Volta Review 60, 1958, p. 304.

Appendix A

6. G. Revesz: *"The Origins and Pre-History of Language"*. by J. Butler, New York Psychological Library 1, 1956, p. 131.

7. A. Van Uden: *"Principles and Practices of a Cybernetical Approach in the Physical Education of the Prelingually Deaf Child"*. In Report of the International Conference on Physical Education and Sport for Prelingually Deaf Children, St. Michielsgestel, The Netherlands. Institute for the Deaf 1962.

8. Mother Nicholas: *"Diagnosis and Management of Language Disordered Children at St. Mary's Cabra, Dublin"*. Teacher of the Deaf, March 1967. England. p. 89.

melodica and the wind organ. This training is more active than passive and it is consistently linked with language and speech. Children who are taught to grasp a musical phrase, or better still play one, will have a better understanding of the melody and rhythm of a sentence as a unit in speech. This will make for more intelligible speech as well as a deeper understanding of language. It will also help towards a more normal psychological development because even an attenuated form of feedback will compensate a little for the sound deprivation in the life of a deaf child.

6. Proper classification in the school for the deaf

Since the change over from manualism to oralism in St. Mary's I have discovered that there are some children who despite ideal opportunities fail to make progress in language learning when pure oral methods are used. Most of these children have additional handicaps. Eight per cent of our school population is made up of these children. They are profoundly deaf and in most cases their intellectual functioning is below average. For them we do not hesitate to use a combined method. They are taught in a completely separate department[8] where they receive specific teaching in language. It is significant to note that even though these children are taught speech and lipreading as well as signs and finger-spelling they tend to use more manual than verbal communication among themselves. However, this type of communication is a more effective basis for language learning in the case of deaf children who have an additional handicap. With proper classification and educational treatment these children can be enabled to communicate adequately through writing with the hearing world.

At the beginning I referred to problems encountered in our efforts to introduce the oral-auditory method at St. Mary's. The task would have been more difficult were it not for the help received from teachers of the Deaf in America, England and Holland. I am glad to have this opportunity of expressing my thanks for the help received from the staff of this school. The late Dr Hudgins and Dr Pratt were generous with their guidance and encouragement. The oral atmosphere at Clarke and the attainment of its past pupils inspired me at a time when the struggle seemed too great.

Appendix B

Deafness or Language Disorder: Differential Diagnosis

Address by Sister Nicholas Griffey to the International Congress for the Education of the Deaf, Stockholm, 1970*

This paper directs attention to the educational training of certain children enrolled at St. Mary's School for Hearing-Impaired Children in Cabra, Dublin, Ireland. The children's enrolments and classifications as deaf or severely hard of hearing were based on their failure to acquire language and speech normally and on audiometric testing at St. Mary's Audiology Clinic. Pertinent information relating to the children's medical histories is noted. Differences observed in the children's responses to teaching as they participated in a programme of oral education appropriate for children with peripheral hearing impairments are identified and reasons are given for incorporating facets of diagnostic teaching into the traditional programme. The teaching procedures of the Association Method as developed by McGinnis are identified as being significantly beneficial to the children who were ultimately considered to be language-disordered rather than deaf or hard of hearing. Recommendations are made regarding the significance of the teacher of the deaf in diagnostic teaching for differential diagnosis. The need for teachers of the deaf to become knowledgeable about and competent in teaching both kinds of hearing-impaired children and St. Mary's efforts to prepare more competent personnel for children in Ireland are noted.

As a central school serving Catholic girls in a wide geographical area, St. Mary's School for Hearing-Impaired Children, Cabra, Dublin, has had the opportunity and the responsibility of providing educational treatment for a wide variety of children. The initial diagnosis for children admitted to the school was one of hearing impairment. Bases for the diagnoses were their failure to respond to and learn language and speech normally and on audiometric testing conducted at St. Mary's audiology clinic. Among the children enrolled were some who were readily recognised as being multiply handicapped.

Founded in 1846, it was not until 1946 that the oral-auditory approach to educational treatment was introduced. In 1950, we became aware of the fact that there were children enrolled in classes for hard of hearing and for the deaf who did not

*Proceedings of the International Congress for the Education of the Deaf, Stockholm, 1970, p. 627–631.

Appendix B

respond favourably to teaching methods found to be effective with their peers. There was empirical and limited clinical evidence to show that their intellectual potential was within normal limits. It was also possible to rule out emotional disturbance and mental handicaps as primary factors relating to the children's poor achievements in language learning and speech. Faced with this paradoxical situation, a closer analysis of the children's functions was begun. This investigation revealed the following kinds of differences in ten children:

1. Lip-reading skills were significantly poorer than those of the deaf.
2. Written language revealed that letters were copied in non-sequential order.
3. Imitation of whole words was poorer than the imitation of single phonemes.
4. Auditory discrimination skills were poorer for whole words than for single phonemes. The children's ability to listen and use their hearing in both test situations and the natural environment was inconsistent and ineffective for learning language and speech.
5. Problem-solving in environmental situations revealed learning potential better than that indicated by standardised psychological tests.
6. Educational attainment level was significantly below that expected on the basis of environmental problem-solving.
7. Some of the children used unintelligible jargon which gave evidence of cadences and inflections akin to those in normal speech. In a few cases, the jargon contained some recognisable words. Others were so mute that their language function resembled that of a profoundly deaf child who has had no instruction. In some, audiological tests reflected inconsistent listening and responses to sound. In others, there were no responses to sound even at high intensity levels. As one teacher puts it: the child is "too deaf to be deaf".

Contacts with professional personnel in the United States and Holland revealed that others were encountering similar kinds of children and such teaching/learning paradoxes. Analysis and diagnostic teaching of the children enrolled at the Cabra school showed that certain specific difficulties were predominant in their function and were the same as those observed by the late Mildred McGinnis at Central Institute for the Deaf, St. Louis, Missouri, U.S.A. Predominant difficulties observed included:

1. Varying degrees of language disorders ranging from mutism to fragmented oral communication.
2. Short attention span.
3. Poor retention and recall for information pertinent to language and speech.
4. Poor memory for both auditory and visual sequences.
5. Inability to use their hearing projectively.
6. Difficulty in monitoring speech accurately in the presence of normal voice quality, intonation and rhythm.
7. Limited comprehension of their own echolalic language.
8. Difficulties in understanding language presented in the normal temporal rate.

These same difficulties have been noted more recently by Monsees (1957), Hardy (1964), DuBard (1967), Eisenson (1968), Stark (1968), Bender (1968) and others.

Because of our observations and experiences, and those reported by other professional personnel, we have concluded that in previous years some of the children enrolled in the Cabra school as deaf were in all probability language-disordered or aphasic.

Examination of medical histories of the total number of children enrolled revealed that a significant number, about 35%, were post-rubella children. Rubella children accounted for 54.8% of those at St. Mary's considered to be language-disordered children. Other aetiologies were related to encephalitis associated with measles, influenza, meningitis, post-convulsive disorders, pre-maturity or anoxia at birth. Some children had negative medical histories. In a few, there was evidence of neurological disorders while it was not apparent in others.

To avoid the semantic problems which have grown out of the professional thinking related to aetiology and pathology related to the condition, we continue to identify the abilities and limitations of the children, putting less emphasis on the diagnostic label. It was the viewpoint among the teachers who work at St. Mary's that longitudinal diagnostic teaching should utilise organised procedures which would help reduce and, if possible, eliminate the specific difficulties observed in the children. A plan of diagnostic teaching to include auditory training, lip-reading, development of comprehension and visual-motor activities was needed. In our search for an approach which would meet these goals, a careful study was made of the unpublished dissertation of Dr Etoile DuBard. Analysis of the Association Method in relation to information theory and motor theory of speech perception served as a framework into which the teaching procedures seemed to fit. It also reflected modifications and flexibility in teaching so as to meet the needs of the children as individuals. As we have continued the systematic use of diagnostic teaching combined with the Association Method, with modifications when and where appropriate, we have observed the children experiencing greater success in learning language, speech and better achievement in academic subjects.

It is our view that the teacher of the deaf can make a major contribution to better educational planning for many children who may seem to be deaf but who, in fact, may have language learning difficulties of a more complex nature. We hold the view that such diagnostic teaching can be of benefit in determining the nature of the child's language learning difficulties and that teaching procedures which will promote better language learning should be utilised.

Because of our experiences and viewpoints, we have taken steps to prepare professional personnel in Ireland to be able to recognise and teach more effectively the child whose hearing impairment may well be more complex than initial tests can indicate. We recommend that teachers of the deaf elsewhere become knowledgeable about the Association Method and skilful in the use of the procedures therein. In this way, we can begin to provide certain children with the kind of educational treatment they need and the chance to acquire the oral communication skills they deserve.

Appendix B

Bibliography

Bender, R.: "Teaching the Non-Verbal Child", *The Volta Review,* Vol. 70, No. 7, October, 1968.

DuBard, E.: *An Analysis of the Association Method for Aphasic Children in Relation to Information Theory and Motor Theory of Speech Perception,* unpublished dissertation, University of Southern Mississippi, 1967.

Eisenson, J.: "Developmental Aphasia", *Journal of Speech and Hearing Disorders,* Vol. 33, No. 1, February, 1968.

Hardy, W. G., "On Language Disorder in Young Children", *Journal of Speech and Hearing Disorders,* Vol. 30, No. 1.

Lydia, Sister M.: *Preliminary Study of the Rubella Children at St. Mary's School for Hearing-Impaired Children, Cabra, Dublin,* unpublished dissertation, Manchester University, 1968.

Monsees, E.: "Aphasia in Children, Diagnosis and Education", *The Volta Review,* Vol. 59, No. 9, November, 1957.

McGinnis, M.: *Aphasic Children,* The Volta Bureau, Washington, D.C., 1963.

Stark, J.: "Teaching the Aphasic Child", *Exceptional Children,* Vol. 35, No. 2, October, 1968.

Appendix C

Oralism versus Signing

Address by Sister Nicholas Griffey to a seminar organised by the Royal National Institute for the Deaf, London, 1975*

1. The deaf child fails to learn language because he cannot hear the rhythmic speech in his environment. Teaching communication to such a child is probably one of the greatest challenges facing an educator today. Glancing through some of the current writings on methods of teaching deaf children, one is bound to be oppressed by the amount of controversy, heated discussion and frustration that exists. The emphasis on manual communication as a panacea for all problems of the deaf can be misleading. Eventually, it will do a great disservice to deaf children. Parents and young teachers are confused. This is a serious situation because we know that successful education of deaf children depends so much on parents and teachers. Science and technology have contributed comparatively little to the field of education of the deaf. There has been no dramatic breakthrough and the teacher is still the key figure in this work. More than ever before, teachers need faith in the ability of the deaf to reach high standards as well as hope in the eventual success of the method used.

2. As a teacher, I have had rather unusual experience because—as many of you know—I have been working in a large residential and day school, where a change has been made from the pure manual method to the oral-auditory technique.[1] I was there when we endeavoured to introduce oral communication into a school where spoken language was virtually non-existent. During and after the transition period, I was helped to gain an insight into the variable factors which seem to help linguistic attainment in deaf children. Through the years I have visited many schools for the deaf throughout the world—good oral schools and bad ones as well as good and bad "combined" schools. It is fair to say that visits to the United States have helped me more than anything else to understand the current emphasis on "total communication" or as I see it "combined methods" for all deaf children. They have helped me to interpret the findings of such researchers as E. R. Stuckless, W. Birch (1966),[2] S. P. Quigley (1969),[3] K. P. Meadow (1966),[4] and M. Vernon (1969).[5]

Since I live in a country where two languages are used in the ordinary schools, I believe I realise the importance of the "mother tongue" in linguistic development as

*Proceedings of RNID Seminar, London, 1975, p. 22–29, reproduced by permission.

1. Nicholas, S. M. (1962). *Classification and Educational Treatment of Deaf Children. The Teacher of the Deaf,* Vol. 1, LX No. 358. December 1962, 329–42.

Appendix C

2. Stuckless, E. R. and Birch, J. W. (1966). *The Influence of Early Manual Communication on the Linguistic Development of Deaf Children.* American Annals of the Deaf, 111, 452, 463.

3. Quigley, S. P. (1969). *The Influence of Finger Spelling on the Development of Language. Communication and Educational Achievements of Deaf Children.* Institute for Research into Exceptional Children, University of Illinois.

4. Meadow, K. P. (1966). *Early Manual Communication in Relation to the Child's Intellectual, Social and Communicative Functioning.* American Annals of the Deaf, 113, 29–41.

5. Vernon, M. (1969). *Sociological and Psychological Factors Associated with Hearing Loss.*

well as the relationship between verbal attainment and mental endowment in the bilingual setting. I have had the advantage of spending the greater part of my life in a school for the deaf. There is no substitute for first-hand experience in our field. I believe that researchers must have had long experience in grappling with the language problems of the young deaf child. They must be fully aware of the attainment levels of a wide variety of pupils who are taught by means of different approaches. Is it not significant that the professionals in the periphery of our field express great dissatisfaction with the standard of education among the deaf? Is this due to lack of experience in the education field? I believe that all workers for the deaf—especially social workers—should spend some time in the classroom, where they will be able to grasp more fully the implications of verbal deprivation resulting from pre-lingual deafness. It is not enough to be able to sign and fingerspell—one must know how a deaf child learns language. Ideally, one must have taught language.

3. I have used the word "communication" rather than "method" in connection with deaf children. The word "method" is currently charged with emotion and so I avoid using it if possible! Deaf children have a vital need to communicate. If we view language in its broadest sense, we will include every form of communication in which thoughts and feelings are symbolised, such as: facial expression, touch, gesture, lipreading, reading, speech, writing, drawing, conventional signs, fingerspelling and pantomime. It is important to keep this in mind because some of our children—for instance, those with multiple handicaps—may have to depend on facial expression and crude natural gestures for communication. These children have a right to this type of communication if they are to reach their highest human level. Likewise those deaf children who can benefit from an exclusively oral education should be given the opportunity to do so. In this way, the latter will be enabled to fit better into a hearing world and will be provided with a wider range of opportunity for educational, social and vocational experiences. They must also be enabled to assist their fellow deaf who may be less fortunate. They have a right to the opportunity to become leaders. They should be helped to reach such levels that they will be in a position to advise hearing people who are working with deaf people. There is a very real danger that in our preoccupation with the problems of deaf children with additional handicaps (who are in the minority), we may forget the needs of the average and the above-average child.

4. My approach is flexible. I do find a place for manual communication in the educational treatment of some deaf children. Happily, in Ireland we have retained a system of sign language which has a limited linguistic structure and one which is used by the adult deaf population.[6] The teachers who use it can sign according to the grammatical and lexical form of the English language. Many of the orally taught pupils learn this system of sign language when they leave school, as one would learn a second language. I have no objection to this as I realise that they may use it when communicating with their fellow deaf. I encourage parents to give freedom of choice in this matter to school-leavers. Once a school-leaver is equipped with good lipreading skills, fairly good speech and the ability to express himself in correct written patterns, I feel I have fulfilled my aims as an educator. However, I never lose sight of the fact that each child is an individual, needing the special care and treatment needed for his particular condition. Is it not true that some language-disordered children have difficulty in learning sign language? I have known mentally handicapped children who have failed to learn fingerspelling and methodical signs. "Total communication" then does not solve all the problems of the deaf, so that we must emphasise the individualistic approach. This is vital because there is far too much stereotyping in our work. The situation of the deaf varies from country to country. In areas of high-density population it is possible to create "deaf communities". The deaf person trained in manual communication can function very well in such a community. This is not the case in my country, for instance, where a comparatively small population is spread across a wide geographical area. The deaf person in rural Ireland must be enabled to integrate into a hearing community, otherwise he will be socially isolated. Of necessity, he must be a good lipreader; he must be able to read and express himself in correct language. His speech may be defective, but, if the school equips him with the ability to express himself in acceptable written patterns, integration will be easier. In 1950 I found that 90% of the past pupils of our school in Dublin wanted Irish deaf children to learn to speak and lipread. Many of them said they would like to lipread because their hearing friends and workmates were not inclined to communicate, either in writing or by means of manual communication. The position has not changed much today.[7] On the other hand "total communication" may be more suitable than oral methods in an underdeveloped country where the average age for a first referral may be 12 or even 14 years.

5. I have referred deliberately to deaf children—that is, those whose hearing loss is greater than 90 dB in the crucial speech range, and whose medical histories suggest either congenital or pre-lingual deafness.

These are children whose impressions of speech are predominantly visual with what cues are available from vibration feeling. It is essential that we bear this in mind because, in the case of reported studies in the use of manual communication already referred to, some of the children had hearing losses that would automatically place them in the partially hearing category. These are children who, when given good auditory training, experience impressions of speech that are more auditory than visual. Naturally they will pay more attention to the auditory stimulus when manual communication is accompanied by speech. I believe that manual communication will not be necessary for them if they receive adequate speech stimulation from an early age. These children are by nature more auditory than visual. To neglect auditory experience because of the visual orientation of manual communication is a great pity. In my work with hearing-impaired children, I have seen some with mild hearing loss who came to rely on manual communication because they were placed in a school for the deaf where signs were used freely. They were in the minority and, to me, it was tragic to find that their residual hearing was inoperative in their communication. The exponents of "total communication" maintain that signs reinforce lipreading and residual hearing when a child who is using a hearing aid is spoken to by an adult who signs and talks simultaneously. They go farther and state that, for the child who cannot

Journal of Speech and Hearing Research, 1969, 12, 541–63.

6. Nicholas, S. M. (1971). *With Other Non-Communicating Children*. Report of the Proceedings of the Third Conference on Children with a Combined Visual and Auditory Handicap. Coventry, England.

7. National Association for the Deaf, Ireland. *Information about the Young Adult Deaf Population of Ireland.*

Appendix C

benefit from amplification, signs reinforce lipreading.[8] My experience in the Cabra school, in schools where "total communication" is used and in oral schools with a strong manual background, have shown me that speech and lipreading skills do not reach a very high level, despite these claims to the contrary. During the transition period in Cabra, I found that our small children were very poor lipreaders because they were thinking in signs and gestures which they had picked up from the senior manually taught pupils. Uncontrolled manual communication like this will foster the use of signs for thought processes to the detriment of lipreading skills. There is scientific evidence available to show that, in the case of verbal learning for the deaf and hearing subjects alike, the system which is acquired first or the "mother tongue" is the one which is used for inner language. This is the one which is retained for thought processes. The situation at Cabra during the transition period was similar in some respects to the bilingual school for normally hearing pupils in which instruction is given in the weaker language. In schools where "total communication" is used, the children use more signs than speech. They do not talk spontaneously. To me this is understandable. Deaf children are keen visualisers and signs are more attractive, more static and definite than speech signals.

When signs are used, only gross visual discrimination is required for receptive communication while, in expressive communication, only gross motor movements are involved. There is also the question as to whether it is possible to pay attention visually to two separate events—signing and speaking. Both rarely synchronise. My experience shows that it takes many years before a teacher has gained sufficient skill in manual communication to enable him to sign and speak at the same rate. Signing deviates considerably from the normal acoustic patterns of the environment. Synchronisation may take place if we slow up speech but this is unacceptable from the point of view of speech and lipreading skills. All these problems are so much present to me that I question the very existence of a "combined method" or "total communication" for young deaf children. "Combined" inevitably means manual. Unless the children in the early years are thinking in speech, the work of the oral teacher is of surprisingly little avail for language learning. Without good auditory and sound perception training and plenty of speech stimulation in and out of school, we can expect poor lipreading skills and speech among our deaf children. I am so convinced of this that I have consistently advocated separate schools—oral schools for those who can benefit from a pure oral education and combined schools for the others. Separate schools are vital if oral communication is to develop. People who advocate "total communication" for all deaf children have, I believe, never taught for any length of time in a real oral school. In the school where the speech is accompanied by signs, I find that communication among the children is mainly manual. In such circumstances I would be tempted to use manual communication but then that would be the easy way out. Oralism makes greater demands on the child, his parents and his teachers. It is easier to be an oral failure than a manual one. Is it not significant that "total communication" is being advocated in the United States where many of the teachers are untrained? A study carried out by the Council on Education for the Deaf[9] showed that 60% of the staff in

8. Mindel, Eugene D. and Vernon, M. (1971). *They Grow in Silence.* National Association of the Deaf, Silver Springs, Maryland, U.S.A.

Appendix C

55 residential schools were ineligible for certification standards. Of the newly employed teachers in day schools in the United States in 1970, less than 20% were trained. I am associated with a school where 63% of the teachers are trained teachers of the deaf and where management is not satisfied with this state of affairs! Is it not true also that deafness is not being diagnosed at a sufficiently early age in the United States? In such circumstances oralism is bound to fail. I look on the current emphasis on "total communication" as a very good solution to a distressing problem. Most people who use it are sincere in their efforts to improve the lot of the deaf population. Is it fair, however, to limit the achievements of some deaf people? I do not think so. They all have a right to the type of educational treatment which will enable them to match achievements with potential. Some children who are given consistent and early speech input and from whom systematic sign language input is excluded do reach satisfactory language attainment levels. They are well equipped to fit into a hearing world. I suspect that they have a better understanding of living English than the manually taught. They have a better grasp of some of the subtleties and innuendoes of speech. Their written expression is less stereotyped.

6. Whatever type of communication is used in the school, the teacher is faced with the problem of teaching language. Manual communication does not enable a deaf child to learn language incidentally. Visit any club for the deaf where "total communication" is used and you will find very few who use correct language forms. Believe me, few teachers in the manual school where I worked as a young teacher had the persistence to sign or spell in correct sentences. There was always the temptation to use the shortcuts employed by the deaf. The syntactic errors that occur among the orally taught deaf are also found among the manually taught. Examination of the spontaneous written expression of a group of the latter showed the following: mistakes in the use of determiners; confusion in the use of pronouns; abnormal usage in the order of adjectives; inability to use conjunctives and relatives; lack of understanding of the passive voice and absence of compound sentences. Language has to be taught to all deaf children. For the child in the oral school success comes through the following:

(a) *Early Ascertainment of Deafness.* Since the child establishes his perceptual habits early in life it is necessary that the deaf child be given amplification as soon as possible so that maximum use can be made of residual hearing. I would like the deaf child to be given auditory experience or sound-perception training in the first year of life. In this way he may become more dependent on auditory than on visual cues in interpreting speech. Teachers of the deaf have daily reminders of the benefits of auditory and sound-perception training. As I look back over the years I can but marvel at what can be achieved by sound-perception training.

(b) *Parent-Centred Guidance Programmes.* These should be developed in such a way that the mother tongue really teaches language to the child. The emphasis is not so much on hearing loss but on the development of hearing perception. The child is bathed in sound. He is constantly exposed to language stimulation. All his efforts at speech production are encouraged and reinforced. The deaf child will inevitably gesture. This is accepted but, as soon as possible, the parents and adults in the

9. *Council of Education of the Deaf Summary,* 1970, U.S.A.

Appendix C

environment clothe these gestures with appropriate language. The "seizing" method advocated by Rev. Dr van Uden[10] approaches normal language development where the mother makes transformations of the child's utterances. Attention is paid to the rhythm of speech which is now considered an important feature of language learning. Oral expressions can be supplemented by drawings and even written patterns in the pre-school years. Auditory training can be linked with receptive language. Parents need to be helped, however, to understand that some deaf children have difficulty in learning language. Working with them, I have got the impression that they can be unrealistic about deaf children. To them, all deaf people are alike—people who can achieve remarkable success in life. They are not inclined to allow for individual differences. Perhaps this is due to the type of publicity given to the deaf.

(c) *Good Oral Schools*, where well-trained teachers who are convinced of the value of the oral approach use electronic equipment effectively. This will mean that the teacher understands the nature and degree of each child's hearing impairment. It presupposes that the teachers in training have had opportunities of working in schools where the standard of oral education is high. It also means that the teacher has an understanding of the equipment used. On becoming a member of the staff of the school, a young teacher should be presented with a well-designed programme. He also requires guidance from senior teachers. How many young teachers are given classes without any direction whatsoever? Teachers in the various department of the school need to meet frequently and discuss their approach to the teaching of language.

From the age of seven years, the deaf child should be helped to extract the rules of grammar from the language he has acquired through conversation and reading. He will not do this without direct teaching. Pattern practice in the use of singular and plural of nouns, in the use of verbs, determiners, word order, prepositions, conjunctions etc. is essential for children who are insufficiently exposed to the auditory aspect of language. Memorisation of oral and written patterns has a place in the approach to the teaching of language. Principles of language structure and their application to reading and writing are being neglected in our schools with the result that reading levels are alarmingly low. This is distressing because a deaf person who is unable to express his thoughts in writing is at a serious disadvantage. Such deaf people may have to spend years in a psychiatric hospital. They are imprisoned souls because they have no language.

In 1971, D. Power and S. P. Quigley[11] investigated the ability of deaf children to recognise correct and incorrect examples of several different synthetic structures. Their ability to produce such structures was also investigated. The findings show that deaf children tend to process sentences according to surface structure. More significant is the fact that the tests did not appear to measure any learning growth—that is, the 18-year-olds did not do better than the 10-year-olds. A similar pilot investigation carried out among orally taught profoundly deaf at a school in Dublin in 1973, where the children are taught grammar in the way already described, showed higher scores for the children in the 13 to 18-year-old level. Highest scores were found among pupils who had studied the use of passive sentences and relative clauses in

10. van Uden, A. J. (1968). *A world of Language for Deaf Children.*

11. Power, D. and Quigley, S. P. (1971). *Testing Deaf Children's Syntactic Competence.* Paper presented to the American Speech and Hearing Association Convention, 1971.

Appendix C

Latin. Language must be taught to deaf children. The out-of-school staff in a residential school need to be convinced of the importance of spoken language and be determined to use it with the children. The co-operation of the parents is necessary also to ensure that the linguistic environment of the home is complementary to that of the school.

(d) *Good Classification.* Without good classification in our schools, deaf children will not reach higher language attainment levels. It seems to me that too much is expected of teachers and pupils where there is a disparity in age, hearing loss and in intellectual functioning among the pupils. It is now well established that some hearing-impaired children have learning disabilities which, if treated early, will enable them to be educated orally.[12] These children do not learn language in the progress, provided their intelligence is within normal limits. Obviously, these children will do better if they are taught in separate classes. Some of them may need fingerspelling and/or signs and, again, this calls for a different approach. It is essential too that their difficulties which may stem from neurological dysfunction be discovered as soon as possible. I have no hesitation in using total communication with children who, because of some specific learning disability—lowered intellectual functioning, cerebral palsy involving the speech mechanism, visual handicap or late referral—have difficulty in lipreading and learning language. I like to see these children treated in a separate school by teachers who were successful oral teachers, who take a short course in the teaching of mentally handicapped deaf and who are prepared to use systematic sign language as well as reading, speech, auditory training, lipreading and writing in teaching. The emphasis on "total communication" has undoubtedly helped these children. Combined schools are more acceptable today than they were in 1950 when I decided that there would always be a need for a manual approach for some children. However, today we need to set up more of these schools so that children who need this type of approach will receive it. Professionals in these centres would build up expertise which could be available to teachers who wish to take postgraduate studies.

To have ideal classification in a school, large numbers are required. In a school population of 327, I found the following classification:

School for Hard of Hearing—122 pupils. All these children whose losses range roughly from approximately 50 dB to 85 dB receive an oral education with emphasis on auditory training. Sixteen children in the group have an additional handicap for which they are receiving treatment. (This does not include manual communication.)

School for Deaf Children—148 pupils. All these children whose hearing losses range from 90 dB to 130 dB are receiving an oral education with emphasis on sound-perception training. Fourteen children in this group have additional handicaps but they do not prevent them from reaching satisfactory standards in lipreading and in written language

School for Language-Disordered Children—30 pupils. All these children are receiving an oral education. The association method is being used with them.

School for Children with Multiple Handicaps—26 pupils. These children have severe hearing losses and they have failed to benefit from a pure oral approach. A combined

12. Nicholas, S. M. (1974). *Language Disordered Children.* Report of the proceedings of the Commonwealth Society for the Deaf (England) Seminar, Sussex University, September 1974, 45–51.

Appendix C

method or "total communication" is used with them.

Unit for Children with Visual and Hearing Impairments—1 pupil. A unit has now been established for deaf children who because of a moderate mental handicap, emotional disturbance and in some cases, partial vision, had been rejected from the above-mentioned school. These severely handicapped children are being taught to communicate by means of natural gestures which have been devised by a group of deaf adults who are experts in the use of manual communication. This unit is developing into a centre for stimulation and on-going assessment of children who have difficulty in learning fingerspelling, conventional sign language, speech and lipreading.

7. To me, there is no simple approach to the education of the deaf. Instead of worrying about methods of communication, I wish we could think of the learning ability of the children. The child is more important than the method. Let us respect the individual and his right to reach his highest human level. Let us try to find the appropriate method by looking for those characteristics which might be predictive of success or failure under different systems.

Appendix D

From a Pure Manual Method via the Combined Method to the Oral-Auditory Technique: Educating Profoundly Deaf Children: Experience in Thirty Years Teaching Deaf Children

Address by Sister Nicholas Griffey to the International Congress on Education of the Deaf, Hamburg, 1980*

As a teacher of the deaf, I possibly have had a rather unique experience, because I have been working in a school which as late as 1946 changed from a pure manual method of communication to the oral-auditory technique. I started teaching in a school which was purely manual and one in which even the moderately hard of hearing used manual communication. The sign language used was a systematic derivative and had a modified linguistic structure. Stokoe (1972) has noted similarities between it and "signed English" currently used in the US. Its inventor—the Abbé Jamet of Caen in France—set out to "pronounce" French in sign language. Later Jamet's system was modified to reflect English syntax by an Irish teacher of the deaf (Bourke, 1848). Basically this manual language consists of:

(a) Natural gestures of basic Irish sign language referred to as Irislan (Nich. Griffey 1978).

(b) One hand finger-spelling—the letters being used the same as those in the US (with the exception of *f, g, h, k, l,* and *p*).

(c) Methodic or conventional signs which are actually based on the initial of a word.

(d) Signs which are a combination of natural gestures and methodic signs.

(e) Signs which are used as linguistic markers. Among the well educated Irish deaf this system is a code for transmitting either the spoken or written form of English. In the pure manual school situation which I experienced as a young teacher, the children did not learn signs themselves. They were taught them by adults. In self directive communication they did resort to gestures but these were quite inadequate for real communication.

At all times emphasis was placed on the adult models of sign language and teachers were expected to be proficient in signing as well as in reading back or

*Proceedings of the International Congress on Education of the Deaf, Hamburg, 1980, p. 255–263. (I have broken the text into paragraphs for the convenience of the reader; the original text had only three paragraph breaks.)

Appendix D

interpreting sign language. A teacher was not given responsibility for a class until he was proficient in the use of manual communication. It was maintained that inadequate models or inability to converse fluently in sign language, constituted an additional handicap for the child.

I mention this particularly, because I see linguistic deprivation today, in schools where total communication has been introduced by teachers and parents who are not proficient in the use of manual communication. Correct adult models and fluent communication are necessary for attainment of acceptable levels of receptive language.

The early expressive manual communication used by deaf children will be made up of inaccurate models but this is acceptable just as approximate speech patterns are used by young children as well as by deaf who are taught by means of an oral/auditory approach. As a young teacher I was expected to sign in conventional English at all times—the order of signs being the same as that of words. I adhered to this—after a long period of preparation—yet, I found that among themselves the children resorted to non-linguistic forms. Their language was pictographic and situation-linked.

Stokoe (1972) refers to a high and low version of American Sign language. The same distinction could be made in the Irish system. Among themselves they used the low version. I must confess that we teachers relied on it occasionally when we wanted to convey a message quickly. Of course, we were then reinforcing patterns which differed considerably from the acoustic language patterns of the environment.

I discovered also that those who used fingerspelling only did not spell in sentences but in isolated words which we teachers referred to as "noun language" because structure words were invariably omitted. Word order was quite inaccurate. I agree with Tweney and Hoemann (1973) who state that "deaf children ordinarily learn to communicate fluently by manual methods—Ameslan—before they acquire competence in English; as a result English is rarely the language of choice for casual conversation."

However, I believe the term "fluent signing" needs to be examined as it is misleading. The children I taught in the pure manual school were fluent in the use of gestures and signs but their language production differed significantly from standard English. Frequent repetition of situational based gestures gave the impression of fluency. There were numerous misunderstandings. Figurative language was rarely grasped.

Some of the current writings on total communication give the impression that once supplemental manual communication is used, the deaf child will understand and will develop normal expressive language. This was not my experience. Language was taught in a very structured way with emphasis on the grammar of the traditional linguists.

Jamet devised a graded set of lessons for class teachers. He advised that from the earliest stages "the deaf child should be surrounded by all those things that surround the infancy of speaking children" (Jamet 1846). He recommended that the child first be taught the conventional signs for things familiar in order "to excite his interest and

Appendix D

engage his attention." Having learnt the sign for a word the child was next encouraged to read the written form, finally he learned to fingerspell the word.

From words the child progressed to phrases and finally to sentences. A set of carefully graded visual aids depicting nouns, verbs and adjectives was also used. He adopted grammatical symbols to indicate the role of a word in a sentence. He used numbers to show the subject, predicate and object as did Sicard but he added symbols for the tenses of the verb as well as the adjective, adverb and preposition. During the formal language lessons correct linguistic patterns were insisted on by the teachers but, as already stated the children resorted to Irislan among themselves.

It was a surprise and a disappointment to me as a young teacher to find that I had to teach language to the deaf child as foreign languages were traditionally taught to hearing children. I thought that because I was using sign language the children would learn the structure incidentally. The main aim in teaching language however was to help the child to express himself in correct written English. He was being prepared to communicate through writing with the hearing world because it was considered more efficient, even by expert signers. When an important message had to be given it was signed and written. Sign language can be ambiguous. Word order is dominated by visual impressions. Certain signs are accentuated by being placed at the beginning of a sentence. This form of thinking militates against the development of rhythmic groups which are so important for the understanding and production of language. I found that my pupils signed in small units. They dramatised their experiences in such a way that the emphasis was placed on the visually perceptible.

It must be said, however, that some intelligent prelingually deaf, educated in this way, were able to read books, write good letters, communicate with their teachers in high version sign language and among themselves in the low version. However, many of the pupils in the school at this time were merely hard of hearing or post-lingually deaf. The tragedy in their case was that their speech and language deteriorated because of the influence of manual communication.

In 1946, it was decided that oralism would be introduced into an environment where the spoken word was virtually non-existent. Speech and lipreading were adopted in order to give hearing-impaired pupils a better opportunity in a hearing society. Education came to be considered within the limits and requirements of their future lives.

A manual world is a silent one. It causes social isolation, especially in Ireland where a comparatively small population is spread over a wide geographical area. Deaf adults who lipread and speak well have a wider range of educational and vocational opportunities open to them. Recent experience in Ireland has shown that they have a higher professional standing than those who are dependent on manual communication. They can communicate more effectively with hearing professionals who work with the deaf. They know deafness from the inside as it were so that much can be gained from their experiences.

Our past pupils—especially those who had a high language level—pointed this out to the school authorities in 1946. In a survey carried out at this time, it was shown

Appendix D

that 95% of the past pupils wanted Irish deaf children to lipread and speak (Nicholas Griffey 1967). Parents who were then becoming more expressive of their views asked for it.

The transition was extremely difficult. Articulation lessons and lipreading were made available to pupils who had already been introduced to manual communication. Auditory training was undertaken with those pupils who could benefit from the fairly limited amplification provided by the existing hearing aids. In fact, a form of "total communication" was used with the senior pupils.

The nursery and junior school children were taught lipreading and speech. Sign language and finger spelling were excluded in their case. Yet, in the out-of-school periods, these "oral" children had some contact with those who were using sign language.

It was obvious that all pupils were more interested in manual communication than in speech signals. They were visually orientated. They were poor lipreaders, because they were thinking in manual communication as they used speech. Instead of the language of signs reinforcing the auditory, it became a "mother tongue".

When teachers no longer used systematic sign language, the children developed an esoteric form of manual communication. This language predominated in thought processes so that language levels were low. Written English was not as correct as when pure manualism was used. Speech was rarely spontaneous and children with a considerable amount of useful hearing, spoke with the voice quality of the deaf.

After some years the school could still be classed as manual. A few intelligent children did however succeed in becoming bilingual but they usually had measurable hearing up to 4 kHz. The hard of hearing did succeed in picking up environmental oral language. The post-lingually deaf likewise made progress in talking but all were retarded in lipreading.

In this connection I find the report of research carried out by Lawson (1978) quite interesting. The study was designed to determine whether hearing-impaired students using total communication spent more classroom time on compliant communications than on self-directive ones. In a discussion on his findings he notes that "in general teachers were using total communication or the manual-dactyl-oral mode while the students were relying more heavily on the pure manual-dactyl mode." He concludes that while teachers were using total communication students were not required to use it and he recommends that the teachers should stress the development of the students' vocal skills. I believe that no amount of emphasis on speech by the teacher will result in the development of an oral atmosphere in the classroom or hostel where a manual code is used to supplement speech.

Observing the communication used among pupils themselves as I have through the years and more recently in the US I am convinced that in the total communication environment the linguistic output is predominantly manual-dactyl. I find it impossible to accept what Delgado says, and I quote: "where sign language is grammatically equal to the vernacular it will not suppress the spoken language" (Delgado 1975). Because of my conviction I advised teachers at the school in 1953 to exclude supplemental manual communication and to place greater emphasis on the speech input, sound perception training and the use of slight remnants of hearing (N. Griffey 1967).

In 1962 screening of hearing programmes was introduced in the Child Welfare Clinics. Preschool children and especially their parents were given help. Gradually an oral atmosphere began to develop in the school. The children were made more aware of sound, more "ear minded". They used their voices as they communicated with each other and with their teachers. Lipreading improved and with it language patterns became more natural, less structured and less esoteric than when either the pure manual method or the combined method was used.

The use of hearing aids also helped to bring about an oral atmosphere in the school. For those of us who taught in schools for the deaf prior to the 1950s there were daily reminders of what can be achieved through auditory training and sound perception training. The experience has convinced me that successful oralism depends to a great extent on a pervasive speech environment for the child as well as consistent emphasis on parent/child and teacher/child interactions. Oral conversation from an early age is vital because a deaf child learns by talking. He must interact with people. In this way he learns language in the experience and the conversation of those in his environment.

It is a great joy to observe the oral language development of some deaf pre-school children today. There is now sufficient evidence to show that provided the speech input is right, hearing can play an important part in language acquisition for large numbers of hearing-impaired children.

Not all children however can benefit from an oral environment and a developmental approach to the teaching of language. In the mid-fifties I found some children with average or above average intellectual potential whose level of linguistic attainment was poor. Investigation showed that they had a language disorder and that they needed a structural approach such as that used by McGinnis (1963).

I found also that some of these language-disordered children together with late beginners and those profoundly deaf pupils with lowered intellectual functioning failed to communicate effectively through speech and lipreading. For them it was decided that the manual code—either Irislan or signed English—should be added to the speech code. Manual communication is more static, more attractive and in some cases has inbuilt concepts so that it is more suitable than the fleeting speech for children who have specific learning problems.

Today I am more flexible in my approach to the teaching of hearing-impaired children, especially those whose hearing is greater than 60 dB at 125 Hz to 250 Hz and greater than 90 dB beyond that. No one method will solve the educational problem of the deaf child. While advocating an individualistic approach I realise of course that it is not possible to provide a teacher for each child. However, with a good classification system in the schools there should be children in each class who need more or less the same approach.

I regret that there is so much controversy today concerning educational treatment of deaf children. Much of it is justified since international studies in language

Appendix D

attainment have shown that many deaf children reach standards which are appallingly low (Wollman 1964; Montgomery 1968; Conrad 1979).

Much of the controversy resulting from the discussions connected with low achievement levels centres round the language code rather than the methods of developing language. The crucial area of disagreement is related to the use or non-use of supplemental manual communication. There is universal agreement that deaf children should learn to speak. But one gets the impression from the current literature (Denton 1965; Vernon and Koh 1970) that if manual communication is used together with speech, lipreading, sound perception, reading and writing, language attainment levels will be raised significantly and deaf children will learn all codes. As has been said this is contrary to my experience. Where total communication is used lipreading skills are poor, and the children do not use their hearing to the full.

To me the methods of teaching language deserve far more attention from the teachers of the deaf who today spend so much time discussing the merits of total communication versus oral, unisensory versus multisensory, the residential versus the day school, or special school versus mainstreaming. The oral/manual controversy has been so much in the foreground that codes have become more important than methods of teaching language.

Observing in schools for the deaf and regarding language as a continuum we find a completely natural or "maternal method" at one end and a pure structure approach at the other. In between there is a mixture of both of these approaches. The natural method is gradually coming into prominence at preschool level.

We are becoming aware that deaf children can be active agents in the language acquisition process because we have evidence to show that they will go through the normal developmental stages of language provided they have the required intellectual potential and that the parents are facilitators of language development. Small deaf children are convincing us that there is a biological aspect to language acquisition. This compelling evidence has led to a world-wide emphasis on early diagnosis, fitting with suitable hearing aids and the provision of parent guidance in the home.

The current findings in the field of psycholinguistics are providing basic information against which the deaf can be compared. Scales of syntactical development norms which have become available as well as the current interest in semantics and the pragmatics of language merit study by and attention from professionals who work with the deaf.

It would appear that in the case of the deaf child on entry to school there is still a tendency for the structural approach to language learning to take over (Brennan 1975; Clark 1975). It is alleged that this emphasis on structured methods causes language retardation among deaf children. Presnell (1973) remarked that in addition to finding that hearing-impaired subjects were delayed in the acquisition of syntax for spoken language, some differences in their developmental sequence of grammatical rules in spontaneous speech as compared with normal children were also observed. He found that the syntactic constructions deviating the most from the normal order of acquisition and usage were the verb constructions. He remarks: "in many schools the traditional order for teaching verbs to hearing-impaired children has been present, past, and future tenses followed by the present progressive tense. Normal children, however, do not learn verbs in the same order as hearing-impaired children in structured situations do."

Is the typical language of the deaf the result of teaching methods used in the schools? Are they analytical? Should not the structuring of language at school level be more a deductive process than an analytical one?

Conversation helps the deaf child in his search for a grammar system—and this is true when either the manual or the speech code is used. Brown et al. (1968) maintain that "the changes sentences undergo as they shuttle between persons in conversations are the data that most clearly expose the underlying structure of the language." This is true in the case of the child who received clear auditory signals but for the deaf child it is unattainable unless parents and teachers direct this normal process of reflection on language already acquired.

Intervention in the form of guided discovery must take place. This calls for a knowledge of linguistics on the part of the teacher and an overall language programme in the school itself.

Reading is one of the most important tools for the development of language structure in deaf children provided it is based on conversation.

There are some children who fail to learn language when a natural approach is used. The number is on the increase especially among pupils of prenatal and perinatal aetiology. For these an analytical approach is recommended (McGinnis 1939; Nicholas 1962; Du Bard 1974). A number of these children may require total communication.

In developing language then in deaf children it would appear that individual children must be assessed and given the method suited to their needs. This necessitates the provision of comprehensive services. It also calls for classroom orientated research which is carried out by experienced and well-trained workers.

To me one of the most important aspects of modern educational treatment of deafness is the proper placement of profoundly deaf children who have intellectual potential. In the past few years I have seen far too many intelligent deaf children between the ages of 10 and 14 who failed to acquire language because they were placed in educational settings which were unsuited to their needs. Not all deaf pupils are subjects for mainstreaming or for placement in small units where one finds disparity in hearing loss and intellectual ability among the pupils. To me an intelligent deaf person without acceptable language levels is a human tragedy.

Let us hope that with improved assessment techniques, comprehensive services, better education of the public concerning the oral way of life where all types of hearing-impaired children receive treatment suited to their needs and better facilities for mainstreamed pupils, more and more children will reach acceptable educational levels.

By way of conclusion I make one appeal: truly a cry from the heart! May we have an optimistic outlook. Let the newcomer to the field feel he has embarked on challenging but rewarding work. This cannot come about as long as his informed

Appendix D

elders continue to hold "entrenched positions" and to erect communication barriers.

It is not the challenge that the effects of hearing loss in children presents; it is the way we face the challenge. Working together, sharing findings and being more open to each other, to the adult deaf and to the parents, our pupils will surely succeed in matching potential with attainment levels. The deaf have a right to this. May they attain it in the eighties!

References

Bourke. *Notes for Teachers*. St. Mary's School for the Deaf, Cabra, Dublin Ireland 1856.

Brennan, M. "Can Deaf Children Acquire a Language" *American Annals of the Deaf* 120, 1975, pp. 463–479.

Brown, R., C. B. Cazden, U. Bellugi. "The Child's Grammar" from I to III. In Hill, J. B., (ed.) 1967 *Minnesota Symposia on Child Psychology*, University of Minnesota Press, 1969.

Clark, M., "A Natural Approach to the Development of speech and Language". *Problems of Deafness in the Newer World. Report of the Commonwealth Society for the Deaf Seminar*, Sussex, 1974 (1975).

Conrad, R., *The Deaf Schoolchild*, Harper and Row, London, 1979.

Delgado, D. L., *Experts Meeting on Education of the Deaf*. UNESCO Headquarters, Paris, France, 1975.

Denton, D. M., *A Study of the Educational Achievement of Deaf Children*. Proceedings of the 42nd meeting of the Convention of American Instructors of the Deaf, 1965.

Du Bard, E., *Teaching Aphasiatics and other Language Deficient Children*, University Press of Mississippi, 1974, Second Edition 1976.

Ewing, A. W. G., E. L. Ewing. *Teaching Deaf Children to Talk*, Manchester University, 1964.

Furth, H., Linguistic Deficiency and Thinking. Research with Deaf Subjects 1964–69, *Psychological Bulletin*, 1971, 75, 58–72.

Howarth, C. I., D. J. Wood. "A Research Programme for the Intellectual Development of Deaf Children". *J. Brit. Assn. Teachers of the Deaf*, 1, 5–12, 1977.

Jamet, l'Abbé. *Notice sur la Vie de M. Pierre-François Jamet*, Caen, 1846.

Lawson, R. S. "Patterns of Communication in Intermediate Level Classrooms of the Deaf". In *Audiology Hearing Education*, 4 (I), p. 19–23, 1978.

McGinnis, M. A., *Aphasic Children: Identification and Education by Association Method*, Volta Bureau, Washington, D.C. 1963.

Montgomery, G. W. G., "A Factorial Study of Communication and Ability in Deaf School Leavers". *British Journal of Educational Psychology*, Feb. 1–68, 38, 27–37.

Nicholas Griffey. The Aphasic Child, *The Journal of the Irish Medical Association*, 1962.

Griffey, N., Speech Methodology used at St. Mary's School for the Deaf, Cabra, Dublin. *Proceeding of the International Conference on Oral Education of the Deaf*, U.S.A, 1967.

Griffey, N., *Irislan*, 1978. Irish National Association for the Deaf.

Presnell, L., "Hearing Impaired Children's Comprehension and Production of Syntax in Oral Language". *Journal of Speech and Hearing Research*, 12–21, 1973.

Appendix D

Sicard, W. C., *Cours d'Instruction d'un Sourd-Muet*, Paris, Le Clere, 1800.

Stokoe, W. C., *Semiotics and Human Sign Languages*, The Hague. Mouton, 1972.

Tweney, R. D., H. W. Hoemann. "The Development of Semantic Association in Profoundly Deaf Children", *Journal of Hearing and Speech Research*, 16, 309–318, 1973.

Van Uden, A., *A World of Language for Deaf Children*, Swets and Zeitlinger, Amsterdam and Lisse, 1977.

Vernon, M., S. D. Koh. "Early Manual Communication and Deaf Children's Achievement", *American Annals of the Deaf*, 115, September 1970, 527–536.

Wollman, D. S., "The Attainments in English and Arithmetic of Secondary School Pupils with Impaired Hearing". *British Journal of Educational Psychology*, Nov. 1964, 34, p. 268–274.

Appendix E

Fifty Years of Teaching Deaf Children

Thomas Watson Memorial Lecture by Sister Nicholas Griffey, Manchester University, 11 May 1988. Sister Nicholas is a patron member of the National Association for the Deaf. She was the Director of the diploma course for Teachers of the Deaf at University College, Dublin, and is a world-renowned authority on the education of the deaf.*

At the outset I would like to let you in on a secret! When I retired from University College, Dublin, in 1986 I had reached the ripe age of seventy years so I decided that I would withdraw completely from lecturing. Yet here I am this afternoon talking in Manchester University. The reason lies in my sense of gratitude to the late Thomas Watson and to his wife, Dorothy, who happily is here with us today—for their help, guidance and friendship since 1946. It is a great honour for me to speak on this occasion.

From the beginning Dr. Watson struck me as one who had given full commitment to his work. As a student I found him approachable, generous in sharing his practical expertise in the area of audiology and language teaching, and utterly dedicated to deaf children whose welfare always came first with him.

His marvellous sense of history enabled him to see approaches to the teaching of the deaf in perspective. From 1947 on, I frequently called on him for help in my work in Ireland. This was generously given. He was a man of integrity and a sincere friend.

Looking to the past is characteristic of people in my age group. This afternoon I am going to look back over a period of fifty years as a teacher of the deaf, in the hope that perhaps my experience may be of some help to you who are actively engaged in what is still considered one of the most challenging fields of endeavour and one which is becoming increasingly difficult.

A study of the past can be of benefit to teachers of the deaf today because issues that have been dealt with one way or another over a period of two hundred years are reasserting themselves and are being debated independently of any historical context. I am convinced that, from a distance, one has the necessary perspective to appreciate the present.

I am often asked if I chose to work with the deaf. The truth is, the work was selected for me. In October 1934 I became a Dominican Sister in Dublin and in the following January I was sent to observe classes in St. Mary's School for the Deaf at

Link, winter 1988, p. 6–10.

158

Appendix E

Dominican Convent, Cabra, Dublin. This school had been founded by two courageous Sisters in 1846 when Ireland was in the grip of famine.

From its foundation until 1952 the school received no State aid. The sisters were voluntary workers who were assisted by selected deaf past pupils who had availed of a course of in-service training which was established in the school in 1854.

As adult role models these deaf people were an inspiration to the pupils and they made such a lasting impression on me that I have always wanted some deaf members on the school staff.

In 1935 the poverty in the schools was obvious but despite difficulties, struggles and privations there was happiness and peace there. The sisters who were outstandingly gifted and versatile were utterly dedicated to a hidden work which was unacclaimed in the Ireland of that time. The Cabra school was better known abroad because it had an international reputation for excellence in the field of language teaching.

The method in use had been devised by a French priest—Père Jamet—who described his approach as a "manual pronunciation of words". It consisted of natural gestures, one hand fingerspelling, and conventional sign language based on finger spelling. When a sign for a particular word was not available finger spelling was used. Signs were invested with grammatical inflections and linguistic markers.

Cabra's first teachers adapted Jamet's system to suit English syntax. They also devised a structured system of language teaching. The spoken word was never used even though some of the pupils had useful hearing. Speech was considered a distraction for the reader of manual communication.

As a young teacher I was advised not to speak for any length of time to a hearing colleague in the presence of the children in case they would feel isolated. So I had joined a "silent community" whose members seemed to function as "outsiders" in a hearing world.

Because of the poverty in Ireland at that time, the children rarely went home. This was a worry to me because I could see that the school had supplanted the family as the centre of the child's life. Yet today, working with elderly deaf as well as young deaf adults who had spent some time in psychiatric hospitals, I can see that lasting friendships formed in the residential schools are such a help. On the other hand I have met deaf adults whose education took place in the integrated setting with the result that they have no deaf friends. Some of them were quite resentful about this.

I would like now to describe the linguistic environment of the Cabra school in the thirties and early forties, because it was probably unique at the time since most schools throughout the world adopted some form of speech teaching following the famous Milan Conference in 1880.

The pupils were not admitted until they had reached their seventh birthday and prior to this neither they nor their parents received any form of guidance. The new pupil was admitted to an environment where all the adults were fluent in the use of natural as well as systematic sign language. From the start the ability of the new pupil to use self devised gestures was closely observed. These were picked up or "seized", as

Appendix E

van Uden would say, and used by the teacher. Emphasis was placed on the development of concepts rather than the imitation of a particular sequence of signs.

Natural sign language is pictographic and situational. Facial expression can convey meaning while one sign suffices for many words. The vocabulary of the pupils in the admission class then was subjective and individualised since it depended so much on gestures. However, as soon as possible, official signs were taught.

In the classroom the aim of the teacher was to evoke expression in I.S.L. from the pupils. This was converted into manually coded English and fed back to the child. Then the pupil was encouraged to imitate and memorise the signed sentence which was backed up by the written form. Finger spelling was deferred until the pupils had acquired some sign language. It was only when they had a considerable amount of receptive and expressive language that daily lessons in syntax were introduced.

From the age of approximately nine years the pupils were given daily structured lessons in language. Imitation, repetition and reinforcement were used in good measure. At that time I knew nothing about short term memory problems but my approach then included remedial techniques recommended today. Language was the main subject on the curriculum and there was much time for it because the school day was a long one.

The sisters at that time did not seem to worry so much about educational attainment as the lack of employment for the deaf in Ireland. However, I was increasingly aware that the transition from the silent deaf community to hearing society was becoming more and more traumatic for our past pupils.

In the early post World War II period winds of change began to make themselves felt. An upsurge of interest in the handicapped developed rapidly. In the list of new words added to our vocabulary could be found:

        rehabilitation
        integration
        audiology
        linguistics.

Parents now became more involved in educational treatment and they were convinced that Cabra had lagged behind through lack of international contact. The result was that those of them who could afford it sent their deaf children abroad for assessment and education because they wanted them to be taught by means of the oral method. Those of our past pupils who went to work in England reported that the English deaf were better prepared for integration because they could lipread. Ninety-five per cent of the past pupils indicated that they wanted Irish deaf children to learn to speak and lipread.

Following visits to schools in England and Scotland and after much discussion it was decided that Cabra would adopt the oral method. The first step towards this was the provision of a teacher who could use this method so in October 1946 I became a student in the Department of Education of the Deaf in this University, I was referred to as the "Swank with the white flannels"! I believe I succeeded in restraining my hands but it has been said that I had "signing eyes". At times that indicative glance could be a life-saver!

In the Department here, and in the schools where I did practise teaching, I found the same dedication as I had experienced in Cabra. The problems in the English schools at that time were many because the children had spent so much time in air raid shelters during the war. Educational retardation was obvious even in the case of children who had a considerable amount of residual hearing.

The emphasis on audiology and speech teaching opened up a new world for me. The children in the schools seemed closer to the normally hearing. They were more integrated in the family and while their written English did not reach the level of the Cabra children, it was more fluent and natural.

I was fascinated with their responses to auditory training even though at that time there was only one group hearing aid in each school. Notice that I used the term "auditory training" which was quickly discarded in favour of "auditory experience" when powerful individual hearing aids became available. That term "auditory experience" brings to mind Tom Watson because he used it so much.

I returned to Dublin in July 1947 where it was my privilege to be the leader of a group pioneering the introduction of new and more modern methods of teaching the deaf. It is interesting to note that the group included four deaf assistant teachers who encouraged me at every step.

We began by admitting four year old deaf children to what we called the "oral class". They were taught by means of speech, lipreading, reading and writing. Signs were excluded in the classroom. Group lessons in lipreading and speech were given to all other pupils who, however, made little progress in lipreading.

I found too, to my great dismay, that our oral pupils rarely used spontaneous speech. The reason was obvious. They were thinking in gestures and signs which they had picked up from the manually taught pupils in the out of school periods. I knew they should be kept separate but we could not afford a new building.

In time the number of oral classes increased. Separate classes were set up for partially hearing but to me the school was still manual. Eventually in 1952 I decided to set up two completely separate departments—an oral department and a department where total communication was to be used.

In the oral school the auditory input became more and more important even though hearing aids were not sufficiently powerful for the profoundly deaf at that time. I fully realised that some children—those with lowered intellectual functioning, those who had received no speech stimulation up to the age of seven or eight years and those whom I termed "visualisers" that is: children who despite average intelligence and adequate stimulation in the early years—failed to speak and lipread. Later I was to discover that some of the "visualisers" had specific language disorders.

In the meantime I was constantly submitting rather ambitious programmes to the Irish Government. In the late fifties and early sixties things began to happen. The Department of Education decided to pay salaries to Irish teachers of the deaf, grants for hearing aids were provided and a national audiology clinic was established. I placed a high priority on early ascertainment of deafness, parent guidance, attainment

Appendix E

and psychological assessment and fitting with hearing aids. It was a very exciting time for all of us.

I had my moments of anxiety but I knew that help was always available from this department. Sir Alexander and Lady Irene Ewing, Dr. Tom Littler and Dr. Tom Watson often crossed the Irish Sea to lecture, to advise and to encourage. At least there were signs of progress. The first thing I noticed was that oral pupils were using spontaneous speech both in and out of the classroom. What a joy to hear deaf children chattering!

Parents reported that they felt closer to their children. The language levels were more satisfactory than they had been before segregation took place. In the early years of oralism at Cabra, I believe we over-emphasised the natural approach to the teaching of language, with the result that the pupils' written English was disappointing. We then began to emphasise written patterns since writing and reading make the whole message potentially available unlike lipreading and signing. However, we were more careful to see that the written form did not supersede the auditory memory. Instead of giving structured language lessons we endeavoured to help the children, to reflect on their already acquired language.

Eventually children from the oral school took state examinations. When the results were available my first glance was at attainment in English because I have always been concerned about literacy levels among the deaf. Employment opportunities improved for our past pupils and it was obvious that the change to oralism had helped towards integration.

In the course of numerous discussions with past pupils it was impressed on me that they wanted to belong to the world of the deaf as well as that of the hearing. I accepted this fully and I never hesitated to use sign language with those who favoured it, though my concern since 1946 has been that the deaf should be integrated as much as possible into the hearing world. The ability to think in speech patterns and to lipread is a prerequisite for this. I found that the pupils who were taught by means of total communication made little progress in lipreading and speaking but they did learn language. On the whole the hard of hearing wanted to be in the hearing world.

So the silent community at Cabra had changed and most of us were happy about the change. It was helpful to be affirmed in our work by parents, the Department of Education and the public.

Then came the sixties which brought social upheaval and ferment. They were the years of the minorities—including the deaf. A spirit of rebellion made itself felt in the world of the deaf. In the United States "Deaf Power" resembling "Black Power" was born. So was the National Theatre of the Deaf.

At the time, research findings stressed the low educational achievement of deaf school leavers. Something had to be done. These factors gave rise to the total communication movement. I was unhappy about it because I knew it would not achieve the educational results promised by its advocates. I was saddened to observe that the movement seemed to set deaf against deaf and deaf against hearing. However, I rejoiced that the deaf were making their own decisions. Their language and culture was being popularised through the international media. The problems of deaf people which are really invisible were being highlighted. Parents whose children required the use of manual methods were finding the decision easier to accept.

Signing is fashionable today. However, I could never regard total communication as a panacea for all the problems of deaf children, their parents and teachers. I was aware that in the total communication environment speech and lipreading would deteriorate. Having made a number of visits to schools in the United States in the seventies and eighties I found that the pupils were more manual than oral. I was reminded of Cabra in the fifties. This is understandable. Signs are more attractive, more static and more easily discriminated than speech patterns.

The small deaf child will not pay attention to speech when it is accompanied by sign because there is a conflict between the auditory and the visual. The visual takes over. Unless the children are thinking in speech both in and out of school oral communication will be stilted and artificial. In such circumstances I would be tempted to use manualism but for me this would be the easy way out. Oralism makes greater demands on the child, parents, and teachers, but I am convinced that it is a better method especially for deaf children who have potential.

When Dr. Markides asked me to address you he encouraged me to indicate where we teachers of the deaf are going in 1988. Even with 50 years behind me it is not easy to predict. However, I am optimistic. When the current controversy dies down—and this will take some time—I believe there will be more and better educational options available to all types of hearing-impaired people. It will be accepted that there is no "one way" of developing literacy in deaf children. Comprehensive services will then be emphasised.

I envisage the development of suitable tests and on-going teaching procedures to enable teachers and parents to select suitable educational environments for individual children. I would like to see parents, teachers and deaf professionals working together to provide ideal opportunities for all deaf children. Constant on-going evaluation of children—especially the under sevens—should be undertaken.

At present it is to be regretted that failure is experienced when children are misplaced. Those who fail in ordinary schools could be successful in good oral schools—or what the Americans call "incontestably oral" schools—where the auditory input is emphasised. "Oral failures" could be successful in a total communication environment. Quite a number of our militant adult deaf have experienced failure in their lives. I hope that in the future we can avoid this.

Today, we can rejoice that there is consensus among a growing number of researchers that language teaching should be the priority of teachers of the deaf. All this has implications for teacher training which I believe should now include experience in the use of manual communication as well as placement periods in schools where total communication is well practised. Teachers now, more than ever, need to be equipped to deal with all types of hearing-impaired pupils. Having experience in a total communication environment a student will have a clearer grasp of its limitations.

The area of adult education of the deaf is opening up and I see more teachers of

Appendix E

the deaf involved. Instead of reducing the period of training for teachers I would like to see it increased because in the final analysis it is the teacher that matters.

Technology and medicine are on our side. I dream of a time when speech will be automatically converted into written pattern in all our schools and colleges for the deaf. Then the conversational approach will take off provided there is good teaching. I hope that in the future cochlear implants will help at least some children. Actually there is much ground for hope. My prayer is, and will be, that all educators of the deaf will work together as well as with parents and adult deaf people and that all will avoid entrenched positions.

My aims if I were still teaching today

If I were teaching today my aim would be to help each hearing-impaired person to reach his/her highest level. I would try to find the appropriate method for the individual. I would look for those characteristics which might be predictive of success or failure under different systems. The level of the child's communication will be determined by his potential and his opportunities. For some pupils it will be oral communication which will enable them to fit better into a hearing world and to provide them with a wider range of opportunity for educational, social and vocational experience.

Uppermost in my mind will be their need to communicate orally eventually with their hearing children. The deaf have a right to this. As adults they are free to use whatever means of communication they wish.

For other deaf children educational treatment may mean manual communication, some speech and written expression. For children with severe additional handicaps it may mean a crude signal system. For all there must be some form of communication.

My philosophy is not easily held today when we are told that every deaf baby must be exposed to the language of the deaf and the deaf culture so that he/she will become a happy, well adjusted and educated adult. I do not accept this. Neither do I believe that reduced literacy levels can be attributed to oralism in schools for the deaf. It looks as if we are now going to make a mistake similar to that made by teachers of the deaf in Milan in 1880.

An American once accused me of being anecdotal but happily, today, the findings of some American researchers are on my side. I would like to quote from them:

In 1978 Jensema and Trybus wrote: "When the use of speech is high, use of signs and finger-spelling is low and vice versa."

In 1984 Quigley stated: "No strongly research-supported directions for educational practice have yet emerged."

In 1986 Luterman wrote: "The methodology dispute has set back the education of the deaf by obscuring other more important issues, such as, the quality of teaching, the effective use of amplification and the effective utilisation of parents."

In 1986 Leo O'Connor wrote: "An increasing amount of evidence reinforces the observation that deaf children cannot process speech, speech reading, and signs at the same time. The research studies that stress the failures of code switching are impressive."

Finally this startling statement made by Stephen Quigley in 1986: "Enough data has been collected over the past 70 years, particularly the past 20, for several tentative conclusions to be advanced regarding the educational achievement of deaf students leaving secondary level education programmes. These findings are interpreted in terms of long standing issues, namely, those related to communication methods, learning environments, and student and test characteristics. Despite decades of educational effort it is argued that the academic performance of the typical deaf as compared with the typical hearing student has not changed since the inception of objective testing. It is further argued that the best overall achievement is associated with a select group of deaf students who have advantageous demographic characteristics (such as high socio-economic status) and have been educated in certain learning environments (for example in private oral residential schools)."

I doubt if socio-economic status would be so important in England or Ireland. With the available early ascertainment of deafness and parent guidance some of our children from working class families are doing remarkably well in an oral setting. A number of them are integrated where they are achieving acceptable levels of literacy, though I must confess that I have come across children who were misplaced in ordinary schools and the results were disastrous.

REFERENCES

Jensema C & Trybus R. (1978) *"Communication Patterns and Educational Achievement of Hearing Impaired Students"* (Series T. No. 2) Washington D.C. Gallaudet College Office of Demographic Studies.

Luterman, D. M. (1986) *"Deafness in Perspective"* p. 264.

O'Connor, L (1986). Oralism in Perspective in *"Deafness in Perspective"*. Luterman, D. M. (Ed.).

Quigley, S. P. (1984). *"Language and Deafness"*.

Quigley, S. P. & PAUL, P. V. (1986). A perspective on academic achievement, in *"Deafness in Perspective"*. (Ed. Luterman, D. M.).

Appendix F

Headstart in Deafness. Early Home Environment

Address by Hilde S. Schlesinger, associate clinical professor of psychiatry, University of California Medical Center, San Francisco[*][1]

O peration Headstart is a program which has become increasingly familiar to all of us through newspaper and television reports. One of the assumptions of Operation Headstart is that some children begin life with their faculties intact, but fail to develop the ability to use their innate capacities because of some deficiency in the early home environment. Compensatory programs have been devised for these urban, "disadvantaged" children. There seems too little disagreement that there is a need for compensation although the what, when, and how of compensation requires further research. Those of us who are interested in the welfare of deaf children would be delighted to see an "Operation Headstart" which might help to compensate for those things which they miss through an absence of auditory contact with their environment.

A comprehensive Headstart for deaf children is to be based upon an understanding of factors important to early development, and upon a knowledge of how those factors are influenced by deafness. Our clinical work and research studies of deaf children at Langley Porter have been designed in the hope of making a contribution to this knowledge so that we may progress toward an Operation Headstart for deaf children.

We feel that the existence of a defect in the auditory apparatus—even if it is associated with some other malformation—does not necessarily block the humanizing interpersonal relationships which are necessary for normal growth and development. The beginning of the life cycle may not be very different for the deaf and the hearing infant. The deaf infant is seen as normal by most parents, who develop expectations that he will develop in a normal way (Downs 1968). Most deaf babies babble, and seem to respond in the usual way to the parents' attention. The fact that the infant is missing out on listening during a critical period of life is not usually perceived by his parents, who have no reason to suspect that he does not hear.

Thus, we might believe that this early period during infancy can be a "Golden Age" for the deaf child, just as it can be for the hearing child:

*Proceedings of the 44th Meeting of the Convention of American Instructors of the Deaf, 1969, p. 250–259.

1. Research supported in part by Social and Rehabilitation Services, grant no. RD-2835.

Appendix F

> When all were content.
> When food came of itself ...
> And spring was everlasting.
> Then did milk and sweet nectar
> Flow for all.
> - Ovid, *Metamorphoses*.

However, this fragment of ancient poetry reflects a mythical belief about the golden age of infancy which has been shared by many behavioral scientists. According to the myth, infancy is golden because the infant is entirely passive; he cheerfully receives and accepts all which his mother offers. As most mothers will relate (either cheerfully or angrily), infants are not passive, despite their complete dependence upon others. Mothers describe babies who are extremely active in utero as well as after birth. The infant is active not only in obtaining nourishment, but in observing the world around him. Observation indicates that this response occurs as early as 18 hours after birth. The infant might be described as being "quietly alert"; the adult might be analogously described as being "attentive."

This state in both infant and adult occurs when pressing needs such as hunger and relief from pain have been met (Fantz, Wolff, and White, cited in Bettelheim, 1967). Bettelheim postulates that an infant will be as active as the environment or his biological equipment permits him to be, and that activity may be of greater importance to his future development than a purely passive satisfaction of his physical needs.

Thus, according to my thesis, infants—whether they be deaf or hearing—need to participate actively with their parent. Furthermore, mothers and fathers need the satisfaction and reassurance of response from their infants, from the very beginning. Frequent and mutually satisfying experiences of interaction between parents and child are of paramount importance for my program of Operation Headstart for deaf children.

It would appear that throughout development the human organism needs to experience a high level of purposeful activity. Both Bettelheim (1967) and Meadow (1967) postulate that the child's activity on his own behalf contributes to optimal solution of developmental tasks. It has long been clear that the infant needs nurturance, protection, and gratification of physical needs in order to establish a sense of trust in the world. It is more recently becoming clear that the infant may also need to contribute to this activity.

Initially, of course, the mother will adapt completely to the infant's needs while he will adapt only to his own needs. The mother will bring a vast repertory of modes to the interaction, while the infant will bring only a few. Similarly, the mother will be the primary initiator of early problem-solving activities. Nevertheless, the infant is not only suckled, it also needs to suckle; it is not only cuddled and loved, it also needs to cling. The infant needs to discover that the world and the people contained therein are basically to be trusted and that they will somehow provide for him. However, the infant needs to discover that not only as a passive recipient, but that his cries will produce

Appendix F

activity which will provide food or relief from pain.

The necessary frustrations of living produce needs that are not always met immediately because mothers are human, and therefore occasionally tired and cross. Thus the child learns at varying ages that the world is not his for the asking, but that he is challenged to do something about it (Bettelheim, 1967). I agree with Bettelheim that all children will experience frustration, but that there may be an optimal time and way for them to experience it. There are some children to whom the world appears to be entirely satisfying but who were denied the experience that what they did made very much difference to anyone—even themselves. These become the good, quiet children who tend to have difficulties later in life when the parent or the world expects independent action from them. Some very active children may not need to "receive" so much from the environment because they learned very early how to promote satisfaction of their needs.

There is another group of youngsters who at some critical time see the world as offering some satisfactions, although in an undesirable or a frustrating way. At the same time they are powerless to influence the environment in a predictable manner through their own actions. These youngsters might be described as having a "predisposition" to autism from birth; by the age of 2, serious emotional disturbance is usually diagnosed. The definition of this illness—autism—is complex, and there are conflicting ideas about it. However, most researchers agree on its descriptive features: The autistic child is a child who does not appear to reach out to its mother or the world about him either physically or emotionally—a child who appears to be preoccupied by his inner self rather than with interpersonal relations.

I have taken some care to describe the possible emotional consequences for a child who is unable or who is discouraged from active participation in the orderly and predictable gratification of his developmental needs, because I feel that some of the vicissitudes of the deaf child's development may be related to a lack of parent-child gratification, or mutual participation in certain developmental tasks. A number of attempts have been made to formulate comprehensive lists of the developmental tasks of early childhood socialization. Most of these concentrate on the tasks which the parent must perform for the child. Meadow (1967) was interested in emphasizing the reciprocal nature of parent-child interaction, and thus elaborated a developmental framework:

Parent's task	**Child's task**
Provision of nurturance and protection, gratification of physical needs creating the setting for ...	... Development of a sense of trust in the continuing fulfillment of physical needs—in the "friendliness" of the physical environment.

Appendix F

Parent's task	Child's task
Provision of affection and warmth in a stable, on-going manner, in order that the child may respond by ...	... Development of a sense of trust in regard to the stable nature of affectionate relationships.
Provision of the opportunity for, encouragement of, and practice in communication so the child may ...	... Develop the habits, symbols, and shared meanings of language; leading to a conception of self as a separate being.
Provision of orientation to socially appropriate ways of gratifying physical needs; plus the setting of limits to the child's expression of these needs so that he may ...	... Learn to control and gratify his needs for food, drink, elimination, etc., in ways which are efficient and acceptable.
Setting limits for the behavioral expression of aggressive impulses so that the child may ...	... Control his aggressive and other expressive impulses or perceive the consequences of lack of control.
Providing the setting, opportunity, and appreciation for unique individual expression so the child may ...	... Express, and find satisfaction in, the unique aspects of his individual self.
Provision of the motivation, techniques, and tools of skill training so the child may ...	... Progress toward the acquisition of necessary physical, cognitive, and social skills.
Orientation of the child to cultural, subcultural and idiosyncratic parental goals and values so he may ...	... Develop a sense of the meaning of "moral judgment."
Allow the child sufficient autonomy so that he may ...	... Develop his own interpretation of these goals and values, provide his own synthesis of them, and be able to apply them with discretion to specific situations.
Recognize the child as a separate, acting, decision making individual, thus...	... helping him to achieve self-identity.

Appendix F

The performance of these "tasks" of socialization are, of course, influenced by many factors which have nothing to do with deafness. One major factor is that of the interaction of the mother's personality and the child's temperament (Thomas, 1968). Deafness need not affect the parent's gratification of the child's physical needs, nor the child's development of trust that these needs will be gratified (task 1). Deafness need not interfere with the parent's provision of affection, nor the child's trust in the stability of affectionate relationships (task 2). Even these seemingly elementary tasks of socialization may, and have been affected by parental reaction to the diagnosis of deafness in their child. The ability of both parent and child to fulfill the more complicated tasks of socialization can be hampered severely by the physical limitations imposed by deafness. Indeed, delay or inhibition of the fulfillment of any of the tasks may well be responsible for the cognitive retardation and psychological difficulties attributed to a large number of deaf adolescents and adults. The difficulties and problems of deaf children are curiously similar to those disadvantaged, poor, or Negro children for whom Operation Headstart has been designed. It may be useful to summarize some of the observations reported in describing these disadvantaged hearing children:

They are children who are said by teachers and administrators to be curious, "cute," affectionate, warm, and independent in kindergarten and the first grade, but who so often become alienated, withdrawn, angry, passive, pathetic, or just troublesome by the fifth and sixth grades.

They are children who have been deprived of a substantial portion of the variety of stimuli which they are physically capable of integrating, and are likely to be deficient in the equipment required for learning. They are the children who are "probably further away from their maturational ceiling as a result of this experimental poverty."

"There is a tendency for these children to be proportionately more present-oriented and less aware of past-present sequences ... to have significantly greater difficulty in handling items relating to time judgments."

They are children whose differences in perceptual abilities and general environmental orientation decrease with chronological age, whereas language differences tend to increase. Although the environment may be full of acoustic stimuli, few are meaningful to the child, leading him to a faulty development of auditory discrimination.

Many of these children may not have learned effective attentiveness, some have even carefully learned inattention. At school inattentiveness often becomes reinforced through lack of understanding (Deutsch, 1963).[2] Riessman (1962) described the disadvantaged child grown to adulthood as follows:

> He frequently feels alienated, not fully a part of society, left out, frustrated in what he can do ... He holds the world, rather than himself, responsible for the misfortune, consequently he is much less apt to suffer pangs of self-blame and can be more direct in his expression of aggression ... Since he sees problems as being caused externally rather than internally, he is more likely to be a poor patient in psychotherapy ... He also tends to have a restricted vocational picture.

2. Barsch (1968) states that, because of the advice of "experts," these youngsters are frequently subjected to a totally incomprehensible verbal barrage, further reinforcing their inattentiveness.

Appendix F

Many professionals who work with deaf children and adults might think that these generalizations had been made about deaf persons. Certainly many authors knowledgeable about deafness indicate similar, if not identical, findings (Rainer, 1963; Vernon, 1962).

It is no accident that the disadvantaged, particularly the Negro disadvantaged, and the deaf share some other characteristics related to psychiatric illness and crime patterns. It is no accident that both are expressing a voluble disapproval of the paternalism of the whites or of the hearing; that slogans of "Deaf Pride" are being seen, along with those for "Black Power"; that the insistence on the need for self-help and grassroots participation is becoming widespread.

If the deaf and the hearing-disadvantaged share some cognitive and psychological problems, they may also share some difficulties in the performance of the developmental tasks of early childhood. There is a growing feeling among those concerned with the disadvantaged that the provision of a richer, more meaningful environment at a critical, early age can help to change potentially "disadvantaged" youngsters into successful ones. Likewise, there is a growing feeling among those concerned with the deaf that the provision of certain early changes in the environment of the deaf infant will diminish or even eliminate some maladaptation associated with deafness.

What kind of program might be instituted which would provide an "Operation Headstart" for the deaf child? Some authors indicate that oral and aural training, provided early and administered properly, will eliminate the linguistic deprivation which creates so many of the deaf child's problems. These authors feel that good oral-aural training will produce a deaf child who "can and does learn language and speech as does the normal hearing child" (Hardy, 1957), or "who will take to lipreading like a duck to water" (Cawthorne, 1967; Whetnall, 1964). Other authors, while agreeing that early intervention is critical, and that speech training is important, do not agree that a purely oral-aural emphasis will provide a sufficient solution for most prelingually deafened youngsters (Brill, 1959; Furth, 1966: Kohl, 1966; Stevenson, 1964; Vernon, 1968).

This group of authors, as well as some others, are becoming more and more impressed with evidence of the relatively better performance of deaf children with deaf parents when compared to that of deaf children with hearing parents. For example, deaf children with deaf parents have been found to show "better adjustment" (Brill, 1960); higher educational level and better command of language (Stevenson, 1964); significantly higher reading scores in fingerspelling and vocabulary (Quigley, 1961). Meadow (1967) found that deaf children of deaf parents have significantly higher achievement test scores and significantly higher teacher-counselor ratings on items relating to maturity, responsibility, independence, sociability, and appropriate sex-role behavior. Furthermore, they received higher ratings for facility in written language, receptive and expressive fingerspelling, absence of communicative frustration, and willingness to communicate with strangers. No differences were fund for speech and lipreading ability.

Appendix F

Thus, some of us who are looking for ways to give deaf youngsters a "headstart" have been looking to deaf families for clues. Clinical studies, experimental evidence, and anecdotal materials all indicate that the interaction of deaf parents and their deaf children may be markedly different from that of hearing parents and their deaf children. These variations may be traced to two sources: (1) Differences in parental reaction to the diagnosis of deafness, and (2) differences in early parent-child communication.

Throughout most of the developmental tasks previously described, the deaf parents appear to encounter more consistently satisfying experiences with their deaf children. The diagnosis is usually more easily accepted (Meadow, 1967), thus freeing the parent to be whole-heartedly responsive to the infant. The distressed, angry, shocked, or guilty hearing mother is frequently temporarily paralyzed. (It is a psychiatric truism that one can give effectively only when one's own needs are effectively met.) Furthermore, the deaf parent tends to have more realistic expectations of the implication of deafness and its manifold effects, and appears to cope more easily with eating, sleeping, toilet training problems; they permit earlier independence and autonomy—integral parts of the developmental tasks. They also have a more intact feeling of parental competence.

The hearing parents frequently are bewildered about the meaning and impact of deafness and vacillate between false optimism or false pessimism which appears to interfere with the consistency of their coping. It has been shown by Merrills (Barsch 1968) that an experimental group of mothers whose children were identified as deficient or different were triggered into authoritarian attitudes with significant increases of directing, interfering, criticizing, and structuring changes of activity of their children.

Another important issue suspected to be of prime importance in the better functioning of the deaf child of deaf parents is the early parent-child communication. Hearing parents frequently make efforts to assist the child in acquiring "normal" communication, efforts which are too often doomed to failure. There is vast parental and professional confusion between speech and language and a consequent over emphasis on the importance of speech. Michaels and Schuman (Ross 1964) report that a majority of parents with defective (mentally retarded) children "hold the belief that the child's major if not his only problem lies in the area of speech." If this confusion exists in the mind of the parents of the mentally retarded it is not surprising to see it equally if more justifiably in the parents of deaf youngsters. Parental expectation of normal speech is erroneous. Clinical experience indicates that the parent who says that his child has a good understanding of spoken language is an expert gesticulator. This parent may not be aware that each of his directives is accompanied by a gesture which gives another clue to the oral message (Barsch 1968). McFarline (Barsch 1968) found that mothers tend to report their children to be more precocious than they actually were. Chess (Barsch 1968) found that the distortion occurred in the direction of socially acceptable concepts of optimal functioning. Hearing parents of deaf children have a high expectancy for speech and distort the

Appendix F

level of its existence.

However, a large proportion of deaf parents use manual communication with their infants from an early age. Despite a paucity of definite facts in this area, it would appear from clinical investigation and our on-going research that the use of manual communication does not inhibit speech, but may actually enhance it (Quigley, 1968; Meadows, 1967; Schlesinger, in progress). Furthermore, it appears to enhance language acquisition at a critical age. With regard to our framework of reciprocal activity of need gratification, the deaf youngster with early acquisition of a symbol system known to him and his mother is more active, meaningfully, and consistently manipulating the environment through the use of language.[3]

Hearing parents who have availed themselves of manual communication systems for their deaf youngsters, as well as the more traditional oral training, have recently joined the ranks of our research subjects. It is too soon to evaluate either the cognitive or the psychological progress of these youngsters. However, there is unequivocal evidence of a high degree of mutual satisfaction, and even delight, in the communicative process itself. These parents seem to us to evaluate their children's receptive communication more correctly. Many other hearing parents exaggerate their deaf child's ability to understand messages. Often they misinterpret perceptual difficulties as stubbornness, willfulness, or playfulness (Barsch, 1968).

Any attempt at mutually satisfying communication will be frustrating if individuals do not share a similar degree of linguistic competence, regardless of the age of the participants and the type of exchange attempted. There is a temptation to withdraw from the encounter, a tendency to distort the degree of receptive understanding by the more competent participant, and a marked negativism toward the expected linguistic mode by the less competent participant. When one member of the communicative pair is unable to obtain the expected degree of competence in the formal language, which occurs only too frequently among prelingually deaf children (Furth, 1966), distortion of perception and negativism toward expression is intensified. Disadvantaged children are frequently said to be "non-verbal." Investigators are finding that these children have a "public" language in which they are quite verbal (Bernstein, cited in Deutsch, 1963), and that this public language must be accepted before the "formal language" is acquired. Negro children only 2 years old revealed constricted verbal responsiveness when examined by white persons (Passow, 1967). Negro adults in one study were fund to give more correct answers when interviewed by a Negro (Pettigrew, cited in Passow, 1967).

There is no comparable research which considers the level of a deaf child's linguistic attainments when he talks to a deaf and to a hearing person. Again, however, we can draw some interesting parallels. Both groups—deaf and racial minorities—are stigmatized. Their means of coping have been disdained for centuries. Both groups are caught in a potentially self-fulfilling prophecy of "underachievement" or failure. Both are presented with an ambiguous request; to act white or to act hearing.

It seems possible that deaf children are reacting to insistence that they "act hearing" by resisting the acquisition of speech, in the same way the Negro children

3. The question has sometimes been raised of whether sign language can legitimately be termed a true language. Ervin-Tripp (1966) defines language as "any symbolic system which is learned, which consists of conventional basic units and rules for their arrangement, and which includes a conventional set of arbitrary signs for meanings and referents." By this definition, sign language does qualify as a language. In any case, it is a viable means of communication.

appear nonverbal to their white examiners. Kohl (1966) speculates that deaf youngsters universally use the sign language. We have found that all the deaf adolescent patients who come to us for therapy have a knowledge of sign language, even though they may deny this initially. It may well be that manual communication is the "public language" of the deaf, and that it must be accepted freely if the deaf child is to learn the formal language of the hearing world. Ervin-Tripp (1966) notes that the introduction of Spanish-speaking teachers into Spanish-speaking classes in New York has resulted in the improvement of the children's ability to speak English. The experience of one administrator of a school program for deaf children is that their speech was more intelligible when they were using sign language simultaneously (Halcomb, 1969).

Experiments indicate ever more clearly that success breeds success, and that even expectation of success breeds success. Deaf children are exposed to the experience of failure too often in their attempts to communicate orally. This frequent lack of success may contribute to a less than optimal cognitive and personal adjustment in a variety of human experiences.

My own experience indicated that there is a disproportionately high proportion of psychiatric casualties among deaf children, and that too many of their parents are deprived of some gratification through the child. This is expressed most frequently during the early years by intensive preoccupation with the child's deafness; by rigid and distorted interpretations of expert advice; by deaf child-centered activities frequently at the expense of marital harmony and sibling well-being. As the deaf child grows older, the early lack of gratification is often verbalized as regret for the "lost years."

It is of paramount importance that more deaf children and their parents be given the opportunity to engage in mutually satisfying developmental tasks of socialization. This could lead, in turn, to more mutually satisfying communication between the deaf child, his parents, and his total environment. I feel that one possible way in which this might be initiated is by encouraging hearing parents to communicate with their deaf children manually during the early years. Such a productive "headstart" in the early environment of the deaf child may well help to eradicate the discrepancy between deaf potential, which is normal, and deaf achievement, which is generally low.

Bibliography

Barsch, R. H., *The Parent of the Handicapped Child: The Study of Child-Rearing Practices*,
    Springfield, Illinois: Charles C. Thomas, 1968.
Bettelheim, B., *The Empty Fortress: Infantile Autism and the Birth of the Self*,
    New York, Collier-Macmillan Ltd., 1967.
Brill, R. G., "A study in Adjustment of Three Groups of Deaf Children," *Exceptional Children*,
    1960, v. 26, pp. 464–466.
Cawthorne, T., "Children with Defective Hearing," In McConnell Freeman and Word, Paul
    (Eds.), *Deafness in Childhood*, Nashville: Vanderbilt University Press, 1967, pp. 3–21.
Clausen, John A., mimeographed paper, 1966.

Appendix F

Craig, W. N., & Silver, N. H., *"Examination of Selective Employment Problems of the Deaf,"* American Annals of the Deaf, 1966, v. 3, pp. 448–498.

Deutsch, M. P., *"The Disadvantaged Child and the Learning Process,"* in Passow, A. H., (Ed.), *Education in Depressed Areas,* New York Bureau of Publications, Teachers College, Columbia University, 1963 pp. 163–179.

Downs, M. P., *"Identification and Training of the Deaf Child—Birth to One Year,"* Volta Review, March 1968, pp. 154–158.

Ervin-Tripp, S., Language Development, In L. W. Hoffman, & L. M. Hoffman (Eds.), *Review of Child Development Research,* New York, Russell Sage Foundation, 1966, Vol. 11, pp. 55–105.

Furth, H. G., *Thinking Without Language,* New York, The Free Press, 1966.

Hardy, W. G., & Bordley, J. E., *"The Child with Impaired Hearing,"* In Smith-Michal. H. (Eds.), *Management of the Handicapped Child,* New York, Grune & Stratton, Inc., 1957.

Holcomb, R., personal communication, 1969.

Kohl, H. R., *Language and Education of the Deaf,* New York, Center for Urban Education, 1966.

Meadow, K. P., *"The effect of early manual communication and family climate on the deaf child's development,"* Unpublished doctoral dissertation, University of California at Bereley, 1967.

Passow, A., Goldberg, M., & Tannenbaum, A., (Eds.), *Education of the Disadvantaged: A Book of Readings,* Holt, Rinehart & Winston, 1967.

Quigley, S. P., *"The Influence of Fingerspelling on the Development of Language," Communication and Educational Achievement in Deaf Children,* 1968.

———, & Frisina, R. D., *"Institutionalization and Psycho-Educational Development of Deaf Children,"* Council for Exceptional Children Research Monographs, Series A, no. 3, 1961.

Rainer, J. E. & Altshuler, K. Z., *Comprehensive Mental Health Services for the Deaf,* Department of Medical Genetics, New York State Psychiatric Institute, Columbia University, 1966.

Riessman, F., *The Culturally Deprived Child,* New York: Harper & Row, 1962, pp. 26–27.

Ross, A. O., *The Exceptional Child in the Family,* New York: Grune & Stratton, Inc., 1964.

Schlesinger, H. S., *"The Deaf Preschooler and his Many Faces,"* International Forum of the National Association for the Deaf, 1969, in press.

Thomas, A., Chess, S., & Birch, H., *Temperament and Behavior Disorders in Children,* New York: New York University Press, 1968.

Vernon, M., *"Suggestions for Parents of Deaf Children,"* The Deaf American, 1968, v. 20, (10).

——— *"What is the Future for the Deaf in the World of Work?"* Silent Worker, 1962 pp. 6–12.

Appendix G

Deaf Studies in the Year 2000: New Directions

Address by MJ Bienvenu, co-director of the Bicultural Center in Riverdale, Maryland, to the Conference on Deaf Studies, Chicago, 1993*[1]

*Proceeding of Conference on Deaf Studies, Chicago, 1993, p. 2–19, in *Deaf Studies III: Bridging Cultures in the 21st Century*, College of Continuing Education, Gallaudet University. Reproduced by permission of the author.
1. I would like to thank Betty M. Colonomos for her valuable input to this paper and her support to make this happen.

Let me begin by saying that I am really thrilled to be here with you once again. As I prepared for this speech, I reflected on what a tremendous task lies ahead for us. It is exciting to consider the wide scope of possibilities available in the area of Deaf Studies. We need to be careful, though, not to fall into the trap of tunnel vision. Let me ask you to imagine that you are looking at a catalog from Harvard University, the University of Washington, or Louisiana State University and in it you see there are courses, or even an entire program, offered in Deaf Studies. Wouldn't it be wonderful to see these universities, which are primarily attended by hearing students, offering courses in Deaf Studies? If we want this to be true in the year 2000, perhaps we first need to reflect back on what has brought us to the point where we are today.

What is Deaf Studies?

In 1991, we met in Dallas, and the question we asked at that time was "What is Deaf Studies?" We were all very excited by the possibilities. We discussed a possible curriculum and how such a curriculum could be developed. There was an exchange of instructional materials and methodologies. But in all of that excitement we focused mostly on content. Many people came to that conference wanting very much to implement Deaf Studies courses or programs, but they didn't feel quite ready to do so. They needed some additional help. They needed to take that next step in understanding the "what" of Deaf Studies, but we can't stay in that place forever. We need to ask a larger question—the question of "Why do we need Deaf Studies?"

Why do we need Deaf Studies?

In Dallas, during my presentation, I explored other minority groups and how they have developed programs for studies of their own culture. We looked at African Americans and why they felt the need to establish such programs. One of the major purposes for creating the Black Studies programs was to send a very clear message that Black people are capable of the same achievements as white people, and that they are deserving of equality in our society. Until that time, they were not recognized nor respected in our society. The same thing is true for women. For many years women were not afforded their rightful place in the history books, or the school curriculum. When women finally started to speak out, they were labeled "radicals." This was the beginning of the feminist movement. It grew out of a desire to eliminate sexism in our society, just as African Americans have struggled to eliminate racism. In Dallas, we also looked at what we could learn from Judaic Studies. For many reasons, Jewish people felt the need to establish a program of studies about their history and culture. Today we have the opening of the Holocaust museum where we can learn important lessons from the past and recognize the place of Jewish people in the world.

There is another minority group currently going through the same process as the African Americans and women—a group whose struggles make the headlines daily. It is the Gay and Lesbian movement. Questions are being asked such as, "Should Gay men and Lesbians be allowed to serve in the American military?" Once again we can learn from this emerging campaign about the struggle to achieve equality in our society. The fight against racism, sexism, anti-Semitism, and homophobia continues. Today you and I are here to talk about why we need Deaf Studies programs. We need these programs to fight against audism.

Looking back to 1988, we remember the very exciting events. For one of the first times, the world realized that we were able to stand up for our rights and accomplish many things. But in 1993 we cannot deny that the stereotypes and the myths still exist. Deaf people are still misrepresented in the media. One of the myths that persists very strongly in our society is that Deaf people are truly disabled. They believe we are lacking intelligence, and that all Deaf people long to become hearing. The "60 Minutes" program on the cochlear implant did much to perpetuate this myth. Hearing parents of deaf children and other non-Deaf people still see deafness as a curable illness. They still focus on the audiological condition and, therefore, cannot understand who we really are. They cannot look beyond the audiogram to see the person behind it. They forget the human being who has feelings and thoughts and abilities and talents.

I do not believe that we started to look at Deaf Studies for these reasons. It may have grown out of the movement to counteract oralism by the use of Total Communication. From that came a myriad of methodologies and philosophies, ultimately ending up in the mainstreaming movement where many deaf children are sent off to be isolated and to suffer further deprivation. This was clear at the conference in Dallas, the one in Washington, and again here today. We still see a tremendous need. In our own center we are seeing more and more people asking about the possibilities of Bilingual-Bicultural (Bi-Bi) education. It is possible that one of the reasons for this movement toward Deaf Studies is a way to pacify or placate those people who are advocating for "radical" change.

Before proceeding, I would like to return to the question of content. Included in the current curricula of Deaf Studies courses are the achievements of "Deaf" people and "Deaf" leaders. I use quotation marks here because I question whom we depict as Deaf leaders in these programs. The majority of these figures do not reflect our Deaf

Appendix G

culture and community. True, someone like Lou Ferrigno is famous, but he may not be an appropriate role model for deaf children. We need to ask ourselves what kind of message is conveyed when we are forced to identify with people like him.

As I noted, I am posing these questions and challenges to you because I want us to look beyond where we have been for the past few years and take a giant leap forward. I will focus on the future for the remainder of our time.

Where should Deaf Studies courses be offered?
Many of you who know me are aware that I usually avoid giving definitive answers or prescriptions for problem solving. Rather, I prefer to stimulate your thinking by posing a few questions to you. Does it make sense in a university with predominantly African American students to offer courses in Black Studies for those students? What about a university where the administration and student body are comprised of women and the power structure is very feminist? Do they need to have Women's Studies in that university? Is that logical? Many of you are probably nodding your head yes. Perhaps this is a reflection of our society. However, the real purpose of those programs in colleges that serve these populations is to teach people how to be active in their community and fight for their causes when they leave college. In mainstream colleges, where African Americans are in the minority or women are not in position of power, those courses are offered so that the student population can understand their situation and appreciate their own cultural group better. With respect to Deaf Studies courses, the ideal situation is for hearing college students to have access to one or more courses in Deaf Studies. There they would learn about Deaf people in very positive ways and come to understand that we are a separate cultural, linguistic minority. That is the ideal. Before I discuss the ideal further, though, I want to take a brief look at reality. Most deaf children know nothing about their own heritage or culture. Because of that, we must have Deaf Studies courses and programs in schools with deaf children. We cannot, however, continue in that vein forever. We need to make some drastic changes.

Schools for the Deaf
For the purpose of this presentation, I will focus on several places where it is commonly thought Deaf Studies programs are appropriate. The first is the school for the Deaf. In general, that environment is Deaf, simply due to the sheer number of Deaf Students. However, the administration and the teaching staff generally are not Deaf. The old philosophies of deaf education have not succeeded, and it is now evident that the schools for the Deaf must undergo major changes. We need to ask ourselves, however, if implementing a course or two in Deaf Studies at a school for the Deaf really solves the problem. Let me draw an analogy that may help you answer this. Suppose you are diagnosed with a serious illness and you are given the choice between two courses of treatment. One course is very easy to pursue. You simply take a small pill. However, you must take the medicine for the rest of your life and it may or may not improve your prognosis. The other course of treatment is harsher and more

unpleasant, but you will be guaranteed a cure. Which would you choose? The latter, of course, as the intensity of the treatment is outweighed by the result. Now, suppose we offer Deaf Studies courses to deaf children and they begin to understand about their own language and culture within the confines of the classroom. They see pictures and stories of Deaf leaders and are inspired by the possibilities for their own successes. Then they leave the classroom and are met by the reality—the reality of mistaken approaches in Deaf education, the reality of poor language policy, the reality of oppression. In their other classes, they are not exposed to the positive environment that they experienced in the Deaf Studies classroom. Understandably, this sends mixed messages to the children. Their school experience is anti-Deaf, except in that one classroom. The information gained from the Deaf Studies course cannot be internalized in that child if it is not being reinforced outside that one classroom. The dichotomy only serves to promote confusion, frustration, and anger. I see people in this room now who are nodding their heads in understanding and agreement.

Up until now we have primarily talked about adding to an existing curriculum. Often when we speak of adding Deaf Studies it is as a special course. The word "special," however, has several connotations and is often interpreted to mean "different." Deaf children should not feel different in a school for the Deaf. The Deaf child should feel s/he is the norm in that environment. It has been one of our long-standing goals in the Deaf community to ensure that that environment is a safe haven for Deaf children. It hasn't happened yet, but the goal is still there. It runs contrary to this goal that such a content area would be singled out for a special course in that environment.

Mainstreaming programs
The second potential environment for Deaf Studies courses is mainstreaming programs. We know mainstreaming is here. I will not add "to stay" because I hope it will not stay. The environment clearly is not Deaf. The administration is not deaf; the teaching staff is not deaf. Again, I will suggest two scenarios and let you decide which would be the lesser of two evils. In the first, a deaf child in a mainstreaming program can take a Deaf Studies course, finding out all of the positive things about Deaf people but is unable to see any Deaf people outside of the classroom. The second option is to not offer Deaf Studies courses in those schools and for the deaf child to go on in a blissful ignorance, only to find out about Deaf culture later on in life when s/he is ready to join the community. I am not sure of the answer myself. I don't know if we should eliminate Deaf Studies courses in mainstreaming programs. It may, however, be cruel to dangle the hope of a Deaf identity in front of these children's eyes. Perhaps it is a Band Aid for a much more serious wound. Then again, something is often better than nothing. I want us to think very seriously about this issue. You and I do not want to abandon those deaf children. We cannot just throw up our hands and accept the status quo. We must do something.

Gallaudet University
The third arena for Deaf Studies courses, and one we cannot leave out, is Gallaudet University. Is the environment at Gallaudet Deaf or hearing? I do not think I will

Appendix G

attempt to answer that question. However, I will ask you to draw your own conclusions. Take into consideration the power structure on campus and whether the administration and teaching staff is composed predominantly of Deaf or hearing people. I believe very strongly that there should be a Deaf Studies program at Gallaudet University. I was very pleased when Dr. Corson announced that one would be added. Many of the students who attend Gallaudet are from mainstreamed programs and have a strong need for such a curriculum. I feel this is a wonderful opportunity for these students, and it is the right time for this to happen. Having a Deaf Studies program on campus is also a public admission that Gallaudet does have Deaf people there. We do have our own culture. We have a language. We have our own history. This program provides official recognition of that fact. Many people feel that if Gallaudet University does not pursue the Deaf Studies program, there will be no need for other places to do the same. Due to its unique position, Gallaudet needs to set the example. Additionally, having this program at Gallaudet means that students can major in Deaf Studies and then go on to teach this subject to others in a variety of settings, including schools, colleges, and interpreter training programs. Deaf children and adults need to learn about their community on a very deep level. We must be careful, though, to avoid introducing this instruction in inappropriate settings. Care must also be given to maintaining the integrity of the curriculum and making those who teach it accountable. The Deaf Studies curriculum should include things about our language, our history, our culture, and also the cultural diversity within the Deaf Community. It is extremely important not to represent the Deaf community as just white Deaf people or male Deaf people. The diverse mosaic of the Deaf community must be included throughout the Deaf Studies program.

The ideal location

As I asserted earlier, the ideal setting for a Deaf Studies program is at universities attended primarily by hearing persons. Educating the general population about Deaf culture and language would help change the patronizing attitude currently held by society toward Deaf people. It would help awaken society to our issues. Maybe people would learn not to give earphones to Deaf people in planes, as Tim Rarus experienced. Maybe I would not be faced with the requirement to use the voice phone in order to gain access to this hotel's exercise room. You understand what I am saying. We all go through this kind of experience on a daily basis. If hearing people take Deaf Studies courses, perhaps our lives as deaf people will improve. Some of the negative attitudes toward us could be eliminated and we could have true equal access. I also believe the education process should start with young people. The sooner, the better. Young people, as we all know, absorb things much more quickly. If we have these courses in high schools and in colleges, perhaps we can eliminate this obsession that hearing people have with curing us or sending us to therapy. Some people today still aspire to become doctors who will cure deafness, or audiologists, or speech therapists.

Before I continue, I need to explain that I have nothing against audiologists. As a matter of fact, I have some very good friends who are audiologists. One of the people who played a critical role in the acceptance of the Bi-Bi movement at the Indiana School for the Deaf is an audiologist. Audiologists are needed for certain kinds of people with hearing losses. There are hard of hearing and deaf people with plenty of residual hearing who would like to have services from an audiologist. Deaf children may also be curious about hearing people and how the ear works. Audiologists can certainly fill that need. So, it is not the career per se to which I take exception, but rather the attitude of many in the field. It is important for the service to be sought by the Deaf person and not imposed on the Deaf person by the audiologist. My point with regard to Deaf Studies courses is that if a person who wants to become an audiologist takes some courses on Deaf history and the community, he or she would have a better understanding of how Deaf people feel about audiology in general, and would understand our negative perception of the field and how it came to be through all of the degrading and unpleasant experiences we have had to endure. This understanding would help these professionals serve us better.

We obviously cannot educate every man, woman, and child in the United States, but we can reach a great many people. With our society increasing its inward examination on issues of diversity, now is the time for us to call for the dissemination of information about our culture. Now, more than ever before, is the time to offer Deaf Studies programs in mainstream universities. Many people would be very excited to know these things about us. Then they would understand that some of our public behaviors are not rude at all, but are, indeed, an expression of our culture. For many years, society, including Deaf people, has looked at hearing norms and rules for behavior as the "right way" and ours as "wrong." Offering Deaf Studies programs at mainstream universities would allow both hearing and Deaf people to recognize, accept, and change our educational system. The Bi-Bi movement would proceed more smoothly if we had many more hearing people who understood us. We might also need to include a course on Hearing Studies in a Bi-Bi school. That would be an interesting idea. It would allow the children to understand hearing people from a less negative perspective.

Fear comes from ignorance. Our fears often come from not knowing what lies ahead. Just as often, though, we are likely to be surprised to find something pleasant and beautiful in place of the nightmare we had anticipated. This is often what we, as Deaf people, experience in society. Many hearing people have not yet had direct contact with a Deaf person. The hearing person we encounter may initially respond with fear out of ignorance. A powerful by-product of fear is oppression. This oppressive behavior toward Deaf people is called audism. One of the ways to rid our society of audism is to provide positive experiences. If information about our culture and language was available out in the mainstream, such as through Deaf Studies programs, many fears would be eliminated.

At this point, some of you may be asking yourselves if I am condemning what we have accomplished thus far or if I believe that we have wasted our time. This is not the case. I think we are doing the right thing.

Appendix G

When should Deaf Studies be offered?
When the question arises as to when Deaf Studies should be offered, my answer is one word: Now. It is 1993, and we have only seven years before the year 2000. We need to examine our goals and decide which steps to take in order to achieve them. It may be necessary for us to realize that creating special curricula in schools for the Deaf is not the right course. The concept behind Deaf Studies must permeate the entire school environment. This means inside the classroom and out; from preschool through graduation. Children need to understand what being Deaf means so that they will be prepared for the future. Remember, as I said before, the Deaf Studies programs we have been using to date were to fill a void. We need to continue serving that need for now, but I hope there will soon be a day when we will not need to take this remedial approach. I am not suggesting that we remove these programs from the schools now. We need to continue correcting the mistakes of the past, but we must also look at the long range. We must adopt a philosophy that is more encompassing. As I said when I started, this will be a very big task. Many people are yearning for a change. The time is right. We are beginning to recognize more clearly that what we have been doing in the past is really not in the best interest of our children. We must change the system. The material heretofore confined to one course or program must infiltrate the child's whole school experience. The school for the Deaf needs to be a safe place for Deaf children; a safe place to be Deaf, to experience being Deaf, to express their feelings and thoughts and attitudes, not just in the Deaf Studies classroom but on the whole campus. When people question the need for deaf studies we need to educate them, not be defensive. We must work together by presenting rational arguments so that people understand the need for Deaf Studies. We will not win everyone over, but we will gain many allies. Naturally, the more people we educate, the easier will be our battle. Even in our own environment, even in our own communities we need to educate people. I am not only talking about hearing people. We need to educate other deaf people and ourselves to understand the many facets of this issue. We benefit when we teach other people about us, and we also come to understand ourselves better. Their questions and their probing will make us think more deeply. We will become more confident and understand on a more intuitive level about these issues and be able to talk about them more clearly.

We also need to look at what Deaf Studies can and cannot do; what problems will it eliminate and which ones it will not. In the 1960s and early 1970s you will recall that Total Communication became popular. Total Communication solved the problem of Deaf children not being allowed to use their hands and bodies to express themselves. It did not, however, solve the problem of providing Deaf children with a native language. We must look at Deaf Studies in the same way, understanding its limitations. Deaf Studies will not solve every problem. We need to identify what other problems must be addressed and how to approach their resolution.

Most of you know that I am known for being honest and direct. Therefore, I must tell you now that I am worried. I am concerned. I have some trepidation about what we are doing. Some schools are working to change their philosophy; others are moving more toward Bi-Bi education. Deaf Studies programs are being implemented in the schools as a temporary measure. My concern is that when we start to push for the real changes, the broader changes, we will regret this decision. People will say that Deaf culture is already part of the school's curriculum. After all, the school does have a Deaf Studies course. This may become our enemy. We cannot be afraid, though, to take this risk. We must try and see where it leads us. The optimistic view is that having a Deaf Studies course in the school will allow people to see that there really need to be bigger changes.

By the year 2000, I predict that we will have won several more battles. It is not possible that we will fall asleep for the next seven years and not move anywhere. We will have a better understanding of our language and culture. In my travels and in my work with many people, I still come across the age old question, "What is ASL?" I don't want to have to answer that question in the year 2000. It is really an unanswerable question. It is similar to asking, "What is English?" As a matter of fact, I usually answer the first question by responding with the second one. People hesitantly offer that English is something you speak; it is a language. I point out that ASL is also a language. I hope that, during the next seven years, we will move beyond these old questions and myths and move on to much more confidence and assurance about who we are and where we are going.

We need to be hopeful that in the year 2000, schools will be providing a healthier environment in which Deaf children will learn about themselves and improve their self image. We should hope that these children will be able to go out into the world with this knowledge and maintain their self esteem. In the year 2000, I would like to see Deaf people feel safe about being Deaf in any environment, not just the kind of closed community in which we see this confidence now. We cannot continue in this way. It is okay to be Deaf everywhere. We need to learn how to accomplish this from other minority groups. Also in the year 2000, I would like to see college students having majored in or holding degrees in Deaf Studies, rather than simply taking one course. That would be a sign of significant progress from where we are today.

Now, please do not be disheartened. I certainly am not. You may be wondering how we are going to accomplish anything given all of these challenges. Let us examine that a little bit.

How should we offer Deaf Studies?
To reach any goal, one must have a plan. This is critical for any movement. Our plan for the next seven years should include not only our own schools and our own environment, but mainstream society as well. It should include trying to get Deaf Studies in mainstream universities, even if it is only one course. Additionally, many of these universities currently put their ASL classes within the Departments of Communication Disorders, Audiology, Health, Educational Psychology, Deaf Education, or Special Education. Deaf people do not have a communication disorder, and it is our responsibility to inform these school of their error. ASL should be in language departments. We can no longer ignore this.

Appendix G

Another way to achieve our goal is to investigate appropriate changes in our school curricula. As you know, there is much talk about the curriculum in public schools within this country being very Eurocentric. This emphasis sends a message to children of other racial and ethnic backgrounds that being white is the norm. It is conveyed that important people and people with power are white, and these children, by virtue of their skin colour or heritage, are not within the group norms and therefore have no power. However, many African Americans and other minority groups are speaking out against this curriculum and advocating for a more balanced representation. Perhaps we can learn from the African American community. Maybe we can make our curriculum more Deafcentric, so Deaf people see themselves as at the core. One way to make a curriculum more Deafcentric is to look at the messages we are currently sending to our children in the schools. If you look on the walls of the classrooms you will see the Capitol, monuments, and the presidents of the United States. Those pictures are fine. But where are our Deaf heroes? Where is Laurent Clerc? Where is Jean Massieu? Where is Fred Schreiber, the first executive director of the NAD? Where is Roz Rosen? Where is Gertie Galloway, the first Deaf woman president of the NAD? Where is Barbara Kannapell, the Deaf sociolinguist? Where is Ann Silver, the Deaf artist? We have so many accomplished Deaf people that we could be showing to Deaf children. We also have African American Deaf people, Andrew Foster and Al Couthen. We also have Asian American Deaf people like Shanny Mow. We need to have not only pictures of Deaf people on the walls, but Deaf people in all different colours. There are wonderful artistic posters available depicting different conferences around the world. These should be included on the walls, too. It would be nice for children to be surrounded by an environment that reinforces and supplements what they are learning in the Deaf Studies classroom. We need to go deeper than the current use of artifacts and superficial items. We need to look at racism, sexism, homophobia, and all of the issues that affect society and that affect Deaf people, too. These changes need to be school-wide.

It is no secret to anyone that I am a strong supporter of the Bi-Bi philosophy. We need to explore the Bi-Bi philosophy further. We will not allow ASL to be eradicated from schools for the Deaf. That is a fact. It is also a fact that Deaf people treasure the English language, too. Deaf people want to have access to books, literature, newspapers, and so forth. We need to have both languages. Having both languages in a school is bilingualism. The Bi-Bi philosophy says Deaf children need to have a native language, ASL, in order for them to acquire this important second language, English. If Deaf children are allowed to have a native language, they will develop a healthy self image. In turn, feeling better about themselves will increase their ability to learn a second language. Increasing their self-esteem also makes it easier for them to succeed in our society. Deaf Studies and Bi-Bi philosophy really need to go hand in hand. We need to learn from both the Deaf community and the hearing community. As I said before, Deaf Studies has its limitations. It will not cure the lack of a Bi-Bi philosophy. We must address the issue of mainstreaming. I feel that we have become a little lethargic about it. We have to do something. We need to think about how to fight the states and how to educate more parents. Putting a Deaf Studies course in mainstreaming schools will not solve the problem. It may even make it worse. This issue of how to implement effective programs deserves serious attention. We need to ask ourselves how we can network and how we can get into the halls of power in mainstreaming schools in order to make these changes. The state school boards are the people we need to educate. They know nothing about Deaf people. Of course, they are always resistant to change initially. However, my experience has been that once you get in the door, you will find that they are not our enemies. We have built up this tremendous fear and this tremendous wall that has not allowed us to take the necessary steps to accomplish our goal. These people are not our enemies. They care about education, and, if we educate them, we can succeed.

Another consideration for this discussion of how to provide these programs is isolationism. Our community cannot remain so isolated. We need to enter into dialogue with other minority communities. The African American community has experienced a tremendous political change. We should ask them how an African American leader can identify with her/his culture, be supported by the members of the community, be acknowledged as an African American, and still be recognized by society as a leader. The feminist movement could also teach us about this. Retaining one's identity while breaking into mainstream society is not an easy task, and we can learn from these people. It is typical in our community that when we are in a non-Deaf environment or we are confronted with outside forces of power, we change our behavior and language. We change what we do so that we appear less "Deaf." Not only is this artificial, but we are sending two conflicting messages. We behave less Deaf, but we speak about being Deaf and accepting Deaf people. If we want to keep our credibility while we are advocating for acceptance of our language and culture, then we must use our language and cultural behaviors when we go out there to educate people. It is understandable why we have made these mistakes in the past, but we need to learn from the successes of other communities about how to shed those coping strategies and move on. We can work in concert with hearing people. Achieving success does not require us to sacrifice our identity in the process. Remember again, it is not a white world; it is not a man's world. It is not a straight world, and it is not a hearing world. We have a right to be there.

Who should teach Deaf Studies?
The last question that we have yet to address is who should be teaching Deaf Studies. I am not sure if we have identified the qualifications necessary for presenting this kind of course material. A logical question to ask is, "Does it have to be a Deaf person?" Maybe initially it does, because we have not yet had the opportunity in our community. At some point, however, perhaps that will not be a limitation that we need to impose. It is possible that the courses could be taught with a Deaf person as the primary teacher and a hearing person as an assistant. We need to be aware, though, that teachers are models. In Deaf Studies classes, Deaf students will want to be able to identify with the teacher. This is not unusual. I do not know how many Jewish people would want to

Appendix G

have someone who is German teach a course in Jewish history or straight people teaching a course on Gay and Lesbian issues. I would guess that not many white people teach African American studies.

One of our realities is that we are moving on the right track. We are still pioneers. That pioneering spirit does not stop in two years or five years or seven years. It continues on. People leave and other people join the movement. We have some setbacks, and we retreat, but we forge ahead, and it continues on and on until we reach our goals. Because we are pioneers, we are going to face a lot of conflicts and barriers. Conflict is not negative. It is only through conflict that we can begin to understand where we are different. It enables us to understand what we may have miscommunicated or that we have some stereotypes or myths that we need to eliminate. If we avoid conflict, we stay where we are. It is safe territory, but we do not move anywhere. It is the conflict that allows us to progress. Of course, conflict is not always comfortable, but once the conflict is resolved, we will feel a lot better, and we will have gained tremendously from the experience.

We cannot be too concerned about ourselves and our jobs nor about making people mad at us. We need to keep the vision clear in front of our eyes. That vision is healthy, well-adjusted Deaf children. They are the bridge to our future.

We have just touched on some of the issues involved in the "what, why, where, when, who, and how" of Deaf Studies. In closing, let me ask you to consider something more. What do we want for our children? What do we want for our future? I would like to allude to Robert Frost's poem "The Road Not Taken". I think that it parallels what I have been saying. We have two roads ahead. We choose one—the one that looks clear and straight. But soon we retreat, recognizing that this is not the way to get to where we want to be. We then take the tortuous path, the difficult road. Perhaps Deaf Studies is on that first road. Yet, once we realize that we must make the difficult journey, we bring our tools, and we prepare to construct the necessary bridges. It will be very hard work, requiring a lot of blood, sweat, and tears. The results, however, are worth it. This is our job. This is our responsibility for the future.

About the presenter:

MJ. Bienvenu is a co-director of the Bicultural Center in Riverdale, Maryland. Born deaf into a deaf family, she graduated from Gallaudet University with a BA in English and an MA in linguistics. She is a strong advocate of the recognition of deaf people as a linguistic and cultural minority.

Appendix H

Stan Foran's Recollections of his Days in the Boys' School, Cabra*

In the mid-1930s I was admitted into St Joseph's, Cabra, and straight away was introduced to sign language, the only medium used in the school. There was what was known as the oral class to cater for those who had some hearing and speech, though outside the classroom its attendees used sign language, like the rest of us.

Early in my time at school, training in speech as a skill was given by a layman to most classes, but after a couple of years he departed for Canada and was not replaced. It will be appreciated that the financial situation was precarious for schools those days.

Conversational sign language was tolerated outside the classroom, though teachers, reasonably enough, strove for us to confine ourselves to grammatical language (as it was called), in order to improve our English skills. Indeed there were some pupils who kept to exact English throughout and into adulthood. Also, some teachers urged us to use writing instead of signing outside the classroom, as a part of on-going training.

I recall that every Monday we had to write out our own accounts of any happenings during the previous week. Then the teacher would discuss our compositions—a useful exercise. Of course gestural sign language was used in the classroom to illustrate the meanings of abstract English or complex language. That was bilingualism in practice then, even if we never heard of that term!

I left school at fourteen years of age, which was common practice then. Continuing education did not cease there, of course: newspapers, books etc. were my means of advancing my English. I would say that my late brother Christy, who was over ten years younger than me, had largely the same experience as I did. He spent nine years at school. Our parents were hearing, and we communicated through finger-spelling and gestural language, a normal practice then. At times writing was needed in certain circumstances, and I can recall benefiting from it.

It is essential that young deaf children are exposed to meaningful communication, provided it is intelligible. For the majority of deaf children lip-reading is not conducive to the acquisition of knowledge as easily (if at all) as through sign language or even writing.

*Dated 24 June 1996

Appendix I

Reading Assessment of Deaf Children

by Trevor James and Erland O'Neill of the Psychology Services of the National Rehabilitation Board, Dublin and Joanne Smyth of the Psychology Department of the New University of Ulster, Jordanstown, Co. Antrim, Northern Ireland 1990.[*]

358 students with severe or profound hearing impairments aged between 6 and 16, and representing a broad cross section of educational histories, were assessed on two reading tests. The results indicated a slow growth in reading skills, with expected superiority of females and students with less severe hearing impairments. The results give some guidance for assessing the achievements of students relative to their hearing impaired peers.

Introduction

Children with hearing impairments typically experience great difficulty in acquiring good reading skills despite special education and training. Deaf school leavers find that the social and vocational opportunities available to them are restricted by their limited attainments in reading and writing skills. Vocationally, deaf people have higher unemployment rates and obtain jobs in lower socio economic classes than would be expected by their intelligence. In social and leisure activities reading is becoming increasingly important as Telephone Decoding devices and subtitling on TV become more available. In the US, the average reading comprehension of hearing impaired in the last year at secondary school is approximately at the same level as the average hearing student of age 8 or 9 (Allen, 1986). Similar results have been reported in Britain (Conrad, 1979).

While hearing impaired children have made gains in reading levels in the past decade, these are more apparent than real. They do not represent a gain relative to their hearing peers who have also improved (Allen, 1986). Thus although the actual level of reading comprehension may have improved, reading ages of hearing impaired children, relative to hearing peers has remained at substantially the same level for the past half century or more (Craig and Gordon, 1988).

Although demographic studies have indicated that a reading age of 9 represents a plateau of achievement for the deaf child, it has been suggested that this may be because of inadequate representation of the more academically successful students at the older age groups (Geers and Moog, 1989). Since the subjects of many of the studies have come from special education facilities, and the more successful students tend to be mainstreamed at younger ages, it is possible that the low scores associated with older students result from a disproportionate number of students with more severely handicapping characteristics remaining in special education.

[*]*Link* Winter 1991

Appendix I

	No.	%
Male	186	52%
Female	172	48%
Profound (hearing loss > 90 dB)	237	66%
Severe (hearing loss > 70 dB)	121	34%
Special schooling	288	80%
Mainstream schooling	70	20%

Table 1. Demographic characteristics of students

The assessment of reading is important in evaluating the progress of children in school. The results of such assessments are normally expressed in Reading Ages. Reading Ages allow a comparison to be made with the average achievement of hearing children at various age groups. This may not be an appropriate method for expressing the reading skills of hearing impaired children since their abilities may progress at different rates from that of hearing children. While it may be important to compare their attainments with those of their hearing impaired peers.

This study attempts to provide normative data on the reading comprehension of hearing impaired school children. As well as allowing comparisons to be made with previous studies in other countries, it will also provide a basis for evaluation of progress in future years.

Method

358 severely and profoundly hearing impaired children were assessed using two reading comprehension tests. These children were identified through the special schools and units for hearing impaired children and the Visiting Teacher of the Deaf Service of the Department of Education in Ireland.

All available children on the rolls of the schools who fulfilled the following criteria were included:

1. had a hearing impairment in the better ear of greater than 70 dB
2. were not diagnosed as mentally handicapped
3. were aged between 6 and 16.

Where possible the level of hearing loss was confirmed by reference to the most recent audiogram. Almost all had a severe prelingual hearing loss but a small number had deteriorating conditions and had had previous mild to moderate losses. Children who were judged by their class teacher to have additional disabilities, including learning disability, were noted and these were excluded from some of the analyses.

Appendix I

Age	N (= 348)	Primary reading mean	Test score SD	Reading age
6	23	10.91	7.71	<6
7	28	13.00	6.23	<6
8	23	20.39	7.36	6
9	19	22.42	8.30	6.3
10	35	22.14	6.69	6.25
11	57	22.98	6.78	6.5
12	43	26.04	8.01	7.25
13	27	28.18	8.06	7.72
14	32	27.93	7.79	7.75
15	40	32.87	6.84	8.75
16	21	29.33	6.11	8.0

Table 2. Primary reading test scores by age

Males and females were approximately equally represented in the sample. Two thirds had a profound hearing loss. Eighty per cent were currently in special schooling (see Table 1). The sample represents a broad cross-section of deaf children, with a wide variety of educational placement histories. There are no comprehensive data on the number of deaf children in Ireland but estimates in 1972 suggested that educational provision should be made for approximately 1 severely or profoundly hearing impaired child per 1,000. Experience elsewhere indicates that these levels have fallen with a suggested incidence of between 4 and 8 per ten thousand school children with a hearing loss of greater than 70 dB. This would mean that there are approximately 300–600 severely deaf children in Ireland, between the ages of 6 and 16.

In the special schools, testing was carried out in groups, by one of the authors (JS) with the co-operation and help of the class teachers. In the mainstream schools, children were individually assessed by a visiting teacher.

The tests used were the Schonell Silent Reading Test A (Schonell, 1960) and the Primary Reading Test, Level 1 (France, 1981). These were chosen for their ease of administration to a hearing impaired group, and provide an overall assessment of the ability to use reading skills for an understanding of words and simple sentences. Although they have been standardised on children of under 10 years of age, previous findings have suggested that this range is appropriate for hearing impaired children.

In the Schonell test, the student has to read a passage and answer a question relating to its content. The Primary test consists of two parts each with multiple choice format. In part I, the student must select one noun from 5 alternatives to describe a picture and in part II the child has to read a sentence containing a gap which must be filled by selecting one word from 5 alternatives.

Appendix I

Age	N	Schonell scores Mean	SD	Reading age
8	23	5.08	4.82	7.6
9	19	5.96	5.41	7.8
10	36	5.50	4.60	7.7
11	61	5.97	4.70	7.8
12	46	7.55	5.47	8.15
13	29	8.10	4.77	8.3
14	32	9.59	4.77	9.0
15	40	11.60	3.88	9.9
16	21	10.00	3.71	9.2

Table 3. Schonell Silent Reading Test scores by age

The examples in both tests were slightly modified to facilitate demonstration and three additional examples were included in the Primary Reading Test to check students' understanding of the type of response required. Students who failed to correctly complete at least two of these examples were excluded from the analyses, as were children who did not attempt any of the questions.

Results

The results are shown in Tables 2 and 3. On both these tests, the rate of increase is very small, with negligible improvements being made between the years 8 and 11. Only scores for 8 year olds and older are reported for the Schonell since many younger children were unable to attempt this test.

When these mean raw scores are converted into reading ages this slow rate of improvement becomes more apparent (Fig. 1). Since separate reading ages are given for the Schonell for girls and boys, the conversion of raw scores into reading ages is based on the mean reading ages of both sexes. Scores on both tests show similar rates of change but the Schonell Reading Ages are consistently about 1 year higher than Primary Test Reading Ages. This may be because somewhat different reading skills are being assessed or it may simply reflect the difference in the year of standardisation of these tests. The Primary Reading Test was standardised in 1977 while Schonell Tests norms apparently date back to the 1950s. However, a reading survey in Ireland in 1981 found the Schonell norms to be approximate, at least for 10 and 11 year old children (Department of Education, 1982). The reason for the slight drop at age 16 is not clear, but there were only 21 in that age group.

Appendix I

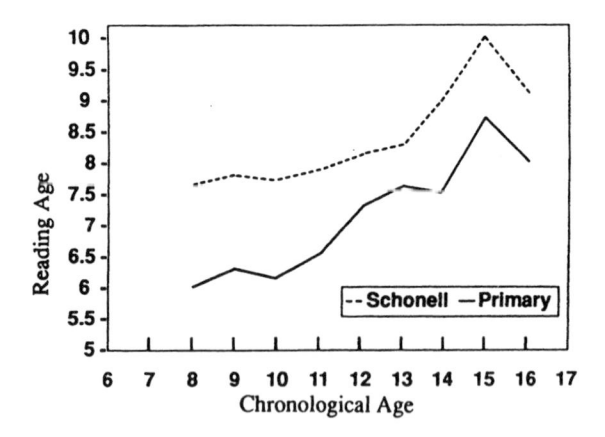

Fig. 1. Growth in reading attainments by age

Comparisons were also made between the scores of severely and profoundly hearing impaired children. At each age level those with the greatest hearing loss had lower reading ages. This is as expected, as severity of hearing impairment has been found to be correlated with reading ability in previous studies.

Among hearing children, girls have normally been found to have higher verbal skills, including reading ability, than boys of the same age (Clarke, 1970). On both tests used, the normative data indicate that girls outperform boys. Analysis of the results confirmed the superiority of hearing impaired girls at all levels. From the age of 8 to 16, they attained scores which were 6 to 9 months above those attained by boys of the same age.

Discussion

The results presented here give some guidance to those who may assess the reading skills of deaf children on the level of attainment that is typical for a deaf child of that age. The results are similar to those obtained elsewhere (Conrad, 1979), showing that the average deaf 16 year old has a reading level of around 9 years, which is below generally accepted standards of functional literacy. Indeed the scores obtained on the Primary Reading Test may well over-estimate the actual reading skills of the children. The test was scored in the normal way and credit given for all correct answers.

However, inspection of the data suggested that the deaf children had tended to guess at answers more often than is normal for hearing children, and thus would receive an artificially inflated score. This is a common finding and deaf children often tackle test materials beyond their understanding and do not self monitor in the way that hearing children do (Webster, 1985). For this reason the obtained scores of deaf children on multi-choice tests are sometimes corrected by subtracting a percentage of the incorrect answers.

The discrepancy between the reading age in the two tests used may be, as suggested, because of different standardisation samples, but it may also reflect a real

Appendix I

difference in the ability of deaf children to read different types of materials. The Primary Reading Test involves the reading of isolated sentences and words whereas the Schonell Silent Reading Test requires comprehension of an entire paragraph. Recently, many authors have argued that hearing impaired readers depend to a greater degree on "top down" reading strategies, such as prediction and the use of prior experience and that these strategies are most useful in the comprehension of whole passages (Banks et al., 1990; Webster, 1988). Reading tests based on short sentences do not provide the context which deaf children use to aid comprehension. It is possible therefore that the greater amount of context available in the Schonell test facilitates comprehension for hearing impaired students.

These data should not be considered to set limits to the achievements of children with severe hearing impairments. Although the mean scores at each age group were considerably lower than those of normal hearing students, it should be noted [that] at least some of the children had attained reading ages similar to their hearing age peers. At ages 8, 9 and 10, for which direct comparisons can be made with hearing ages within one year of their chronological age. It is possible, therefore, for children with severe and profound hearing impairments to attain much higher reading levels than the demographic data would indicate.

Acknowledgements
Thanks are due to the principals and teachers of the schools concerned for allowing the testing to take place, to the visiting teachers for all their help and co-operation, and, of course, to the students themselves.

Allen T., (1986). A study of the achievement patterns of Hearing Impaired students 1974–1983. In A. Schildroth & M. Karchmer (eds.) *Deaf Children in America* I(161–206) San Diego: College Hill Press.

Banks J., Gray C. & Fyfe R. (1990) The Reading Abilities of Severely Deaf Children: A Developmental Study using the Edinburgh reading Test. *J Brit Assn Teachers of the Deaf* 14, 2P.

Clarke M. M. (1970) *Reading Difficulties in School.* Penguin.

Conrad R. (1979) *The Deaf School Child: Language and cognitive function,* London: Harper and Row.

Craig H. B. & Gordon H. W. (1988) Specialised Cognitive Function and Reading Achievement in Hearing Impaired Adolescents. *J Speech and Hearing Disorders,* 53, p. 30–41.

Department of Education (1982) *English in the Primary School: Survey Report,* Department of Education Curriculum Unit.

France, N. (1989) *Primary Reading Test,* NFER-Nelson.

Geers A. & Moog J. (1989) Factors predictive of the development of literacy in profoundly Hearing Impaired Adolescents. *The Volta Review,* Feb.–Mar., p. 69–87.

Schonell F. (1960) *Silent Reading Test A.* Oliver and Boyd.

Webster A. (1985) Deafness and Reading II. Children with severe hearing losses. *Remedial Education,* 20, 3, p. 123–128.

Webster A. (1988) Deafness and Learning to Read I; Theoretical and Research Issues. *J Brit Assn Teachers of the Deaf,* 12, 4, p. 77–83.

Appendix J

Survey of Past Pupils on their Education in Irish Schools for the Deaf.

Opinion poll by Irish Deaf Society, sept 1988.

	Results
1. Which School did you attend?	
(a) Deaf School	94%
(b) Deaf/Hearing School	6%
2. At what age did you start School?	Yrs: 3 4 5 6 7 23% 25% 26% 17% 15%
3. Were you—	
(a) Boarder	76%
(b) Day Pupil	17%
(c) Both	7%
4. At what age did you leave school?	Yrs 15 16 17 18 19 20 10% 27% 28% 21% 9% 5%
5. Were you satisfied with your Education?	Yes 50% No 46% Fair 4%
6. By what method of communication were you taught?	Oralism 52% Sign Language 28% Total Communication 20%
7. Did you find it easy to lip-read?	Yes 35% No 21% Fair 44%
8. How was your lip-reading skill?	Very well 48% Fair §3% Poor 21% Hopeless 21%

Appendix J

9. Looking back, what method of communication would you have a preference for?	Total Communication Oralism Sign Language only	78% 7% 16%
10. Do you like sign language?	Yes No	99% 1%
11. Are you ashamed to use sign language?	Yes No	8% 92%
12. Do you feel at ease lip-reading?	Yes No Fair	49% 48% 3%
13. Do you feel at ease doing sign language?	Yes No	85% 15%
14. Is your speech—	Fair Good Excellent	44% 44% 12%
15. Do you feel that you lost out in education because of the wholly oral method of communication?	Yes No Do not know	69% 29% 2%
16. How is your grammar now?	Fair Good Excellent	40% 45% 15%
17. Were you—	Born Deaf Became Deaf at a young age	70% 30%
18. Do you think Total Communication should be incorporated into the education system in Schools for the Deaf?	Yes No Do not know	86% 11% 3%
19. Do strangers understand your speech?	Yes No Sometimes	38% 52% 10%

Appendix J

20. How do you communicate with hearing people?	By speech	42%
	In writing	42%
	Both	16%
21. Having been a boarder—do you now wish you were educated in a Deaf Unit in your home town?	Yes	37%
	No	52%
	Do not know	39%
22. Did your parents object to sign language when you were at school?	Yes	19%
	No	42%
	Do not know	39%
23. Do your parents object to sign language now?	Yes	11%
	No	69%
	Do not know	20%
24. How did you get a job when you left school?	Self	27%
	Parents	15%
	NRB	38%
	Friends	14%
	Others	14%
25. Do you feel that speech was wasted on you?	Yes	50%
	No	48%
	Sometimes	2%
26. Did you feel that too much time was wasted on speech training?	Yes	57%
	No	40%
	Sometimes	3%
27. Do you think that speech should be treated as a medical problem and should be taught by choice after school hours?	Yes	67%
	No	31%
	Do not know	2%
28. Did your education prepare you for employment opportunities?	Yes	37%
	No	63%

29. Do you agree that teachers of the deaf should have experience in communicating with the deaf before being allowed into the classroom?	Yes No	94% 6%
30. Should the past pupils have a say in the running of schools for the deaf?	Yes No Do not know	82% 11% 7%
31. Do you agree that deaf students' rights come first, before parents' rights?	Yes No Do not know	65% 10% 25%
32. Were you informed on current affairs, politics etc. when you were at school?	No Yes	72% 28%
33. Do you agree that there was a lack of social communication between teachers and deaf pupils at school?	Yes No	64% 36%
34. Did you think there was not freedom of information at school?	Yes No Do not know	57% 41% 2%
35. Do you communicate well with your family?	Yes No Fairly	79% 17% 4%

Appendix K

Irish Deaf Society Questionnaire

Prepared for the Forum on Education of the Deaf, 1991, but not accepted by NAD because of question no. 5.

QUESTIONNAIRE

THIS QUESTIONNAIRE IS DESIGNED TO HELP EVERYONE TO SEE IF THERE SHOULD BE ANY IMPROVEMENT FOR THE NEXT FORUM.

1. Are you able to follow the speakers through the interpreters?

    A Very Good ☐   **B** Good ☐   **C** Fair ☐   **D** Poor ☐

2. Do you understand the purpose of the Forum?

    A Yes ☐   **B** Fairly Well ☐   **C** No ☐

3. Would you like to see more Deaf participants in the Forum?

    A Yes ☐   **B** Don't Mind ☐   **C** No ☐

4. Do you feel the present speakers are willing to listen to your views?

    A Yes, always ☐   **B** Sometimes ☐   **C** No, not always ☐

X 5. How often would you like a Forum of a similar kind to occur?

    A Annually ☐   **B** Semiannually ☐   **C** Quarterly ☐   **D** Monthly ☐

6. If you have any other comment about this Forum, please comment?

_____
_____
_____
_____
_____
_____

Thank you and have a nice weekend!!!

Appendix L

Are the Deaf ready to take their place in the hearing world? - Another view*

Through my own fault in forgetting to renew my subscription, I did not get the Journal of Winter 1991. Only recently I heard reference to it and particularly to an article by E. J. Crean. I have now seen it and as a person who spent the first 47 years of my life as a hearing citizen and the past 13 years as a profoundly Deaf person I would like to make some comments.

My first reaction on reading the essay was a growing amazement at the ease which he was knocking the parents, friends, relatives and servants of Deaf children: the Irish Government, principal of St. Joseph's, the NAD, Beechpark School, Department of Education, RTE, the Gaeltacht, the Catholic Churches, a former Minister for Education, and God knows who else with scant regard for the rules of fair comment or indeed for the laws of libel. I was appalled.

There should be no place for this type of offensive attitude in the debate on the development of the Deaf in Ireland. It is okay to have confrontational discussion in the Courts of Law or the Dáil where the participants are professionals and there is a judge or Ceann Comhairle to see that rules of procedure are observed. It is entirely out of place among people who come together in voluntary organisations. It can too easily deteriorate into abuse and insult. All concerned including the Deaf will be the losers. It is great to see the Deaf community speak up for itself but no one group should make its point by running down the work of others. It is useless for Mr. Crean to say it gives him no pleasure to say these things after he has said them. That is patronising, a word he objects to in another part of his essay.

If there is a fog area between the Deaf community and hearing people, each side must examine it to see whether they have contributed to it, when Victor Hugo spoke of Deafness of the mind, he was addressing both sides. While the gap is mainly on the hearing side, Deaf people are not immune to the syndrome of deafness of the mind. I know this from my experience in both worlds.

There is of course an abundance of truth in all that Mr. Crean says about the problems of the Deaf. There are many difficulties to be overcome in education, social integration, employment and other areas. There have been many successes, including the marvellous achievement of Mr. Crean and his family in pursuing his son's education to University graduation in the face of major obstacles. I remember seeing his son's picture in one of the last year's *Journal* and felt very proud for him and all Deaf people in his breakthrough. He is now adding to the glory by doing a University

*Letter from Pat Quinlan, Director of the National Association for the Deaf, published in the Irish Deaf Journal, summer 1992, in response to an article by E.J.Crean published in the previous issue of the Journal.

Appendix L

degree himself. He should be more positive about this in his essay and develop the idea of notable achievements by the Irish deaf. This is what impresses the world at large.

I would also make the point that comparison with other countries should be treated with caution. The USA has certainly some enviable features in providing for minorities but it also has its Los Angeles which we saw recently. Also there are many countries which are far below Irish standards. We can be proud of our record and have confidence in our ability to make progress in time.

Finally I have to speak about one more issue in which I have direct involvement and strong views, namely the continued obsession of the IDS and its supporters with antagonism towards the NAD. I have been a member of NAD since I became Deaf and I became a director eight or nine years ago. I have also followed the progress of the IDS since its formation and have given it any support and encouragement I can. To my knowledge NAD has made many efforts, without avail, to reach a happy relationship between the two organisations. Mr. Crean's essay reaches a new low of understanding and misrepresentation about NAD. This must stop immediately before people's patience runs out, if it is not too late already. There is real danger of a head-on clash which could cause a set back for all the Deaf and their supporters for years to come. Nobody wants that and we must see that it does not happen.

Let me one more time try to set the record straight about the similarities and differences between them.

The National Association for the Deaf (note carefully the preposition "for") is a national umbrella organisation catering for the problems of all hearing-impaired people including born-Deaf, hard of hearing, Deaf old folks, and Deaf people with other disabilities and their families and supporters. It has attracted the most eminent public figures as founders, chairpersons, and members over the years. It is right up-to-date in having a distinguished lady chairperson at the moment. It has 26 branches throughout the country. It is entirely a voluntary organisation with no State aid except for specific projects such as Minicom aids which all goes to Deaf people. It pays its way, including office rent, and other expenses from fund-raising activities. Yes, it received a totally unsolicited legacy in recent years, which is a tribute to the association's good standing. It will be used solely to further the cause of the Deaf.

The Irish Deaf Society which Mr. Crean calls the national association of the Deaf (note the different preposition "of") is a more recent body comprised of one section of the Deaf community, namely those for whom sign language is their preferred form of communication. They do not represent me as a deafened person nor the hard of hearing nor other groups connected with the Deaf. They do very good work within their own sphere of activity and this is appreciated by all.

So it is clear that NAD and IDS have much in common but also different aims and purposes. The position is the same in the UK, where RNID is the national umbrella group and BDA is the association of the Sign Language Deaf community. On Mr. Crean's own figures, the IDS aspiration would be to represent 16,000 Deaf persons while NAD would represent the 200,000 people who are quoted in the Government

Appendix L

Green Paper of recent years as being affected by hearing loss to an extent that creates problems for them in communication in their day to day life. All these people including members of IDS benefit from the work of NAD. So why can we not get a friendly working arrangement between the two? I am still hopeful that it can be achieved with good will on both sides.

I hope Mr. Crean and the Journal's readers will find some food for thought in my comments. I wish him and the IDS every good luck in their work.

Education reform*

Here is some good news for the Deaf which I am sure will cheer you up. Last January 25th, my son Brian and myself had a meeting with the Minister for Education Mr. Noel Davern to discuss an article of mine on Deaf education which was published in your journal last winter. The article contained proposals on how to go about reforming the existing system and putting it under the control of the Deaf. (It would not mean getting rid of any of the hearing people, but it would mean putting the Deaf in control so as to make sure that it is run in the best interest of the Deaf. The Deaf could hardly make a worse job of it than the hearing. The hearing have had it for over a hundred years and produced only two Deaf teachers of the Deaf). The minister was so impressed that he got his officials to set up a meeting with a delegation from the Deaf community. We organised and assembled the delegation which included Mr. Johann Wesemann Director General of E.C.R.S. and Mrs. Eileen Lemass.

Brian and myself with help from Fergus Dunne, proposed the agenda for the meeting and got it agreed by both parties. The meeting took place in the Department of Education Head Office on 2nd February 1992 and was followed by one with the Brennan Committee on 13th March 1992. This was the first time an official delegation from the Deaf community and the ministers' officials sat down together to discuss proposals aimed at giving the Deaf community control of the education system. The ball is rolling now! That's the good news. The bad news is the *Irish Deaf Journal* ignored it as a news item, even worse in the AGM report it criticised the Minister for not attending the meeting! Such disrespect to the Minister is very embarrassing to me and very damaging to the development of the Deaf community. Surely it makes more sense to judge a person by what he does, rather than his staged appearance. You will hardly be taken seriously by the Department of Education unless you can show enthusiasm and representative support behind you. I would find it impossible to be of further assistance unless I get that support.

What the N.A.D. are really tops at, is ignoring opinions from the Deaf community. The video on the Deaf Education Forum shows some of it and must be seen to be believed. The hearing delegates got twelve times more time than the Deaf delegate. One Deaf person made a statement in the form of a question and was abruptly told "no questions", yet questions from hearing people were courteously answered. There was only one Deaf delegate allowed, he was instructed not to exceed five minutes, while some of the hearing and non-sign language people got from fifteen to thirty

*Letter from E.J.Crean, published in the Irish Deaf Journal, Autmun 1992.

Appendix L

minutes, etc. etc.

If the N.A.D. was controlled by people elected by the Deaf community, people with the language, culture and experience, a feature which makes the community unique and identifiable, it would have been a very different forum. The true political message would then come through.

In order to reply properly to Mr. Quinlan's letter, we must look at some of the terminology in the Deaf world. For instance the term "Deaf" could mean one or more Deaf persons of any level of deafness, cause, age etc. It could mean Deaf persons living in a hearing environment, schools etc. I know a few people going Deaf due to ageing, or perhaps neglect and they know as much about the Deaf community as Robinson Crusoe on his desert island. The term Deaf sometimes means the Deaf community- that is people who from infancy are more at home communicating in sign language. Indeed it might help to prevent misrepresentation if we had a law stating that only organisations controlled by the Deaf would be allowed to use the word in their title. I think it would be a very reasonable and logical claim - there is already a corresponding law in commerce to protect consumers.

The Deaf community grew naturally out of the friendships made in the schools for the Deaf in the last century. Before those schools, the Deaf lived a very isolated life, scattered around the hearing environment with little or no means of communicating with other Deaf people or the hearing and unable to express their feelings.

We must be most grateful to these institutions for the foundations they laid for the Deaf community, both as a society and individually. It was the greatest single event in the history of Deaf culture.

The Deaf community is a relatively new occurrence in Ireland, only recently emerging from the institutional shadows. They have their own language which is the principal characteristic of an ethnic or natural grouping. They are like a nation within a nation. The Deaf community is quite powerless to extend its own "border". The border is really formed by the hearing people and is most common in the Deaf person's own family. The border can be extended only by the hearing people learning the language.

Thankfully the border is extending rapidly in countries where the language is encouraged and is on the school curriculum like any other language. This is particularly noticeable in the U.S.A. The result is you do not find the hang-ups and stigma that you find in Ireland. The major consequence of deafness is the inability to keep up in the classroom, playground and home - hence the need for a proper sign language environment from day one.

There is no doubt that Deaf community people, are generally far happier socialising with people of their own language.

Another matter that is beginning to get attention is the superior right of a Deaf child, over its parents or guardian, to have an environment, language and education suited to the community it is naturally growing into, yet the establishment are still keeping the parents of Deaf infants apart from the Deaf community.

Appendix L

Of course the culture of the Deaf community is in its infancy - it is hardly a hundred years old - and has a long way to go to catch up.

Nobody has a right to stand in their way as Parnell said in reference to Ireland's struggle for independence "No-one has the right .... no one shall say so far and no further".

Clearly, there is a whole world of difference between Deaf community people and the individual who lives/socialises in a hearing environment. The Deaf community is a unique living, evolving and developing culture, with a track record of independent existence. The idea of providing an "umbrella" as the N.A.D. maintain, it hostile rather than helpful to Deaf community development. It also highlights one of the weaknesses in their social philosophy. In my opinion this is the root cause of the bad relations between the organisations bearing the title "Deaf".

Mr. Quinlan says "the I.D.S. benefit from the work of the N.A.D." Well, when the demon money comes into play, it is difficult to avoid conflict. For instance are funds distrbuted fairly between sections of the Deaf? How does the N.A.D. determine which section the donor wishes to benefit? Are all sections satisfied with the decisions? Can all the facts be verified? Who decides if there is a dispute between the parties? A viewing of the Forum video inspires no confidence on the matter of justice and fair play from the N.A.D.

Mr. Quinlan mentioned that the N.A.D. "attracted the most eminent public figures as founders, chairpersons" etc. Attraction is not the word I would use to describe the relationship I observed between them and the Deaf community.

I am not well up on all the activities or aims of the N.A.D., but I wonder if Mr. Quinlan is correct when he says they claim to represent all the Deaf in Ireland. Surely it is not possible to represent people legally - until one is properly and democratically elected. The only people the N.A.D. can legally represent are the people who appointed them.

The denial of voting power and the exercise of the democratic and human rights to control their own affairs might be a suitable system for parental control of an infant family or for situations where the controllers have more ability than the controlled - characterised by the powerful father and the helpless child.

There are few cases where it can be morally justified. It was very common in all countries until this century. For instance men of no property were not given a vote until the last century, and women were given the vote in this century. There are many other examples. The proper term for this is paternalism - "Father knows best".

It generally creates an environment that appeals to people who like to take the easy way out and have things done and decisions made for them.

It is a philosophy that suits the N.A.D. and rather than being "right up-to-date" as Mr. Quinlan professes, it belongs to the past.

Mr. Quinlan's attempt to mock my recital of facts about the situation in Deaf education in Ireland does little for his credibility as a player in the field of reconciliation. One must start by putting all the facts on the table and to go on from

Appendix L

there to study the areas of conflict. Discussion and agreement on solutions come later.

I have written to the Patrons of the N.A.D. making proposals on how to get the process of reconciliation started. They are in a very influential position and therefore carry a heavy responsibility, and indeed a duty, to resolve the impasse.

Finally, I think a panel of arbitrators should be established to settle disputes. Parties in dispute could take their case to mutually agreed arbitrators for a binding decision. Conflicts would then be treated objectively and hopefully resolved fairly and quickly.

I am sending a copy of this letter to the N.A.D. for circulation to the other Deaf organisation for publishing so that everyone will have the chance to contribute to the debate.

The Deaf in society: a final word*

I am very glad to have an exchange of views with Mr. E. J. Crean on this subject. It was useful to me and I hope it was for him and your readers.

Some people tell me I don't really understand the Deaf. I can agree fully with this as I am no expert. However, I have been a long-time observer of the human scene, both hearing and deaf. I know too well that there is a wide gulf of lack of understanding between the two and I want to see it narrowed and closed if possible. I can also see that in these tense situations, even the most well-intentioned people can inadvertently run the risk of widening the gap. It was this fear that inspired me to respond to Mr. Crean's original article. I am one hundred per cent in support of the Deaf in their struggle for full rights in a mixed community. I admire their language, their culture, their clubs, their achievements, and have got great personal sustenance from their friendship and company. They will continue to develop and broaden their influence through these structures but they must not retreat into them or adopt a "them and us" attitude to the hearing world. There is a considerable number of people out there in the hearing world who have the interests of the Deaf at heart and are anxious to help. They give their professional time as well as their voluntary time to organise support groups, raise funds, publicise the problems and use their influence in our favour. We must not spurn them or undermine their good work. We must appreciate them and co-ordinate our own work with them.

Finally can I again assure Mr. Crean that the NAD is a fully legal and democratic body. It is a voluntary organisation set up by its members. It has a constitution, a legal set of rules, an elected Board which is appointed at the public AGM in the Dublin Deaf Centre each year. There is also a set of trustees. It is totally answerable to its members for all its actions. There are about 1,000 registered members. It draws support from all sections of the deaf community. It has had many deaf members on the Board, including three at present. It is crystal clear that the vast majority of the deaf appreciate its value and want to continue in operation.

I recognise that Mr. Crean has a strong feeling of grievance about the treatment

*Letter from Pat Quinlan, Director of the National association for the Deaf, published in the Irish Deaf Society Journal, winter 1992.

Appendix L

of deaf people at some meeting organised by NAD. I have no knowledge of it and cannot comment. But I can say that like all human organisations, the NAD can make mistakes. The IDS also makes mistakes. It has been wisely said that any man who never made a mistake never made anything. In human experience people don't dwell on mistakes. They try to learn from them, remember the good things and get on with the job. Could I again plead with him and with the IDS to accept this situation and to recognise all the good work that both organisations are doing. There is no need for federation, arbitration or whatever. All we need to aim for is good neighbourliness where we live in harmony and avoid treading on each other's toes.

I have now made my point more than enough. I am grateful to the Journal for the opportunity and will no longer intrude on your space.

Every good wish to all the deaf and to their organisations.

Appendix M

A letter to the press from Grover Odenthal and some replies, November 1986

The following letter was published in *Contact*, March–April 1987, with a request for responses from readers.

Are we oppressed?

Dear Editor,

I am an American deaf person who visited Ireland this summer. I am writing at the request of the hearing parents of a deaf friend who grew up in Dublin. I had commented to them on what I perceived to be oppression of deaf people in Ireland. I am not referring to the general intentions of Irish people which happen to be good, although often patronising.

Rather I am concerned about the availability or the lack of social services for deaf people. These social services include provision of sign language interpreters in legal and medical situations as well as in higher education, assistance with mental health and vocational problems (provision of professionals trained in deafness and able to communicate effectively with deaf people) and sign language access to government facilities. There are many more instances but enough here to illustrate my point.

In other countries such as Denmark, Sweden, Finland, Norway, the United States and Canada, extensive social services are provided. It has been shown that the provision of services is far more cost-effective than if not provided. That is, the resultant burden on the employment and social welfare systems is hardly cost-effective.

A society which allows its deaf members to participate more equitably in the society's activities is promoting the ability of theses people to be productive and well-functioning individuals. Unlike other countries there are few deaf professionals in Ireland. Neither the cost-efficiency nor the humanitarian aspects of such an approach need be pointed out.

In America the situation is far from ideal, but we are fighting for further advancement with the major thrusts being provided by such entities as the National Association of the Deaf (NAD), an organization for and by deaf people. According to deaf people I met and spoke with, the NAD in Ireland (run by hearing people for deaf people) does not accomplish much in meeting the needs of deaf people in its advocacy efforts.

It stands to reason that the Irish Deaf Society (the true NAD?) should be recognized as bona-fide spokespeople for the Deaf population. This is more than amply demonstrated by the work and accomplishments of the NAD's of those countries I have mentioned earlier. That is, deaf people are themselves far more able to determine and meet the needs and make decisions regarding the affairs of deaf people.

Grover Odenthal,
Cheverly, Maryland

Appendix M

Are we oppressed? Readers reply ...

Niall McCarthy, Chairman of NAD:
I have read the letter from Mr. Grover Odenthal, as published in the March/April issue of *Contact*. Mr. Odenthal criticises N.A.D. as not accomplishing "much in meeting the needs of deaf people in its advocacy efforts." I regret that during his visit to Ireland Mr. Odenthal could not, apparently, find time to meet any directors or officials of N.A.D. to discuss its activities, including, incidentally, support, financially and otherwise, of *Contact,* since its inception.

Pat Quinlan (deafened):
The letter from Grover Odenthal from America is very interesting. It is always useful for us, as the poet said "to see ourselves as others see us." He sure paints a bleak picture of us. He finds the Irish people patronising, the Irish deaf oppressed and non-professional, and the N.A.D. incompetent. It must have been our terrible weather last summer that gave him such a gloomy impression. I will try to give him a more balanced picture.

Grover tells us that social services for the deaf in Ireland fall far short of what they are in America. I can fully accept this but I would point out that America is the wealthiest and most developed country in the whole world and can naturally look after all of its citizens much better than a small less-developed country like Ireland. Grover is fortunate to live in such a flourishing country and I wish him the best of luck. But it does not mean that the deaf in Ireland are badly treated or oppressed.

We may not be in the top league of social services but we are also far from the bottom and could name many countries which are much worse off than we are. The Government and people of Ireland have a very good reputation for providing social services for those who need them within the limits of the money available.

Enormous advances have occurred over the past thirty years when economic progress was good and the deaf benefited from their share with better education, training and vocational services.

Unfortunately in the past few years the country has been hit with a deep economic recession and there are now 250,000 people unemployed dependent on the State for support. This has forced a temporary halt to the expansion of social services to all groups including the deaf. In the meantime there is plenty that can be done through our own organisations, N.A.D., I.D.S., H.F.O.D., and all the other groups and committees.

The surprising part of the letter for me was that Grover should find himself drawn into efforts to discredit the N.A.D. and to create a divisiveness in the Irish deaf community. With all due respects to him this is a bit much from a person who has spent a short holiday here and never even spoke to the N.A.D. It also does no credit to whoever prompted these views to him.

All groups working for and with the deaf are doing excellent work and if any one group wants to make its case at home or abroad it must do so on the strength of its own policies and achievements and not by running down what other groups are doing.

Appendix M

Surely everybody must realise that in these difficult times we need a united front in the deaf community and we cannot afford the luxury of arguing among ourselves.

The solution has to be found here in Ireland and not in letters across the Atlantic Ocean. We have democratic institutions with plenty of scope for different views and the means of reconciling them. I do not know the details of the confrontation between the I.D.S. and N.A.D., but I do know they can be solved by good will and co-operation.

I join with the Editor and other commentators in urging them to sit down together in a genuine spirit of reconciliation and reach a working arrangement. Then we can apply ourselves in a united fashion to the real issues of building our new Deaf Centre and improving the social services so that the next time Grover Odenthal comes to visit he will see us in a much more favourable light.

Ann Murphy (partially deaf/blind):
With reference to Grover Odenthal's letter may I have a say? It is a grave error, I feel, to draw comparisons between Ireland and the wealthier countries particularly the U.S.A. Ireland is not a wealthy country by their standards, and at present is in serious economic difficulties, necessitating many unfortunate cut-backs for the common good of all.

Also this is a small country and it is not yet clear if there are sufficient deaf people to warrant the provision of such luxury services, no matter how wonderful they would be. In the U.S.A. there is a law which guarantees easier access for deaf people. No such law exists here. Before we campaign for a change in the law we need to study and decide whether we could afford the consequences of such a law. Due to these and other important factors, I for one cannot claim to be "oppressed". So what if some people are patronising? Let them patronize.

When we review the past 20 years we have to admit that progress has been made in many areas, even if it has been slow, for example, there have been improvements at schools for the hearing impaired which continue all the time; today parents of deaf children receive far greater guidance and emotional support than did my parents in the early 1960's; we have an increasing number of voluntary interpreters; public services personnel including hospital nurses, are far more aware than before of our communication problems and show greater consideration and patience.

It's unfair to knock the N.A.D. so much who like all of us have made mistakes, and who have certainly accomplished quite a bit even if they have not succeeded in securing what is most desirable to us. Some deaf people assume very wrongly that the N.A.D. gives greater priority to someone like myself, with an additional handicap, but that is just not so. If the N.A.D. went into liquidation tomorrow I feel sure that many people would be unhappy.

It may well be better if the I.D.S. and the N.A.D. work alongside co-operating with each other for the overall good of the Irish Deaf, our relatives and friends and the media.

For the past five years I have been closely involved with physically disabled people, who you might also call "oppressed" because they lack the wonderful aids and services that their counterparts in some countries have. They and disabled people, and others, are all busily agitating for better facilities.

In a sense our hopes and dreams can be compared to the struggle for Irish freedom. Our ancestors fought for years and years to bring about an Irish Republic and finally it came to be. So too, bit by bit, will circumstances for us improve. Therefore let us not bemoan what we lack today, but campaign and keep campaigning fairly for better services for all; let us be proud to be Irish and accentuate the positive.

From a deaf reader:
It is a question that only "the deaf in Ireland" themselves know; there is no way an outsider could pass judgement on this issue, after a flying visit to Ireland and indulging in one sided off the cuff comments. It reflects badly on the person(s) who asked for such an inaccurate letter to be written. We in Ireland are quite contented to allow steps to be taken in the right direction leading us to a better position in life, knowing that our deaf population is at a level where many other large organizations have priority when it comes to "cap in hand" with the government.

The tactics of novelty minority groups, that would only draw disdain from the powers that be, will only take us back a step. The proper solution can never be less than a total presentation on any issues to bring about a change which would benefit the deaf. So let us all band together with all the influential people, hearing and deaf, to make a just and sound case for our cause.

C. Foran (born deaf):
I was hugely amused reading "Are we oppressed?" in the last issue of *Contact*. Can't that American guy see the great majority of us have houses of our own, jobs and facilities for our different types of recreation—a good number of us have cars and can afford holidays in the sun and so on.

I say to him, come over here again and do a proper investigation of the true facts and judge for himself. Or get lost.

An incensed deaf reader:
Are we oppressed? What an insult to the Irish Deaf. It doesn't require a Sherlock Holmes to see that the letter was really written by a crackpot here using the American dupe as a cover. So this letter deserves nothing but contempt.

The attack on the N.A.D. seems to point to certain culprit(s). Life is fine for us as it is. Don't spoil our lives with these half-baked ideas of what should be done for the deaf.

Finally, Editor, please spare your readers such stupid letters or articles.

Anon. (deaf):
Are we oppressed? I read this article at first with anger at the comments, then with sadness that a visitor should come to Ireland and just seem to meet a few people, then return to U.S.A. with the view that we are oppressed. Far from it, the deaf in Ireland

Appendix M

are too busy getting on with their daily lives, running a home, jobs, children, clubs etc. Most visitors to Ireland remark on the very happy atmosphere they find among the deaf here.

It is also with great sadness that the hearing parents of the deaf friend could not talk to the many fine bodies we have here to help people. Schools, N.A.D., Parents groups, N.R.B., I.D.S. etc. I know for sure that most of the deaf here put problems of the deaf at the bottom of their priorities in life. That those parents gave their negative views to a stranger is mystifying.

Mr. Odenthal compares us to socialist countries such as Sweden, etc. I think we Irish are more independent and would not like to be cared for by the state from the cradle to the grave. Also we do not have the resources like U.S.A. So next time you visit Ireland, do meet as many deaf as you can and the many bodies that are associated with the deaf.

A partially deaf reader:
In reply to the letter under the heading "Are we oppressed?" Yes—in certain areas of our life, but in the year of 1987 who is to blame? Ourselves. We have seen organisations take on government over difficult issues and in many cases won their case.

So we should make better use of services of the fine organisations we already have to get our rights.

I find the remarks made by the American writer quite offensive. That unwise person should just come here for a short stay and obviously speak to a very few people, and then on such a poor basis pass judgement on us. In regards to his comment on the NAD, I don't think he ever visited the NAD offices or talked to any NAD official. Otherwise he would have been told of the achievements that organisation had won for us in its two decades of existence. Oh, yes, we had no such organisation until 1964 or thereabouts. It had campaigned for more deaf members, but a more personal approach would have got better results.

Eileen McCaul (teacher of the deaf and also an interpreter with the deaf):
I would like to comment on the letter from Grover Odenthal in the March/April issue of *Contact*.

I agree totally that the social services for the Deaf in Ireland, as outlined in the letter, are far from satisfactory. I have worked to provide too well that many areas are very neglected. However, there are some points in the letter with which I do not agree and some areas where, I think, the writer needs some more information.

Firstly, I wonder about the use of the word "oppression". My dictionary defines oppression as "subjection by cruelty, force etc., affliction or torment." Are deaf people oppressed? It is possible that there are deaf people who have been treated cruelly, forcefully, or have been tormented by representatives of the social services, but the writer, during the visit to Ireland, perceived the situation of deaf people here as oppression. As your title asks, "Are we oppressed?"

Appendix M

The writer makes the point (paragraph 2) that the availability or lack of basic social services is proof of this oppression. Here, I would like to stress the writer's word "availability". As I see it, the problem is more one of restricted availability rather than of lack. In fact, the story on the page opposite to the letter shows very clearly that Christy Foran got plenty of help from Government agencies in his very creditable success in finding his current job.

Many deaf people have, in fact, interpreters when coping with legal, medical and mental health problems. Again, I emphasise that these facilities are certainly not adequate, but they are not, as the writer suggests, completely lacking.

All deaf people have access (by sign language, speech, lipreading, or by writing a letter) to information re Social Welfare Entitlements, Tax problems, Housing etc. through the Community Information Service. This service is funded by the government and is operated completely by deaf people.

The provision of adequate facilities in Ireland is in many cases a question of money. The burden on the employment and social welfare systems is a very wide one in Ireland—affecting many more groups than the Deaf Community, and involving many more factors than Communication.

The question of the small number of deaf professionals in Ireland is also a very complicated one; it could be the subject of a deep and wide ranging study. Certainly there is need, as the writer points out, for big improvements in facilities for deaf people in Ireland. The National Association for the Deaf, as well as providing a social worker for the deaf, does, in spite of what the writer was told, work in a valuable way, informing the general public about the deaf community. This work is helping to break down the patronizing attitude of some members of the general public. The Irish Deaf Society has, I feel a very important and unique role in expressing and seeking to improve the situations of deaf people whose rights are being infringed. The writer, however, does not contribute to the achievement of these improvements by the statements in the last two paragraphs of the letter.

The answer to many of the problems outlined lies in co-operation between the various bodies involved in deaf interests, not in claiming that any one body has the monopoly of ability to solve the problems.

An Irish proverb says "There is strength only where there is co-operation."

The members of both the deaf and the hearing community have a contribution to make in the very important aim of providing better services so that deaf people (in the correspondent's words) may participate more equitably in society's activities.

Thank you for the hospitality of your magazine in allowing me space to express my views on this topic.

Frank Toomey, London:
I would like to comment at length on Mr. Grover Odenthal's letter, which appeared in the March/April issue of the splendid voice of the Irish Deaf, namely *Contact*. It would appear to me that Mr. Odenthal has used the incorrect word in describing the social

Appendix M

and employment aspects under which the deaf in Ireland live.

"Oppression" is a word which can be applied to peoples whose lives have been made much more difficult by the policies used by harsh regimes. In the past, it could be said that the 6 million Jews who perished in Hitler's "final solution" were oppressed. People resident in the iron curtain countries are also oppressed in being denied the freedoms which we in the West take for granted. They are denied freedom to practise their religion, which Marx said is "the opium of the people".

Mr. Odenthal, therefore, cannot be correct in his use of this harsh word. But he does make some interesting comments in his letter, which I feel cannot go without criticism. As one who lived and worked in Ireland for three years, I feel I am in a unique position to do so.

For the deaf and hard of hearing themselves, for the various groups plodding on in the field of sport, social activities, drama and so on, I have nothing but admiration. What has been accomplished? Mr. Odenthal certainly may take for granted all that has been achieved, but I myself feel that what the various deaf bodies have done has been nothing short of remarkable.

For a start, we have *Contact,* in my opinion, one of the finest communication magazines for the deaf to be found anywhere. Here, you have news, views, photos, important spiritual guidances, in short, everything which one could wish for.

Then, I must turn to the achievements of the Irish Deaf Sports Association, in the field of athletics generally. We have seen various teams go from strength to strength, and some of Ireland's swimmers now rank as world class, no mean tribute to the organisers.

In the field of drama, there have been countless productions and suffice it to say that the expertise, dedication and diligence that the deaf employ each time ranks among the best available.

Inevitably, along the way, and during the three years which we lived in Ireland, I have seen much in-fighting or dissension from among the ranks. This was apparent in the removal from his post of one of the co-founders of the IDSA prior to the Los Angeles Games for the deaf and his reinstatement shortly afterwards. This aroused widespread criticism and did not serve to create unity at the time.

I would also fully endorse the views of the Editor of this magazine that whatever has been achieved has only been done so at the enormous effort; and I would say to the IDS—"Try to bring about a unity of purpose, since to an outsider or the general public, it could look as if one section of the deaf is pulling one way and the other in a completely different direction."

Mr. Odenthal makes the point that the Social Services are not providing sufficient help to the deaf and hard of hearing generally and I would entirely agree with him on this issues. The National Rehabilitation Board does not have enough clout in being able to make potential employers of the deaf more aware of the qualities which the deaf possess.

At least one of your readers has harped on the unemployment problem as being the reason why potential employers will not engage the deaf. I would say to your

Appendix M

readers, unemployment is not to blame; indeed I myself have seen young persons of normal intellect with no disabilities flitting from job to job in a period of high unemployment. These people have very little experience or qualifications—indeed, their only gift seems to be one of eloquence, or as many would say "They have been to Blarney and kissed the Blarney Stone."

One cannot always apply the above to the deaf—they do need interpreters, persons who are prepared to voice to employers the enormous potential of a deaf employee. It is in this respect that the NRB and the Government must shoulder much of the blame for their failure to make an impact.

Christy Foran must be congratulated on his determination and resilience, but under no circumstances should anyone be compelled to wait a year before locating a new job. It's all very well saying "Fair enough, if there is no work, I can live off the state," a situation which can only add to one's difficulties.

We now turn to the question of hearing-aids, batteries, environmental aids for the deaf, telephone amplifiers and so on. There is absolutely no reason whatever why the hard of hearing of Ireland cannot have a free hearing aid if he or she possesses any degree of residual hearing. In this respect Ireland lags behind most other Western Countries.

It is widely known that the cost of components for a hearing aid is really very little—less then 1/8 of the total cost of the aid itself. Here again the Government and Social Services are to blame—I say to the deaf "Do not be fobbed off with taunts of no money being available to pay for these aids." There is and you can win if you present a united front.

It is also a frequent moan on these pages that the deaf/H.O.H. community are being harassed in the field of motor insurance, in that an additional premium must be paid by them before they can take to the road. Some companies will not grant insurance under any circumstances until a doctor's certificate has been obtained. This is wrong and drives a wedge through one of the basic principles of democracy—the deaf are being singled out as being more of a threat on the roads than a person with all his facilities.

The foregoing examples number only three, so Mr. Odenthal, during your stay you witnessed much, but your choice of word is wrong—it is not "oppression", but rather "discrimination". On no account could the blame be placed at the NAD's door—this is a very fine body of people—I really do think that the NAD and all of the other organisations working for the deaf should amalgamate somehow, so that a united front can be presented to the persons in Dáil Éireann who have steadfastly resisted change for the deaf community for too long.

Those readers who have so magnificently responded to Mr. Odenthal's remarks and adopted the "I'm all right, Jack" attitude should bear in mind that there is still much to be achieved if the Irish Deaf are to reach the standard of services in many other countries. They should remember that it takes courage and determination as well as patience to make the bureaucrats in the power see the light. And the fight must be carried on till what is rightfully yours has been gained.

Appendix M

Comment by editor of *Contact:*

We consider Mr. Odenthal's letter having been adequately answered and we thank the writers of the above letters for taking the trouble to pen them. Though, here it must be pointed out that among the members of the NAD Board of Directors are two born deaf, one hard-of-hearing and one deafened.

We regret having to accede to the requests from most deaf writers for anonymity so as to protect them from automatic verbal thuggery from certain quarters with vested interests.

By the way, it may be as well mentioned here that the moves to set up an independent body to run what is intended to be a statutory interpretation service in this country are held up by the demand from the IDS for control of the service, which is, of course, unacceptable. Also, they seem incapable of respecting other organisations' right to operate without interference in their fields of concern.

Thus the image of the Irish Deaf is brought into disrepute, and no self-respecting deaf person should tolerate this state of affairs any longer.

These words are written by the one who originated the group (Deaf Action Group) which eventually led to the formation of the IDS with the aims to identify deafness-related problems and to co-operate, where asked for, with other organisations.

We certainly did not envisage the IDS going further than that, for which there is absolutely no need. Incidentally, we are disappointed that they had not heeded our advice given a few years ago to thoroughly research all aspects of any issue (which can take years) before they start to promote solutions ... Their approach to certain matters cannot be described other than immature.

We cannot afford duplication of services which will only injure the Irish deaf in the long term. We say to the IDS: "Please, do not mess up the scene. And listen to the calls made in the above letters, and to the IDS Chairman who, at a private meeting last year, advocated union with the NAD." This sane course should be taken without further delay.

The name of the Irish Deaf was certainly saved from further injury when the daily newspapers refused to print Mr. Odenthal's letter which was sent to them by the IDS last November.

Appendix N

Irish Sign Language Project*

In 1988 the Irish Deaf Society began the process of seeking EC funding for a research project on Irish Sign Language. The IDS sought the assistance of the Linguistics Institute of Ireland (ITE) in achieving this aim. The IDS and ITE collaborated in producing a proposal which was sent to Brussels via the National Rehabilitation Board and the Department of Labour. IDS and ITE were partners in this joint proposal. Neither group was identified as "Lead" organisation although it was clearly an IDS initiative. The IDS relentlessly pursued funding for the proposal for the Irish Sign Language project until the objective was achieved when the EC (DG V) confirmed funding for such a project on 26th February 1993.

Between 26th February 1993 and the launch of the project on 7th December 1993, effective control of the project had passed from IDS/ITE to ITE. This occurred against the wishes of the IDS. The nuts and bolts of how this occurred will in fact never become transparent. As things stand the NRB insists that IDS was involved at all stages of the development of the project; the IDS will never accept that it voluntarily gave control of the ISL project to ITE, even to the point of disputing the contents of minutes of meetings.

The fact is that the IDS started out as a joint partner with ITE in this project in 1988 and ended up in 1993/94 being unable to participate in any meaningful way in the project.

The IDS sees the following points as being relevant to the way the project progressed to its current status:

1. **March 1993:** After DG V approved the proposal, NRB insisted that the IDS agree a "common strategy" with the National Association for the Deaf (NAD) for the project.

2. **April 1993:** The NRB invited NAD and IDS to a meeting where the NRB insisted that NAD would have a role in the project. IDS concedes to NRB wishes to include NAD but dissents from NAD having equal status. Working Group (Steering Committee) with representatives from NAD, IDS, ITE and NRB established.

3. **September 1993:** Funding for the project was allocated to ITE, after which the project became an ITE project. ITE ceased to function as a partner with the IDS in the project.

To elaborate on the above points:

(1) The NRB was making a political decision by insisting on the NAD being involved in the project. A "common strategy" was never agreed. The NAD had no previous experience of the project proposal because they had not been involved, whereas the IDS had initiated the proposal and had spent five years working to get it off the ground. The IDS believes that the NRB did not have the right to insist on the inclusion of NAD.

*Report compiled by the Irish Deaf Society, January 1995

Appendix N

(2) The IDS did not wish the NAD to have equal status on the project with ITE and IDS. The Director of ITE is on record saying that he did not want a steering committee to run the project. Equally the IDS did not want a steering committee but instead wanted the project to be run by the proposers (ITE and IDS). ITE adopted a neutral stance saying that it did not want to get into an argument with NRB, but the IDS could pull out of the project if the organisation was so unhappy.

(3) ITE urged the IDS to "go along with NRB" until the funding was allocated. Verbal assurances were given by ITE to IDS that once the money was allocated, ITE and IDS could get back to working together again as they had done in the years before the project had been approved. However since the funding was allocated, ITE has all but ceased to have any relationship with IDS.

NRB

In relation to the inclusion of the NAD in the project the NRB said in the Spring of 1993 that they wanted all of the Deaf Community to benefit from this project and that both Brussels and the Department of Enterprise and Employment (formerly the Department of Labour) were gravely concerned about this. The implication of this was that all of the Deaf community would NOT benefit if the project went ahead as envisaged in the proposal. There was absolutely no basis for this projection.

In our direct communications with DG V and Department of Enterprise and Employment personnel, this issue was never raised. Furthermore the person with responsibility for the project file in DG V was adamant that the funding allocated had been for a project which would be jointly run by the proposers.

By insisting on the inclusion of the NAD in the project the NRB politicised the project and undermined the position of the IDS. The NAD and the IDS have diametrically opposed views on certain issues of Deaf politics and one of them happens to be in the area of communication (the use of spoken language, Irish Sign Language, signed English, oralism, lip-reading etc.). In short, to impose the NAD onto an ITE/IDS Irish Sign Language project was not a good idea.

ITE and funding

ITE offered to "help" with providing matching funding for the project. The original sum sought was approx. £80,000. NRB got this figure increased to approx. £160,000. The IDS was alarmed at the idea that the funding would be solely allocated to ITE. Nonetheless, ITE repeatedly gave assurances to the IDS that once the funding was allocated, IDS would be treated as an equal partner in the project. Feeling there was no other option, IDS placed its trust in ITE. ITE reneged on those assurances.

IDS

The IDS experience in relation to this project, following its approval by DG V, has been that of frustration, humiliation and rejection.

Appendix O

"Dialogue of the Deaf: What Gallaudet Won't Teach"

by Lew Golan[*]

Gallaudet University officials don't talk much about it publicly, but an internal study revealed that 70 percent of the undergraduates at Washington's liberal arts university for the deaf cannot read a college-level textbook and that employers are increasingly dissatisfied with the English skills of Gallaudet graduates.

To help students improve their reading and writing skills, the university set up a project called English Literacy 2000 and brought me to the campus as a guest speaker last spring. Drawing from my experience on both sides of the desk–as a totally deaf person in a variety of professional positions and as a business executive who has hired and promoted people–I painted a real-world picture of how reading, writing, and critical thinking are key factors in getting better jobs and promotions.

But campus militants have been denouncing the literacy project as a conspiracy to oppress deaf people and to eliminate American Sign Language (ASL). There was virtually no advance publicity, so no more than 20 students showed up.

Yet programs like these are much needed because Americans who are deaf and whose English is poor are doubly disadvantaged in the job market. Unfortunately, this message is not getting through to many Gallaudet students; they are now demanding that their exams be given in ASL, which is a separate language, instead of in English. Most drop out before graduation–and those who do graduate take an average of seven years to do so.

I. King Jordan, president of Gallaudet, has said he believes the university can best prepare students for the job market by providing an empowering environment in which they may blossom and prosper without feeling like outsiders. The university's new "Vision Implementation Plan" calls for maximum use of visual learning and communication (sign language) and a reorganization of various procedures to improve academic progress.

But is a sheltered, academically undemanding, sign language milieu the best form of higher education for the deaf? The militants (who are becoming increasingly prevalent among both students and faculty) say yes–that it is a form of affirmative action. Some Gallaudet faculty members say no–that it is intellectually dishonest and leaves graduates unprepared for the real world. The militants are part of a minority of deaf people who base their identity on the use of American Sign Language, who view

[*]Lew Golan was senior vice-president and head of creative services at the largest marketing communications agency in the United States and executive vice-president at another. He has been a newspaper editor, advertising copywriter, television scriptwriter, creative director, computer guru, social and political activist, and kibbutznik. He is the author of Reading Between the Lips: A Totally Deaf Man Makes It in the Mainstream, and was the keynote speaker at the Bell Association's 1994 Convention in Rochester, New York. This editorial is reprinted from the Washington Post, 10 March 1996, with permission. See pp. 92-3 for comment on this article.

217

themselves as having their own culture, and who capitalize the D in Deaf to distinguish themselves from the 90 percent of deaf people who are not "culturally Deaf."

It is true that ASL permits fast, accurate, and comfortable communication among people who sign. For those who are fluent, it is a full, rich language. And the culturally Deaf community provides a supportive environment in which its members feel more at home than they do in the hearing world.

But the unqualified adulation of ASL as the be-all and end-all for deaf people ignores the flip side: ASL is virtually useless in the mainstream, because almost no hearing people sign. The trade-off for the feel-good environment is that it isolates deaf people and limits their horizons.

In school and on the job, the ability to speak and lipread opens many additional opportunities in the mainstream. Deafness itself is not an impenetrable barrier to integration; the barrier, if any, is when there is an inability to communicate with hearing people.

The culturally Deaf are not a homogeneous group; many of them believe, as I do, in different strokes for different folks. But the narrow-minded arrogance of the militants tars them all with the same brush of intolerance and clannishness.

Militants constantly disparage Heather Whitestone, the deaf woman who was Miss America of 1995, for giving parents the idea that perhaps their children, too, will be able to speak and lipread. Yet the fact is that many totally deaf people are succeeding to various degrees in the mainstream—educationally, professionally, and socially—by communicating orally as she does.

If the activists want to isolate themselves in a sign language community, to reject oral communication and English, to reject medical and technological advances that mitigate or, in some cases, even eliminate deafness—that's their business. But when they try to force their values on other deaf people, especially children, that's something else. Unfortunately, that is what is going on right now as ASL activists push their agenda in statehouses throughout the country.

The core item on the sociopolitical agenda of the Deaf cultural movement is bilingual, bicultural education. This means using ASL as the language of instruction in the classrooms from preschool on up. The BI-BI advocates permit no spoken English in the classroom—disregarding the fact that most parents want their children to speak English; that many children learned English before becoming deaf; that most of the hearing-impaired children are hard of hearing, not deaf, and can speak English quite well.

Since there is no written form of ASL, the textbooks (if any) are in English. What the proponents do not say is how a child whose preschool language is ASL will suddenly become proficient enough in English to read the textbooks with any degree of understanding.

State residential schools based on sign language are the traditional incubators for the culturally Deaf. Today, because of declining enrollments (fewer than 10 percent of deaf students go to state schools), state legislatures are talking about closing them down.

Some lawmakers are also concerned about the well-known negative effects of the environment at state residential schools on many students. These include immaturity, naivete, intolerance, a lack of the attitudes and people skills needed for employment and independent living, a lack of intellectual development, and dependence on welfare.

The goals of those who are pushing for special state laws are both ideological (to perpetuate the Deaf community by recruiting more ASL users) and financial (to appropriate more money for the state residential schools). They claim that other educational methods have been failures. As evidence, they point to surveys by Gallaudet covering 60 percent of the country's deaf students, which indicate that the average reading level of 16- and 17-year-old deaf students is third grade.

But what about the uncounted 40 percent, most of whom communicate orally by speaking and lipreading? A survey commissioned by the National Institutes of Health found that a sample of profoundly deaf oral students in the same age group averaged an eighth-grade reading level (five grades above the national deaf average), and 30 percent were above the 10th-grade level.

Nevertheless, without any proof that an ASL-based education would be any better, the militants are trying to make it the law of the land for all children with hearing losses. In Maryland, a proposed bill (fortunately defeated in committee) called for all deaf children to be fluent in ASL and educated in ASL classrooms. Similar "educational bills of rights" have been introduced in other states, including Indiana, South Dakota, California, Louisiana, Washington, Virginia, North Carolina, Utah, and Texas. In Minnesota, a law pushed through by militants requires all teachers of the deaf to be proficient in ASL and for half of their continuing education hours to be in Deaf culture studies or ASL. This, and the repeated bashings they get from the culturally Deaf, have moved many dedicated teachers to leave the profession altogether.

In the 1970s, Jerome Schein's landmark survey, "Deaf People as a Population," provided substantial evidence that deaf people as a group are underemployed. More recently, Janet MacLeod-Gallinger's seven-year study, "The Career Status of Deaf Women" (1992), corroborated the existence of underemployment among deaf people, especially women. Employers say that the biggest obstacle to the hiring and promotion of a deaf person is when there is an inability to communicate adequately, if at all, on the job.

It is irresponsible to minimize or eliminate the teaching and use of oral skills in the classroom. With early identification and early intervention, significant numbers of prelingually deaf children are being taught to speak and lipread. In addition, most

Appendix O

deaf children have some residual hearing that can be enhanced wit the proper technology. A relatively new technique, "cued speech," uses hand shapes around the speaker's mouth to help young lipreaders differentiate among similar-looking sounds.

Hearing aids are constantly being improved. And cochlear implants are having unpredictable but often dramatic results in giving deaf people some usable hearing.

After being totally deaf for 55 years (since the age of 6), I myself received a cochlear implant a few months ago. I can hear and identify many environmental sounds, and the feedback of my voice has made my speech somewhat more pleasant and understandable. Although my ability to understand spoken words by hearing alone is still minimal, it has been slowly but steadily improving. The most successful implantees (about 20 percent) can understand spoken words over the telephone, and almost all can lipread and speak better.

But ASL militants are against such advances, especially for children. They claim that in a community in which everyone is deaf and communicates in ASL, deafness is not a disability and is not something that needs fixing. This is self-delusion.

Regardless of whether a child signs, he will maximize his opportunities for an independent, productive adult life by developing whatever speaking and lipreading skills he can. Some children are up to the greater challenge, with various degrees of success; some are not. Each child is different.

The important thing is to have all options available for deaf people with different needs and capabilities—not a restrictive mandate that takes away freedom of choice, that bars access to opportunities in the mainstream. Those who give lip service to English reading and writing skills, and who deliberately reject spoken English, are biting the tongue that feeds them.

Response to Mr. Lew Golan from Dr. I. King Jordan
Gallaudet University president

As President of Gallaudet University and as an educator for many years, I share Mr. Golan's deeply held concern about literacy in America today. I do not, however share his conclusion that literacy level among Gallaudet students is a unique and special problem. Quite the contrary, in fact.

Ongoing research of institutions of higher learning across the country shows exactly the opposite. Throughout the land, college and university presidents and faculty members are addressing the lack of adequate reading and writing skills of entering students. That is necessary because too many American high school graduates read well. As Secretary of Education Richard W. Riley has said. "the most urgent task" for secondary schools is how to improve the teaching of reading

(Washington Post. March 13. 1996). Post-secondary institutions are implementing, in a variety of ways, programs geared toward giving new college students an optimal start in the academic world.

Gallaudet is no different from any other college or university in this regard. We may, however, be a bit ahead of the game, because individuals who are born deaf learn English differently from those who have hearing. Gallaudet has been in the forefront of enhancing literacy skills for its 132-year history. We have always accepted "at risk" students and given them the opportunity to meet our graduation requirements.

We are proud of our record and of the fact that other colleges and universities are learning from us. For example, the use of networked computers to enhance English language instruction, a technique which originated on our campus, is now being adopted elsewhere. Like other institutions of higher learning, we have also embraced such curriculum concepts as writing-intensive courses, in which students are introduced to cycles of carefully guided and continuous skill-building approaches that encourage reading, critical thinking, and writing opportunities to support mastery of course content.

The English Literacy 2000 program, which strives to link reading and writing skills with all components of academic life. is so important at Gallaudet that it is administered directly through mu office; through that program, the University is funding a number of research projects to develop innovative literacy-related pedagogies.

Again, Gallaudet is no different from any other college or university. We all want our graduates to have the skills and knowledge that employers expect from workers. All of us who are involved in higher education have a vested interest in making this happen. And, I emphasize here, we do it in English. Gallaudet students, like all other University students, must read and write in English to take part in university education, in scientific dialogue, and in learning and participating in the diverse culture of America.

Now, in one regard Gallaudet is different from other colleges and universities; all of our undergraduate students are deaf or hard of hearing. I have said repeatedly that we can best prepare our students for the job market by providing an empowering environment. That is true. While they are at Gallaudet, deaf students are totally free to explore academia, to learn about themselves, and to set forth on the road to accomplishment. They can do that because Gallaudet provides them with a `level playing field` that affords them a rich collegiate experience. On our campus, the President of the Student Body Government is deaf; the members of the world-famous Gallaudet Dancers are deaf; the peer counsellors in the residence halls are deaf. Both in the classroom and outside the classroom, our students have unlimited opportunities to develop leadership skills—by being leaders.

As the world`s premiere university for deaf students, Gallaudet must pay attention

Appendix O

to the fact that if one cannot hear, one depends far more heavily on visual means for receiving information. Sign language is the most visible method of visual communication. It is not, of course the only one. Speech and lip reading, hearing aids, and cochlear implants, as well as enhancement systems such as audio loops, have proven helpful to some individuals with hearing loss, and all of these technologies are available for Gallaudet students who wish to take advantage of them. And many do. In 1995, our Hearing and Speech Centre logged more than 1600 student visits. But communication is so broad and diverse that we cannot link it to any specific method. If a student is taking a class in history or small group dynamics, I am far more interested in whether he or she has mastered the concepts for these classes, than exactly which communication method or tool he or she chooses to employ. Is the student qualified to enter a graduate program in history? Can the student lead a group through the decision-making process? Can he or she exert leadership in solving problems? Can he or she make presentations, conduct interviews, and demonstrate the kind of skills that today's employers are looking for? Surely an employer would rather have a gifted deaf programmer who can sit down and write an innovative program than one who is mediocre, but has excellent speech skills.

When I talk about empowerment, I am talking about the studies that show the tremendous success of Gallaudet graduates in obtaining professional employment and about the fact that more than 50% go to earn graduate degrees. I am talking about not about what they have learned in the classrooms, but about the confidence they have developed as members of this community. Both serve them well as they move into the larger society. Regardless of what skills an entering student brings, regardless of what communication style may choose or prefer, our goal at Gallaudet is to help all our students realise their full potential and use every method and tool available which will assist them in achieving their goals.

This is the American dream. And the dreams of Gallaudet students are no different from the dreams of university student everywhere.

Glossary

American Sign Language (ASL): the natural language of the deaf community in the United States and Canada.
aural-oral method: a variant of the *oral method* in which communication is through sound only: lip-reading is not allowed.
British Sign Language (BSL): the natural language of the deaf community in Britain.
Catholic Institute for the Deaf (CID): an organisation founded in Dublin in 1845 by the Vincentian priest Thomas McNamara; it assumed responsibility for providing educational services for the Catholic deaf of Ireland in the two schools in Cabra, Dublin.
deaf community: "A group of people who live in a particular location, share the common goal of its members, and in various ways, work towards achieving these goals. A deaf community may include persons who are not themselves Deaf, but who actively support the goals of the community and work with Deaf people to achieve them." (This definition, proposed by Carol Padden, has the approval of the National Association of the Deaf in the United States.) The deaf community in Dublin has set up the Irish Deaf Society and holds to its aims rather than those of the National Association for the Deaf.
Deaf Studies: courses provided by deaf educators to inform hearing students from all walks of life of the culture within deaf communities, of *sign language,* of deaf people in history, and of deaf humour and art, to develop positive attitudes to deafness in society, and to raise the self-esteem of deaf people individually.
European Union of the Deaf (EUD): an organisation founded in 1985; its membership comprises the national associations of the deaf in most European countries and includes the Irish Deaf Society as the official national association of the deaf in Ireland.
finger-spelling: a system of hand-shapes to represent letters of the alphabet for spelling out the words of a speech language; commonly but incorrectly called *sign language.*
International Congress on Education of the Deaf (ICED): an organisation that traces its ancestry and its ethos back to the Milan congress of teachers of the deaf in 1880.
Irish Association of Sign Language Interpreters (IASLI): an organisation founded in 1994 by the former voluntary Interpreter Group and some

Glossary

graduates of the Horizon One training course organised by the Irish Deaf Society. They are introducing an awareness of good practice and the ethics of interpreting.

Irish Deaf Society (IDS): an organisation founded in 1981, with a board of directors made up exclusively of deaf people, working for the improvement of the quality of life of the deaf through education, information, and deaf empowerment. Affiliated to the World Federation of the Deaf.

Irish Deaf Sports Association (IDSA): an organisation founded in 1968 with help from the Cabra schools but now independent of them and run by the deaf.

Irish Hand Alphabet (IHA): the form of *finger-spelling* used in Ireland.

Irish Sign Language (ISL): the natural language of the deaf community in Ireland.

Irish Sign Language and Interpreting Training Agency (ISLITA): an organisation founded by the Irish Deaf Society in the nineteen-eighties. It follows an approach to the development of Irish Sign Language similar to that successfully pioneered by the British Sign Language Interpreter Training Association at the Centres for Deaf Studies at Durham and Bristol Universities. It was responsible for initiating the successful 1992–93 Horizon One training course for ten interpreter-trainees in conjunction with Bristol University and Trinity College, Dublin.

mainstreaming: the education of a deaf child in the local hearing school, sometimes misleadingly called "integration".

methodical signing: an artificial variety of sign language invented by non-deaf educators and others in which signs represent the words of a speech language, as well as grammatical concepts such as gender, number, tense, etc., as distinct from natural *sign language,* which arises spontaneously among deaf people.

National Association for the Deaf (NAD): an organisation founded in Dublin in 1962 by Sister Nicholas Griffey, associated with the Cabra schools and their commitment to oralism, with a board of directors exclusively of non-deaf people until 1979 and a majority of directors still non-deaf. It works for the improvement of the quality of life of the deaf through its influence in the education and political fields, modelled on the RNID.

National Association of the Deaf (NAD): an organisation founded in the United States in 1880 by and for deaf people.

oralism/oral method: the theory and practice of education for the deaf exclusively or mainly by means of amplified sound and lip-reading, whereby children are taught to express themselves through speech; also called the German method.

Royal National Institute for the Deaf (RNID): an organisation founded in London in 1911; essentially a parents' organisation concerned with the perceived deficit of hearing loss and with their desire to make their deaf child as much like a hearing child as possible.

St Mary's School for the Hearing Impaired: the central school in Cabra for all Irish Catholic deaf girls, founded in 1846 by the CID and run by the Dominican nuns. (To avoid confusion, I have used the more easily recognisable term "Girls' School" to distinguish it and the boys' school.)

St Joseph's School for Deaf Boys: the central school in Cabra, for all Irish deaf boys, founded in 1857 by the CID and run by the Christian Brothers.

signed English, signed French, etc.: the application of *methodical signing* to particular speech languages.

sign language/signing: a language of hand shapes and face and body movements that evolves naturally in a deaf community, as spoken languages evolved in hearing communities; not to be confused with *finger-spelling* or *methodical signing*. It is the natural language of the majority of the deaf; like spoken languages, it comes up from the homes, work-places and streets rather than down from experts. Sign languages have their own syntax with distinct grammatical and semantic structures: most signs represent complete ideas rather than just letters or some spoken words. Sign language is now recognised as the official language of the deaf in a few countries.

Sign Language Association of Ireland (SLAI): an organisation founded in the nineteen-eighties under the umbrella of the National Association for the Deaf and St Patrick's College, Maynooth. With the support of the NAD it runs a network of classes on *methodical signing*, which holds back the natural growth of *sign language* and the deaf community.

total communication (TC): a combination of *sign language, finger-spelling,* speech and hearing for expression and reception, a policy that endorses the right of every deaf child to communicate by whatever means are found to be beneficial. In reality it does not yet exist, except in the rare cases where teachers are proficient in Sign Language.

World Federation of the Deaf (WFD): an international organisation founded in 1950 with its head office in Helsinki; 116 countries are now affiliated. It is an organisation run by the deaf, working for the establishment of human rights, principally the free evolution of natural sign languages, and for deaf control of deaf education. Ireland, through the Irish Deaf Society, became a member of the WFD in 1986.

Bibliography

Atkinson, Norman, *Irish Education* (Allen Figgis, Dublin, 1967).
Boyd, William, and King, Edmund, *The History of Western Education* (A. and C. Black, London, 1975).
Campbell, Joseph, with Moyers, Bill, *The Power of Myth* (Doubleday, New York, 1988).
Cebe, Juanita (ed.), *Deaf Studies: What's Up?: Proceedings of a Mini-Conference at Gallaudet University, Washington, 1991* (Gallaudet University, Washington, 1992).
Cebe, Juanita (ed.), *Deaf Studies III: Bridging Cultures in the 21st Century: Proceedings of a National Conference on Continuing Education and Outreach, Chicago, 1993* (Gallaudet University, Washington, 1993).
Corish, Patrick, *Maynooth College, 1795–1995* (Gill and Macmillan, Dublin, 1995).
Corkery, Daniel, *The Hidden Ireland* (Gill, Dublin, 1925).
Crowe, F., *Lonergan* (Geoffrey Chapman, London, 1992).
Cullen, E., *The Origins and Development of the Irish Vincentian Foundation* (Three Candles, Dublin, 1933).
Curtis, L., *Apes and Angels: the Irishman in Victorian Culture* (Smithsonian Institution, New York, 1971).
Department of Education, *The Education of Children who are Handicapped by Impaired Hearing* [*report of the Committee on the Education of the Hearing-Impaired*] (Stationery Office, Dublin, 1972).
Deuchar, M., *British Sign Language* (Routledge and Kegan Paul, London, 1984).
Dewey, John, *Experience and Education* (Macmillan, New York, 1938).
Dewey, John, *Art as Experience* (Paragon, New York, 1979).
Durkheim, Émile, *Moral Education: a Study in the Theory and Application of the Sociology of Education* (Free Press, New York, 1973).
Ewing, A. (ed.), *Proceedings of Conference of Heads of Schools for the Deaf and Partially Hearing* (University of Manchester, Manchester, 1969).
Gannon, J.R. *Deaf Heritage: A Narrative History of Deaf America*. Maryland, USA: National Association of the Deaf. 1981.
Gardiner, D. (ed.), "Second International Catholic Conference on Religious Education of the Hearing-Impaired" in *Towards a Living Eucharist* (Henesy House, Manchester, 1983).
Gergen, Kenneth, *The Saturated Self* (Basic Books, New York, 1991).
Gregory, Susan, and Harley, Gillian (eds.), *Constructing Deafness* (Open University Press, Milton Keynes, 1991).
Griffey, Sister Nicholas, *Irislan: Manual for Basic Irish Sign Language* (National Association for the Deaf, Dublin, 1979).
Griffey, Sister Nicholas, *From Silence to Speech: Fifty Years with the Deaf* (Dominican Publications, Dublin, 1994).
Groce, Nora, *Everyone Here Spoke Sign Language: Hereditary Deafness in Martha's Vineyard* (Harvard University Press, Cambridge, Mass., 1985).
Hodgson, K., *The Deaf and Their Problems: a Study of Special Education* (Walter, London, 1953).

Bibliography

Hurd, Geoffrey, *Human Societies: an Introduction to Sociology* (Routledge and Kegan Paul, London, 1973).

Jackson, J. Hughlings (ed. Henry Head), *Hughlings Jackson on Aphasia and Kindred Affections of Speech* (Macmillan, London, 1915).

Johnson, A., *Human Arrangements* (Harcourt Brace Jovanovich, New York, 1989).

Kagan, Jerome, and Segal, Julius, *Psychology: an Introduction* (Harcourt Brace Jovanovich, New York, 1988).

Kyle, J.G. *Sign language: The Study of Deaf People and their Language*, (Cambridge University Press, 1991)

Lane, Harlan, *The Wild Boy of Aveyron* (George Allen and Unwin, London, 1977).

Lane, Harlan, *When the Mind Hears: a History of the Deaf* (Random House, New York, 1984; Penguin, London, 1988).

Lee, J. J., *Ireland, 1945–1970* (Gill and Macmillan, Dublin, 1979).

LeMaster, Barbara, "When women and men talk differently: languages and policy in the Dublin deaf community" in C. Curtin, H. Donnan and T. Wilson (eds.), *Irish Urban Cultures* (Institute of Irish Studies, Belfast, 1993).

Lenneberg, Eric, "Prerequisites for Language Acquisition": *Proceedings of the 1967 International Congress on Oral Education of the Deaf*, Lexington, NY, and Northampton, Mass., 1967.

Lonergan, Bernard, *Method in Theology* (Darton, Longman and Todd, London, 1973).

Luddy, Maria, *Women and Philanthropy in Nineteenth-Century Ireland* (Cambridge University Press, Cambridge, 1995).

McDonnell, P., *Patterns of Communication among Deaf Children* (IDS, Dublin, 1991).

Mahshie, Shawn Neal, *Educating Deaf Children Bilingually: With Insights and Applications from Sweden and Denmark* (Gallaudet University, Washington, 1995).

Meadow, Kathryn, *A Developmental Perspective on the Use of Manual Communication with Deaf Children: Proceedings of RNID Seminar*, London, 1976.

Montessori, Maria, *The Montessori Method* (1912; reprinted Schocken, New York, 1964).

Montessori, Maria, *The Absorbent Mind* (Clio Press, Oxford, 1949).

Moores, Donald, *Educating the Deaf: Psychology, Principles and Practices* (3rd ed.) (Houghton Mifflin, Boston, 1987).

National Association for the Deaf, *Forum on the Education of Hearing-Impaired Children in Ireland, Dublin, 1991* (videotape).

Ó Buachalla, Séamus, *Education Policy in Twentieth-Century Ireland* (Wolfhound, Dublin, 1988).

O'Connor, J., and Seymore, John, *Introducing Neuro-Linguistic Programming* (Aquarion, London, 1993).

O'Dowd, Michael, *"The History of the Catholic Schools for the Deaf, Cabra"* (MA thesis, University College, Dublin, 1955).

O Láimhín, J., *"Co-education: a Review and Further Investigation"* (MEd thesis, University College, Galway, 1987).

O'Neill, Fergal, *"The Social and Emotional Adjustment of Hearing-Impaired Irish Children in Special Schools"* (MPsychSc thesis, University College, Dublin, 1993). Orpen, C. F.

H., *The Contrast between Atheism, Paganism and Christianity Illustrated on the Uneducated Deaf and Dumb as Heathens Compared with Those Who Have Been Instructed in Language and Revelation and Taught by the Holy Spirit as Christians* (Goodwin, Dublin, 1828).

Phoenix, Susan, *Interim Report on a Pilot Survey of Deaf Adults in Northern Ireland, 1988* (Northern Ireland Workshop with the Deaf, Belfast, 1988).

Pim, Jonathan, *On the Necessity of State Provision for the Education of the Deaf and Dumb, the Blind and Imbeciles* (Royal Irish Acadamy, Dublin, 1846).

Purcell, Mary, *The Story of the Vincentians* (All Hallows College, Dublin, 1973).

Rogers, Carl, *On Becoming a Person* (Houghton Mifflin, Boston, 1963).

Sacks, Oliver, *Seeing Voices: a Journey into the World of the Deaf* (University of California Press, Berkeley, 1989; Picador, London, 1990).

Steinem, Gloria, *Revolution from Within: a Book of Self-Esteem* (Corgi, London, 1993).

Stoker, Charlotte, *On the Necessity of a State Provision for the Education of the Deaf and Dumb* (Thom, Dublin, 1868).

Stuckles, E., *An Interpretative Review of Research on Manual Communication in the Education of Deaf Children: Proceedings of RNID Seminar, London, 1976.*

Stumph, Samuel, *Socrates to Sartre* (McGraw-Hill, New York, 1988).

Supalla, Samuel J., "Language Access and Deaf Children" in *ASL in Schools: Policies and Curriculum,* Washington: (Gallaudet University, 1992)

Swan, Ethna, "Report of the Study on the Dublin Schools for the Deaf" (Survey by the Catholic Institute for the Deaf, 1994).

Thackeray, William Makepeace, *The Irish Sketch Book* (Chapman and Hall, London, 1857).

van Uden, Anthony, "Proceedings of the Second International Catholic Conference on Religious Education of the Hearing-Impaired" in D. Gardiner (ed.), *Towards a Living Eucharist* (Henesy House, Manchester, 1983).

Vernon, M., *Communication and the Education of Deaf and Hard-of-Hearing Children: Proceedings of RNID Seminar, London, 1976.*

Whyte, J., *Church and State in Modern Ireland, 1923–79* (Gill and Macmillan, Dublin, 1980).

Wilcox, Sherman (ed.), *American Deaf Culture: an Anthology* (Linstok Press, Silver Spring, Maryland, 1989).

Index

Explanations.

References in the text some sources, such as Sister Nicholas Griffey, Harlan Lane, Donald Moores and Father O'Dowd are scattered throughout the book, and are felt to be too numerous for 100 per cent listing.
The letter "n" immediately following a page reference indicates a footnote.
The foreword, introduction and the appendixes have been indexed
Definitions of technical terms may be found in the Glossary.

Academy of Medicine, Paris, 16, 17
Ackers, Benjamin St.John, 22, 30
Adams, John Quincy, 11
Agricula, Rudolf 1433-1485), 3
Alexander Graham Bell Association of the Deaf, see Bell
Allibert, Eugene (deaf pupil and teacher), 17
Allied Irish Banks, 68
American Sign Language (ASL), 1, 36, 38, 40, 86, 90-3, 150, 217-220
Amman, Johann Conrad (1669-1724), his belief in divine quality of speech and its influence on oralism, 7
influence of his books on growth of education of the deaf, 8, 12
Andersson Dr.Yerker, 95
apathy, in deaf children, 170
in the deaf community, 105-7
aphasia, Dr.Hughling-Jackson's research, 116
discovered in Cabra girls school, 116, 137-140, 153
Arnold, Rev. Thomas, 26, 27
Ashley, Lord, 48n
audiology clinics, 50
audism, 181
average deaf child neglected, 142

Babel of Sign Languages Ireland, 37
Baker, Henry (1698-1775), started first British school, 10
Balestra, Abbé Don, 23-7, 30
Beechpark, School for Deaf Boys, Stillorgan, 58, 94, 113, 114, 124
origins, 50
Bebian, Roch-Ambroise (1789-1834), 18
Belfast Telegraph, 76
Belfast, 70, 71

Bell, Alexander Graham, 31-2, 64, 82, 86 8, 110, 119
his contribution to the Royal Commission, 32
his American Association to Promote the Teaching of Speech to the Deaf (later The Alexander Graham Bell Association of the Deaf), 32n, 88
his attitude to deaf community, 31-2, 88
Bertier, Ferdinand, 18
Bi-Lingual/Bi-cultural education (Bi-Bi), 177, 181, 183, 184, 187, 218
Bienvenu, MJ, 114n, 120n, 176-186
Binet, Alfred (1857-1911), 29
Bishops' Conference, 71
Bonet, Juan Pablo (1579-1629), 4, 5, 12
Bordeaux School for the Deaf, 13
Bourke, Fr.John, 70
Braidwood, Thomas (1715-1806), father of family dynasty of schools in Britain, 10, 29, 36, 79, 80, 82
Breslin, David (deaf historian), 76
Bristol University, 67, 68
British Deaf Association, 75, 120n, 200
Bulwer, John (1614-1684), 6

Cabra establishment, xiv, 46, 69
attitude to deaf people, 70
educational expectations, of the, 47, 55
"educational treatment" in the, xv, 47, 60, 132, 139, 160
Cabra schools for the deaf, international reputation, 1, 42, 59-60
original and new names of the, 40,
rationale for change-over to oralism, 53-7
segregation of deaf pupils, 144, 161
staffing problems in the, 111
Carnegie, Andrew, 32
Cardano, Girolama (1501-1576), 3, 7

230

Castleknock College, 38
categories of deafness, official, 51
Catholic Congregation of the Mission to Ireland, 3, 8
Catholic Institute for the Deaf (Cabra), 30, 36, 39, 40, 46, 48, 49, 50,
    and mainstreaming, 113 reasearch by the, 123-130
Catholic Institute for the Deaf (St. Louis, Missouri), 110, 138
chaplaincy of the deaf, 70-3, 106 hegamony of the, 72
Charles I, 5
Charles II, 6
child frustration, avoidance of, 166-175
Children of a Lesser God, 76
Christian Brothers, 37, 40-5
    at Milan Congress, 22
    request for finance to visit foreign schools, 40
    tour of British schools, 50
Christian Observer, 80
Clare Champion, 21n
Claremont School for the Deaf, Dublin (1816-1971), 35-7
Clarke School for the Deaf, 58, 86, 89, 110, 129
Clarke, John, 86
Clerc, Laurent (1785-1869), 18, 80-2, 99, 184
co-education, 82
Cochlear implants, 48n, 164, 177, 220
Cogswell, Alice, 81
Cogswell, Dr.Mason, 79
Colonomos, Betty M. 176
combined method, see total communication,
Condillac, Etienne (1715-1780), 8, 11, 16
Congregation of the Missioneries, see Vincentions
Congress of Milan, see Milan Congress
Connecticut Asylum for the Education of Deaf and Dumb Persons (later American Asylum for the Education of Deaf and Dumb Persons). see Hartford School
Connell, Dr.Dermot, Archbishop of Dublin, 72
Contact magazine, 65n, 66, 74, 75, 206-214
convent ethos, 43-4, 50
Cork school for the deaf(1822-1846), 38
Cosgrave, Liam, 49
Cosgrave, W.T. 49
Covarrubias, 3
Crean, Brian, 51, 61, 69, 113
Cronbach, L. 59

Cullen, Dr.Paul, Archbishop of Dublin, (later Cardinal), 38, 40, 44
cultural conditioning, see apathy
curriculum, xiii,100-102, 184nd education for life,

Dalgarno, George (1628-1687), Scottish teacher, 7
Davern, Noel, Minister for Education, 69, 201
Davis, Thomas, his opinion of denominational education, 39
de l'Epée, Abée Charles-Michel. see Epée
de Valasco, Luis (remarkable deaf student), 3, 5
    Valasco family, 3
deaf children of deaf parents out-performing deaf children of hearing parents, 171-2
deaf clubs, 75
deaf community, 59, 74-6, 120-2, 143, 199-220
    participation in politics, 65
    deaf folklore, 76
deaf people, opinions on:
    co-education, 128
    education through Sign Language, 125, 126, 195-197
    mainstreaming, 127-8
    oral education, 194-197
    oral teachers, 197
    lip-reading, 194
    see also Desloges
Deaf Pride, and Deaf Power, 74, 162, 171
Deaf Studies, 22n, 120, 176-186
    how they should be taught,184-5
    who should teach them, 185-6
    where they should be taught, 178-9
    why they should be taught. 176-178
    see also Trinity College, Dublin,
deaf teachers, oralism's effect on deaf teachers, in America, 85 (diagram), 86,
    in Cabra, 107,
    see also Allibert; Clerc; Massieu,
Deaf, the, generosity of Irish people towards, 40
deafness, the consequences of being deaf in former times, 2, 9, 11
Denison, James (deaf teacher), 25, 27
Department of Education, 42, 46-7, 53, 55, 60, 61, 62, 68-9, 76, 101, 107, 113, 114-5, 124, 127, 161, 189, 201
    lack of understanding of language acquisition, 60
    on arrangements for Protestant pupils, 36
    Report on Education of the Deaf (1972),

47, 57, 60
Special Education Review Committee (1993), 68-9
White Paper on Education Bill (1991), 62
Desloges, Pierre (deaf author,1749-?), 9
Dewey, John, 44, 89
    on use and misuse of teachers' experience, 103
Diderot, Denis (1713-1784), 8
Digby, Sir Kenelin (1603-1666), his account of deaf Spanish student (Luis de Valsco), 5
discrimination, 21-22, 62-5, 69
    against deaf parents, 64
    against Protestant pupils, 36
    against deaf people, 2, 22-9
Dominican nuns (Cabra), 37-45, 47, 50, 53, 55, 65, 75, 96, 104-116, 122
    tour of British schools, 48, 57
Dowley, Fr.Philip, 38
Dublin Deaf Association, 72, 75
Dunne, Fergus, 63, 64, 69

early intervention, 57, 112
    importance of, with oral education, 46
Elliot, Richard, 25
Encyclopaedia Britannica, 40n, 105n
England, Rev. T.R., 38
Epée, Abbé Charles-Michel de l' (1712-1789), 17, 39-40, 51, 70, 81, 89, 99, 105 his background, 10 his offer to Heinicke to come and see his school, 11,12
    satellite schools opened due to, 12-19
esoteric signs, 15
Eugenics, 32
European Union, 215-6
European Union of the Deaf (formerly ERCS), 68
Ewing, Sir Alexander, 47, 48, 50, 52, 58, 110, 162

feed-back from deaf adults, lack of, xv,55
first book on teaching the deaf, see Bonet, Juan Pablo,
First Congress of the Irish Deaf Society, 105
Fletcher, Louise, 119
Flynn, Sister Peter, 48
Foran, Stan, 41, 50, 54, 187
Forum on the Education of the Deaf (1991), 62-4, 68, 123, 201
Frank, Adolphe, 24
French Academy of Medicine, 16
French Academy of Sciences, 24
French Enlightenment, influence of, on education of the deaf, 4, 7-8, 11, 35, 89

French Revolution, 13
Fuller, Sarah, 86

Gallaudet University, 90-3, 120, 180, 217-220
    revolt by students, 91
Gallaudet, Edward Miner (1857-1917), 22, 28, 31, 34, 83-8
Gallaudet, Sophia, 83
Gallaudet, Thomas Hopkins (1787-1851), 12, 51, 79-82, 105
Golan, Lew, xiv, 92, 217-220
Griffey, Sister Nicholas (1916-), 12n, 21, 29, 41, 43, 47, 55-6, 64, 70-3, 94, 126, 131-165
Groce, Nora, 2
Gustaston,G., 119

hard of hearing, 213
Hartford School for the Deaf, Connecticut, 80-5
Heinicke, Samuel (1723-1790), 9,11,12,19, 53, 105n
    his method revealed, 13 his refusal to submit oral method to tests, 11-13
Henry IV, 5
Higgins, Paul, 121
Higginson, John, 79
Hobbes, Thomas (1588-1679), 6
Hodgson, K.L., 1n, 39n
Holder, William (1616-1698), 6
Hooker, Thomas (1586-1647), 79
Howe, Samuel, 84, 85,
Hubbard, Gardiner, 86, 88
Hubert, Brother, 22

Illinois Test of Psycholinguistic Abilities (diagram), 59
Indianna School for the Deaf, 181
Industrial Revolution, 18, 44, 101
Institut du Bon Sauveur, Caen, 40, 115, 129
Institute of Industrial Research and Standards, 58
integration. see mainstreaming
International Catholic Foundation for the Service of Deaf Persons, see chaplaincy of the deaf.
International Congress for Oral Education of the Deaf (1967), 131,
Interpreter Group, 68
interpretive services, 66-8, 211
Irish Association of Sign Language Interpreters, 68
Irish College in Paris, 30, 38
Irish Deaf Journal, 75

Irish Deaf Society, xiii ,xiv, xvi, 56, 61n, 62-4, 69-7074, 76, 95, 105, 121, 123, 127, 199-216
  attempt by, to reform education system, 68-70
  conflicts of, with Cabra estabishment, 62-7
Irish Independent, 21n, 130n
Irish Language, neglect of, in schools for the deaf, 102
Irish National Institution for the Deaf and Dumb. see Claremont School for the Deaf
Irish Press, 48n
Irish Sign Language (ISL), 'high' and 'low' versions of signing, 104, 150,
Irish Sign Language Research Project, 65, 215-6
Italian schools for the deaf in 1880s, 23-9 passim
Itard, Dr.Jean-Marc (1774-1838), 8, 14, 15, 118
  medical experiments and result, 16
  oral teaching experiments and result, 17

James, O'Neill and Smyth survey, 111-2, 188-193
Jamet, Abbé Pierre-François, 18, 40, 70, 150, 159
Johnson, Samuel (1709-1784), 10
Jordan, Dr. I. King, xiii, 220-222
Joseph II, 11

Keane, Niall, 65, 130n
Kehoe, Dr.Patrick. see Cork School for the Deaf
Keller, Helen, xiv, 86
Kinniburg, Robert. see Claremont School
Kyle, Dr.Jim, 68

Lane, Dr. Harlan, 10, 22n,
language acquisition by the deaf, as understood by the Dept. of Ed, 60-1
Late-Late Show, 119
Lemass, Eileen, 69
LeMaster, Dr.Barbara, research into Irish male and female languages, 41, 42, 54, 56, 57n
Lenneberg, Dr.Eric, 3, 89, 108n
  research into education of the deaf, 58
Lincoln, President, 83
linguistic deprivation of deaf children, 171
Linguistic Institute of Ireland (ITE), 215-6
Link magazine, journal of the Irish NAD, xvi, 54, 65n, 67n, 73n, 74, 75, 158n
lip-reading myth, 119-120, 130

Lonergan, Fr.Bernard, 97, 103, 104
Louis XVI (1754-1793), funding for Epée's school, 11
  funding for oral teacher, 8
Louis XVIII, 14

McCarthy, Justice Niall, 62, 65, 66, 67, 207
McCullough, Bob, 76
McDonnell, Brother, 30
McDonnell, Pat, 69
McDonough, Fr.Peter, 96
McEvoy, Sister Carmel, 58
McGettrick, Brother, 53,
McGinnis, Mildred, 137, 138, 153, 155
McGrath, Brother G.J., 110
McNamara, Fr.Thomas, 30, 38-40, 72
McQuaid, J.C. Archbishop of Dublin, 49, 53,124
  his promotion of oralism, 50
Macaulay, Zachary, 10, 80, 81
Maginn, Francis, 120
Magnat, Marius (organiser of Milan Congress), 23
Maguire, Frank, 116
mainstreaming, xiii, xv, 53, 95, 104, 112-5, 127-8, 177, 179, 180, 185, 217-220
Manchester University, 48, 50, 58, 129, 158, 160-1
  contribution to oralism in Ireland, 48, 50, 58, 158,
  teacher training dept. 52
Mann, Horace, 23, 83-5
Marie-Antoinette, 11
Markides, Dr.Andreas, 163
Martha's Vineyard, a model of integration, 2, 81, 91, 96, 121
Massieu, Jean (deaf teacher), 13, 15, 80, 120
Maynooth College, 39, 40, 41, 68
Meadow, Katherine P. 90, 142, 167-9, 171-2, 173
media, xviii accounts of oralists' messages, 21n, 48n, 84, 88, 111n
medical experiments, see Itard,
method, definition of transcendental. see Lonergan,
Milan Congress 1880, 20, 22, 33, 62, 93, 94, 99, 159, 164
  resolutions, 22
Miller, Jonathan, 89
Montessori, Maria (1870-1952), 17, 43, 89, 116, 118
Moores, Dr.Donald, 3n, 59–86
Mottez, Bernard, 29
multi-handicapped children, 115-9, 139, 142, 155

233

myths and falacies about deafness, 1, 177
Napoleon I, 14, 19, 35, 85
National Association for the Deaf (Cabra), xvi, xviii, 54, 62-80, 73, 75, 88, 104, 124, 158, 199-216
National Association of the Deaf (US), 28, 64, 65, 75, 88n
National Convention on Education, (Irish), 64n
National Deaf Children's Society, 47, 52
National Institution for Deaf Mutes, Paris. 11, 14, 15, 18
National Parents' Council for Special Schools for Mentally Handicapped Children, 118n
National Rehabilitation Board, 188, 212, 215-6
natural language of the hands. see Bulwer
Nelson, Doris, 62
New York Institution for the Deaf, 41
NRB, see National Rehabilitation Board,

Ó Fiaich, Cardinal, 38n
Ó Murchú, Éamon, 64
O'Dowd, Fr.Brendan, Cabra historian, 3, 30, 36, 40, 49, 53, 57, 109, 115
  limitation of his research, 37
O'Farrell, Fr. 71
O'Malley, Donough, 57
O'Neill, Rose, 43n
O'Reilly, Dr.Tony, xviii,129n
Odenthal, Grover, 66, 67, 206-214
Operation Headstart, see Schlesinger,
oral 'failures', 60, 62n, 131, 143, 163
oral education (oralism), media involvement in, 21, 66, 67
  medical involvement, 47
  more suited to German and Spanish languages, 4, 12
  revival of, in Germany in 1830s, 13
  revival of, in Britain in 1860s, 29
  attitude to use of signs in oral schools, 20-21,55
  short lived results with, 21
oral schools, attitude to past pupils, 72
  back-up experts, 47, 180-1
oral teachers, classroom experience, 56
  knowledge of Sign Language, 55-6
Orpen, Dr.C.E.H. 35-6
Owen, Rev.C.M., see Royal Commission,

parent-infant interaction, 167
parents' expectations, 55, 172
Parstall, Gerard, 4n
past-pupils comments, 40
Paul-Dubois, Louis, 107

Periere School of Paris, 23
Periere, Eugene. (1831-?), 22, 26
Periere, Jacob Rodrigues. (1715-1790), his sensational successes, secrecy of his method and dubious reputation. xiv, 8, 9
  his conflict with Epée, 11-12
  see also Desloges
Phillip IV, 3
Phoenix, Dr.Susan, 105-6, 111n
Pironio, Cardinal, 71
Ponce de Leon, Pedro (1529-1584), 3-5, 71
Pope Pius VII, 14
Protestant proselytism, 72
Protestants' choice of schools in Republic of Ireland, 36
Purcell, Mary, 72n

Quinlan, Pat, 199-205, 207-9

Radio Telifis Eareann (RTE), 71
Ramirez de Carrion (1579-?), 4, 5
reading skills, 188-193
religious institutions of education, 42-5
Report of Department of Education, see Dept. of Ed,
research and surveys on the deaf,
  in America, 59
  by Christian Brothers, 50
  by Dominican nuns, 48,
  by Dr.Hughling-Jackson, 116
  by IDS, 194-8
  by National Rehabitation Board, 188-193
  preferred interviewees, 106
  see also Binet; Itard; Lenneberg; Moores; NRB; Phoenix; and Swan,
Review Committee on Education of the Hearing-Impaired, 62, 63, 68, 124
rhythm in speech therapy, 116, 136, 151
Rousseau, Jean-Jacques (1712-1778), 8,16
Royal Commission, Report of (British), (1889), 20, 22, 29, 52, 72, 75
  comment on the Cabra boys' school pupils, 33
  minority report (in it) by clergymen, 32-3
  recommendations, 32-4
Royal National Institute for the Deaf, 55, 64, 68, 75, 88, 92
Royal Society, 6, 7
Ryan, Matthew, 70

Sacks, Dr.Oliver, 90, 91, 96
Schlesinger, Dr.Hilde, 127n, 166-175
Second Congress of the Irish Deaf Society, 96
Second International Conference on Religious Education of the Hearing-

Impaired, 53, 111n
Seguin, Dr.Edouard, 8, 17, 118
Sicard, Abbé Roch-Ambroise (1742-1822), 40, 68, 70, 80, 81, 105n, 109, 120
   his influence in the spread of education, 14
   his showmanship, and the honours bestowed on him,14,19
   his ambivalent attitude to Sign Language, 13,15, 18
   how the deaf saved him from execution, 14-15
Sign Language Association of Ireland (SLAI), 67
Sign Language, oral education allegedly undermined by, 32
   superiority over oral method for teaching, 37
Sign of the Times, 76, 98
signing schools, experiences of past pupils,
   in America, 83, 85, 91
   in Britain, 95 in Cabra, 187
   in France, 14, 17
   in Sweden, 95
Sint-Michielsgestal school, Holland, 48, 51, 52, 70, 110, 129
Sleigh, Rev. W.E., see Royal Commission,
social isolation, 54, 108
social services, 54, 73
Society of Friends, 30
Special Education Review Committee, see Dept. of Ed,
special schools for the deaf. see Bulwer
speech training neglected in some signing schools, 21
Spencer, Herbert, 32,
St. Joseph's School, Missouri. see Catholic Institute for the Deaf, St.Louis, Missouri
St. Vincents Centre for the Deaf, 72
St.Gabriel's School, Sidney, Australia, 110
Stoker, Charlotte, 30
Stokoe, Dr.William, 56, 89
Stuckless and Birch, 90
Sullivan, Anne, 86
Supalla, S.J, 18
Swan Dr.Ethna, xiv,123-130
Sweeney, Fr.Dermot, 71

Tarra, Abbé Giulio, 25-26, 28
teacher training, for oral teachers, 52
   for signing teachers, 51
teachers' experience, 56, 102, 142

teaching through writing, 3, 6, 7, 58
Teaching Machines, seminar on, 58 see also Agricula; Covarrubias; Cardona; Lenneberg and Ponce de Leon;
Time Magazine, 21n, 48n
Total Communication (or the combined method), 92, 129, 132, 141, 143, 145, 146, 147, 154, 155, 144, 150, 152, 162, 163, 177, 182
Trinity College, Dublin, xiv, 68, 74
   classes in Irish Sign Language, 74

United States, 49, 54, 75
University College Dublin, 107
   teacher training course, xv, 52-4
   library, 53, 123,

Valladolid, 3, 71
van Asch, Gerrit, 29
van Eyndhoven, Fr. 70
van Uden, Fr.A, 47, 48, 56, 102n, 110, 111, 146, 160
Vernon and Koh, 90, 154, 171
Vincentians, 38-9, 72
visiting teachers of the deaf, 52, 62, 63, 112-3, 189
vocational education, 38, 82

Wall, Brother, 58
Wallis, John (1616-1703), 6
Walsh, Dr. Archbishop of Dublin, 30
Washington Post, 92, 217
Watson, Dr.Thomas, 158, 161, 162
Watts, W.J., 58
Wesemann, Johann, 69, 201
Whaley, Daniel, 6
White, Bruce A., 92
Wild Boy of Aveyron, 14, 15, 17
Wilde, Dr.William, 31
Wilde, Oscar, 31, 44
Williams, Robin, 110
Wilson, Fr.Des, 38
Woodward, Allen and Schildroth, 90
World Congress for Improving Welfare of the Deaf, 23
World Federation of the Deaf, 65, 68, 95, 121